PLEASURE AND PRIVILEGE

Olivier Bernier

PLEASURE
AND
PRIVILEGE

Life in France,
Naples and America
1770–1790

FOREWORD BY
LOUIS AUCHINCLOSS

Doubleday & Company, Inc.
Garden City, New York
1981

Engravings numbered 4 and 12, courtesy of The Metropolitan Museum of Art.
All others, courtesy of The New York Public Library.

ISBN: 0-385-15780-0
Library of Congress Catalog Card Number 79–6174
Copyright © 1981 by OLIVIER BERNIER
Foreword Copyright © 1981 by LOUIS AUCHINCLOSS
All Rights Reserved
Printed in the United States of America

First Edition

BOOK DESIGN BY BENTE HAMANN

CONTENTS

*The author wishes to express his gratitude
to the New York Public Library
without whose admirable research facilities
this book could not have been written.*

FOREWORD

The privileged French of the late eighteenth century have always seemed to me the most privileged class in history. Not only did they live in the lap of luxury—that state was available to the vulgarest eras—but they were willing to face the hard fact that the truest pleasure involves the strictest discipline. Ennui makes an easy victim of the sybarite unless he has cultivated good taste, and the sybarite of Paris in the 1770s and 1780s made good taste his god. It ruled him in everything: in decoration, in architecture, in clothes, in cooking, in decorum, in conversation, in friendship, in love. Why have I left out art? Because art was implicit in the whole thing; art was life itself, the good life. There was as much art in the making of a doorknob or a truffled *foie gras* as in a painting or a tragedy.

Today we tend to put art in a category of its own. Art belongs in museums, in concert halls, in libraries. Art is for leisure time. To look for art where it doesn't belong is to be "arty." And what is that but to be superficial—like those silly French aristocrats with powdered hair who fussed over sauces and made faces in the mirror? It's a relief, isn't it, to learn from Olivier Bernier that those people made a bloody mess of it? Taxing the poor and torturing criminals while they shed tears at sentimental comedies? If the guillotine way was a bit rough, they had certainly asked for it!

But the uneasy feeling still remains, in some of us anyway, as we face the glory of the Wrightsman eighteenth-century rooms in The Metropolitan Museum of Art (although Bernier doesn't think much of these) that we should have been all thumbs in such a chamber. And wouldn't the privileged of other eras have been all thumbs too? Wouldn't Augustus, or Lorenzo the Magnificent, or even Mrs. Astor of the Four Hundred? Isn't there something about a life where everything was exquisite that leaves us a bit awestruck?

Olivier Bernier helps us to avoid being overpowered—or even resentful—by supplying us with such a wealth of detail that we actually enjoy the illusion of being French in what Talleyrand deemed the most delicious of eras. Bernier tells us what these people ate and drank, where they shopped, what coins jangled in their pockets, how they sued each other, and how they made love; he follows them through their days and nights, at parties, in palaces, and on their travels. And he explains how every section of their society was pitted against every other in such a complex, interwoven pattern that no force could have saved it from ultimate disaster.

Our old image of the era, a fancy engraving after Greuze or Vernet or Robert, or maybe a combination of all three, begins to shape itself into something more like a photograph. But at just this point Bernier performs another remarkable stunt. He simply explodes our illusion of reality by following his portrait of France with contemporary pictures of Naples and of the American colonies; the first a kind of parody of what we have just seen; the second a species of idealization.

Naples was an *opéra bouffe* to Paris's *comédie larmoyante*. It might have seemed to a Talleyrand as his Paris would have seemed to us: too rich, too highly colored, too artificial. Queen Marie Caroline was a crude version of her younger sister, Marie Antoinette. It was a mad world, even more bound to explode; it made Paris seem as sober as Rome of the ancient republic. It was the dream of a "bad" Frenchman.

The thirteen colonies, on the other hand, were the dream of a "good" one. They approached, at least to oversophisticated European eyes, the rustic simplicity and democracy that Rousseau had made so fashionable to his multitudinous readers. If French society was to go any further downhill, it might go the Neapolitan way, but if it was to purge itself, might it not become America?

Of course, it became neither. Revolution in 1789 paved the way for a century that was to have little enough to do with the Paris, the Naples, or even the Philadelphia of 1788. But, having read Bernier, we have at least an idea of how massive the change was to be.

Louis Auchincloss

PREFACE

In the last twenty years of the Ancien Régime in France (1770–90), cultural trends which had been developing for more than a century came to a final, brilliant bloom before disappearing forever. PLEASURE AND PRIVILEGE is both a description and an analysis of this society, with its glamor and weaknesses, its comforts and difficulties. And since most European nations took their cue from Paris and Versailles, the major part of this book is devoted to life in France.

For much the same reason, the author has chosen to look at Naples and America from a French point of view. Why Naples? Because it was the first great European tourist center, a Monte Carlo of the eighteenth century which also happened to have the newly excavated ancient Roman cities of Pompeii and Herculaneum in its back yard. As a result, a new antique-inspired style of architecture, interior decoration, and fashions in costume and coiffures swept Europe and America, thus adding major cultural significance to the pleasures of an exotic landscape and people.

As for America, no book describing France under Louis XVI could ignore it: the War for Independence was a key political issue creating a first but lasting division between liberals and reactionaries; it was a fashion, long and enthusiastically sustained; more, for many followers of Rousseau, America was a continent peopled by good savages, men and women both virtuous and unspoiled who might show the way to a better world. The French came, fought in the war, and went home to publish their diaries and memoirs. PLEASURE AND PRIVILEGE therefore depicts a new French look at America, while still pointing out the errors of fact and interpretation sometimes made by these enthusiastic travelers.

"Only those who lived before the Revolution know how sweet life can be," Talleyrand wrote many years later. PLEASURE AND PRIVILEGE is an attempt to resurrect this dazzling yet utterly comfortable way of life so that the modern reader may understand, and perhaps share, Talleyrand's feeling, while wondering whether there are not more parallels between the France of Louis XVI and the United States in the 1980s than he might at first have supposed.

LIST
OF EIGHTEENTH-CENTURY
ENGRAVINGS

To A. and E. v. W.

PLEASURE AND PRIVILEGE

I

PARIS AND
VERSAILLES

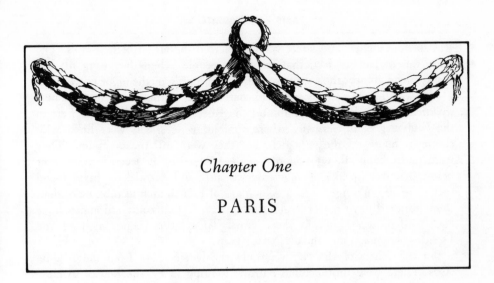

Chapter One

PARIS

London was cleaner, Rome more ancient, Venice more magical, Vienna cozier; you might eat better in Lyon, trade better in Bordeaux, sleep better almost anywhere; it was dirty, noisy, expensive; but if you had asked almost anyone where he or she most wanted to go, the answer would have been Paris. More than the capital of France, more than the largest city in Europe, Paris was the center. Its influence radiated all over the world. Its books, its fashions, its habits, all were avidly sought and copied. Living in Paris was a privilege, a subject of conversation, a cause for envy, something so rare and thrilling, in fact, that Sébastien Mercier, a Parisian lawyer, sat himself down and, over a period of five years (1783–88), lovingly composed the eleven volumes of his *Tableau de Paris* after apologizing for its brevity. Paris, it seemed, was almost the entire world.

It was a huge city, for the eighteenth century, with its population of over eight hundred thousand, and it grew steadily throughout the years 1774 to 1790. It had long ago expanded beyond its medieval fortifications, and only recently a new wall had been built with, every so often, a tax collector's pavilion. No one thought of defense, it was just a question of collecting the full amount of the high impost due on any goods that entered the city. At each of these pavilions carts and coaches waited in long lines as clerks unloaded and searched them thoroughly, even probing any suspicious packages with long metal needles.

Once inside, what was the city like? Bustling and noisy, all the travelers say. Countless carriages clattered down cobblestoned streets, going at breakneck speed and preceded by running footmen shouting, "Make way, make way!" Carts and drays rumbled in and out of the markets, cattle mooed on its way to the butchers and street vendors pierced the air with their cries. The noise was so bad, in fact, that well-to-do people, when they were ill, had straw spread all over their street so they might have a modicum of peace.

Most of the city's streets were old, narrow and tortuous. There were new *quartiers,* on the Right Bank around the Rue Saint-Honoré, on the Left in the Faubourg Saint-Germain, where straight, wide streets were lined with the town houses of the very rich, but they were still the exception. They were multiplying, though; more people were rich, it seemed, than ever before—Mercier speaks of monstrous wealth and scandalous luxury—and they were all building. It was a golden age of French architecture; more than three hundred town palaces, each set between a front courtyard and a huge back garden, were built in those years. Today, they house most of the French government and the diplomatic corps.

But the center of the city was only slowly emerging from the Middle Ages. There were innumerable narrow, twisting lanes, the houses so close they barely let in the light, the pavements covered with garbage and excrement. Over them, here and there, towered a Gothic church or a medieval fortress: the Temple, built by the Knights Templars in the fourteenth century, the Bastille, that fortress become prison, and the Tour de Nesle, by the river. Now and again there was a great open space: the Place Royale (now Place des Vosges), near the Bastille, the Place des Victoires, built by a courtier of Louis XIV and adorned with an equestrian statue of the Sun-King, the Place Vendôme, the Place Louis XV (now Place de la Concorde). Little by little, medieval houses were replaced by new, tall five-story apartment houses faced with stone, their wide windows opening onto the sun. Government buildings were going up too: the Halle au Blé, the Mint, many others, which were giving Paris that monumental look it has retained ever since.

There were no sidewalks; pedestrians were constantly forced to squeeze against the walls to let the traffic through—and everyone, in Paris, seemed to have a carriage. Accidents were commonplace and often bloody. People were run over or knocked down, like Jean-Jacques Rousseau, by the lackeys or the dogs running in front of the coach. There was even a fixed rate for injuries —so much for an arm, so much for a leg, so much for a life. Doctors drove in black four-wheelers, dancing masters and smart young men in light, two-wheeled gigs; the rich rushed past in ornate carriages pulled by four horses (six if it was a Prince of the Blood Royal). Adding to the confusion, thousands of cabs, often driven by drunken coachmen shouting hoarsely, scooted in and out of the stream. Water was supposed to run down a sort of open gutter in the middle of each street, but these conduits were generally clogged by filth and refuse so that a black, clinging, stinking mud spread everywhere: it left indelible stains on your clothes, so it was not a good idea to walk around except in a few specific areas.

It was dark at night. New oil lamps with reflectors had just replaced the old system of candles in lanterns, but they were lit only on moonless nights

—about a week in every four. The system was universally decried: not only was moonlight dim at best, not only did it not reach down tall, narrow streets, but it was also frequently hidden by clouds; and then total blackness prevailed.

Still, with all the rush, mud, noise, and stink, Paris was a cheerful city. Street vendors, crying their wares, sold everything, it seemed: milk, water, vinegar, pastries, forbidden books, lemons, oranges, fritters, chestnuts, ratbane, oysters, vegetables, flowers, porcelain, lanterns, drinks, herb teas, knives, candles, brooms, sauces. Street singers strolled here and there; church bells rang; people scurried about their business and pretty girls in short skirts (mud!) ran, carrying a variety of baskets. The shops were often new, always filled with a variety of goods of such quality that they were sold all over Europe. And then there were the promenades, areas where people went just to stroll, see, and be seen: the Tuileries gardens, for instance, or the new boulevards ringing the city where you could ride your horse in the middle or walk under a double row of chestnut trees on the side. If you wanted to look at—or display—the new fashion in carriages, you went to the Cours la Reine; and, if you weren't too easily shocked, you could smile at the obscene graffiti which seemed to cover every wall.

It was easy to find your way. Uniquely, all the streets had names and the names were engraved on every corner house; even better, all the houses were numbered; and further, you could actually buy a map of the city. You might not want to walk, in which case you could either rent a cabriolet, a light, two-wheeled carriage, for ten livres[1] ($30) a day plus fodder for the horse (but including the stable fee) or you could take a cab for one livre ten sous ($4.50) an hour, although these were often dirty as well as dangerous. On the other hand, all the cabs were numbered (an innovation unique in Europe) and there was a central lost and found office where you might, and often did, recover your lost property. If you wanted looking after, you could for forty sous a day ($6.00) rent a servant who would dress you, do your hair, look after your clothes and bring you your food. Of course, you might hire the wrong servant and be robbed; but then you went to the Bureau de Sûreté and complained: in almost no time, it seemed, the police, helped by an extensive network of informers, would come up with your stolen treasures.

Society met in private houses, but Paris was also a city of public gatherings. There were some four hundred and fifty cafés where you could sit, read the newspaper and discuss current events; perfect strangers might join the discussion and you could spend hours in happy (or sometimes boring) debate. Then there were the promenades where you could watch women, and men, wearing the very latest fashion, while prostitutes, standing on chairs, lifted their skirts high and displayed their most secret charms. There

[1] It is almost impossible to establish a true equivalence between the livre and the dollar; money has very different values in pre-industrial and post-industrial societies. Still, a livre was probably roughly equivalent to about $3.00.

were the new galleries of the Palais-Royal, built around the garden of the duc d'Orléans's town palace. There, protected from the weather, you would find smart shops, good restaurants, many cafés and, again, an assortment of whores tugging at every man's arm.

The very idea of the restaurant was a new one, and it hadn't quite caught on yet. There were many old-fashioned taverns where the gluttony of the habitués was often so great there would be almost nothing left in the dish when it reached the stranger. You could also go to the fowl market, near the Pont Neuf; there, a huge vat full of capons was always on the boil. You would buy one of these fowls and go wash it down with a glass of wine at a nearby café. If you were broke, you could go to any number of little inns where, for ten sous ($1.50) you would be given roast veal, roast mutton, beef stew, lentils with fatback and a salad, all quite palatable. If, on the other hand, you were well to do but liked your privacy, you could buy a complete hot meal from a pastry cook and have it brought to your house or hotel by a servant. Paris had many renowned pastry cooks and their food could compete with that of the best houses. There were a few restaurants where the décor, the food, the service were of high quality, but not many Parisians went to them; they started to flourish only when the Revolution, by closing down so many houses, put the great chefs out of work.

If you had spent enough time in a café, eaten a good meal and were anxious for something to do, the possibilities were endless. If you liked animals and rare exotic plants, you could go to the Jardin du Roi; if the weather was warm, you could go to a bathing house on the Seine; if you liked art, you could (already) go to the Louvre where, although it was not yet a museum, most of the King's collections were kept, so that you would see paintings, sculpture, rare books, coins, medals, engravings and objets de vertu. If you liked furniture, you could go to the Garde-Meuble, on the Place Louis XV, where the King stored quantities of excess furniture; and, while you were at it, you might take a look at the Queen's dresses, a number of which were always on public display. Then, if you liked to see grand houses, you could visit just about any you cared to see. The great nobles, and even the members of the royal family, felt an obligation to the public. Any well-dressed person could ask the concierge for a guided tour. The private apartments were only shown if their owner was away, but the rest of the house was always accessible.

Finally, of course, there was the theater. First and foremost came the opera, housed in a brand-new oval hall, much admired by all travelers. In the seventies and eighties its repertoire was in the midst of a great change. Lulli and Rameau were giving way to Gluck, Piccinni and a number of young French composers. The Queen backed Gluck because he was Austrian and she enjoyed his French-style operas; people who didn't like the Queen backed Piccinni's Italian style just to annoy her. The audience was always glamorous, the boxes filled with courtiers dressed in silk, brocade or velvet, glittering with diamonds, dripping with costly lace. On the stage the greatest, most famous singers and dancers would perform along with a large, mostly feminine corps de ballet—convention demanded that every opera have at least two ballet interludes. People chatted and visited one another, listening only to the arias. It would never have occurred to anyone that he ought to sit still for a whole evening!

The Comédie Française was the other great theater. Founded by Molière a century earlier, the company kept its early repertory alive: the plays of Racine, Corneille, Molière were still constantly performed, as were those of newer dramatists like Marivaux and Voltaire, even, finally, Beaumarchais. The Comédie Française could make or break a playwright's reputation and was the scene of Voltaire's quasi deification when he came back to Paris in 1777. Mademoiselle Clairon, the greatest actress of her time, crowned a bust of the author, placed center stage, with a garland of roses while the old man, sobbing and blowing kisses from his box, listened to an interminable ovation. The actors despised naturalness. They strutted, declaimed and exaggerated every emotion. They wore powdered hair and hoops for plays set in ancient Rome or contemporary Turkey and refused to change, but remained popular nonetheless.

There were a few other theaters of lesser importance. The Comédie Italienne, once the repository of the commedia dell'arte, was giving up Pierrot, Harlequin and Columbine for a new, modern repertory. The Théâtre de Nicollet was for the dance only; at the Ambigu-Comique child actors performed in pantomimes and fairy tales; the Théâtre des Variétés Amusantes put on new, light, amusing plays. And at the very bottom of the scale, open theatricals of a licentious character were offered on platforms scattered along the boulevards.

There were other, grimmer spectacles: the capital executions on the Place de Grève. They were well attended, not just by the poor but by men and women of rank who stood on open balconies and stared at the hangings, floggings and mutilations. Casanova, during his stay in Paris, joined a group of courtiers who went to watch the execution of Damiens[2]; noticing the emotion of the lady standing before him as the would-be assassin's hand was urned off, he proceeded to lift her skirt and spice the pleasures of sex with those of seeing a man disemboweled, drawn and quartered. The lady, it appears, was thoroughly satisfied. That took place in 1757; but in the seventies and eighties the Marquis de Sade was conducting his experiments and writing books which achieved an early, if limited, popularity.

Yet this taste for blood and torture was not reflected elsewhere in the life of the city. Paris was an eminently safe place in which to live; you could walk anywhere, at any time. Robberies were few, and the culprits usually apprehended within a few hours. Prostitutes were watched and controlled—

[2] He made an unsuccessful attempt on Louis XV's life.

in fact they often served as police spies. As a result, the French archives abound in precise and sometimes comical descriptions of the sexual habits of a variety of famous men, including the old Maréchal de Richelieu, still going strong in his eighties, and various members of the royal family. Commerce was watched just as sternly, with the police keeping an eye on the price and quality of the various goods for sale. It seemed as if the watchful eye of Monsieur Lenoir, the Lieutenant de Police, was everywhere, but there was no feeling that you were living in a police state. Although arbitrary arrests were legal, they no longer took place. When the Bastille, that infamous fortress-prison, was stormed in 1789, it contained a half dozen prisoners too senile to be let out to wander on their own.

In one respect, however, the failure of the police was spectacular: forbidden books and pamphlets circulated freely and constantly. All printed matter had to be approved by a board of censors. The two news sheets, the *Journal de Paris,* which related day-to-day stories of life in the capital, and the *Mercure de France,* limited to literary matters, were both strictly controlled, as were all books and plays. Even the *Almanach Royal,* in which everyone, from the Princes of the Blood to the lowliest apothecary, was listed, along with his exact rank, address and hours of reception, bore the censor's stamp. But anything could be printed in Amsterdam, for instance, and smuggled over the border; as usual, forbidden books were in great demand, so great, in fact, that the King himself owned many a volume that he had officially banned.

But what if you had seen all the plays, read all the books, were neither hungry nor thirsty, what if you were bored? Then you could just look out your window.

At seven in the morning the gardeners drove their carts away.

At nine you saw the barbers, hairdressers, coachmen and café waiters running about.

At twelve lawyers and notaries appeared on their way to the Palace of Justice.

At two carriages rumbled through the streets, taking people to dinner.

At five-thirty there was a deafening noise as everyone rushed to the theater.

At nightfall the workingmen made their way back to the faubourgs where they lived.

At nine people were coming out of the theaters and driving here and there. The prostitutes came out.

After midnight there was the noise of carriages going home.

At one you heard the farmers bring their produce to market.

At two the turgotines, those new, narrow, fast stagecoaches named after Turgot, the Controller General of Finances, rushed through the streets on their way out of the city.

At six the bakers came in from Gonesse, bringing in their bread, and as the day started again the street vendors came out, joined now by a new-comer, the lottery salesman, whose tickets were avidly sought for; this new game, imported from Italy, was immediately popular and immediately profitable for the government.

All was well so long as you were healthy. When you fell ill, if you were rich your doctor would attend you every day, your apothecary would concoct his finest preparations, your surgeon would come by every day to bleed you and, if you were strong enough, you actually survived; if not, you at least had the comfort of dying at home. But for the poor illness was a real disaster. The only hospitals were those run by the Church; they were places of filth and degradation, with stinking wards, unwashed, tattered linen, several patients to a bed and virtually no medical care. The Hôtel-Dieu, the principal hospi-tal, remained exactly as it had been in the Middle Ages and people tried as best they could to avoid being taken to it. It was not by accident that Marat, who started his surgical career there, became a fervid revolutionary. The only exception to this was the splendid Hôtel des Invalides, built by Louis XIV for the injured veterans of his wars. Here old soldiers received lodging, food, treatment, and respect as well.

The poor, healthy or ill, led miserable lives, in Paris and everywhere else; the rich could buy themselves more luxuries, more refinements than any-where else; but the person of moderate fortune who insisted on living in the capital was doomed. Not only was everything much more expensive than in the provinces, but much more was expected of you.

It started with a carriage. "Walking, which in London is so pleasant and clean that ladies do it every day, is here a toil and a fatigue to a man and an impossibility to a well-dressed lady," wrote an English visitor, who added, "Paris is an ineligible residence for persons who cannot afford to keep a coach, a convenience which is as dear as at London" (where it was no-toriously ruinous). Then there was the problem of dress. An embroidered silk or velvet suit cost from $2,000 to $3,000—an expense not everyone could afford, especially when you added lace for collar and cuffs, silk stockings, ex-pensive and fragile shoes adorned with gold buckles. What could one do? Why, dress in black and pretend one was in mourning for some recently de-ceased European monarch. Needless to say, the excuse wore thin and the black suit came to represent a visible and humiliating social distinction.

And then food was so costly. Fish was impossibly high because so much of it was bought by convents; fowl was reasonable only when the court was away from Versailles—some two months a year. When finally you had to give a dinner party or lose face, the many dishes brought in from the pastry cook's cost a small fortune; if, on the other hand, you were lucky enough to be a single man, and knew a few people, you could (and many people did) dine out every day, without special invitation; but then you had to amuse your host and hostess, not always an easy task. Even salt, as heavily taxed as gasoline is today, and perhaps even more indispensable, cost over sixty livres

($180) for a little over a pound. Water itself was sold by twenty thousand water carriers; there was no running water. It seemed as if, everywhere you turned, everything cost more than you could afford.

Still, Paris was a well-run city. The new corps of firemen had recently put a stop to the fires which once ravaged whole streets. There was a special tax to support the very poor. Depending on your income, it was thirteen, twenty-six or fifty sous a year ($1.95, $3.90, $6.50), and it was paid by everyone.

Then, each trade was organized in a guild which, beside monitoring quality and price, helped members when they were sick or too old to work; the guilds also took in young men so as to teach them the trade. As a result, there was no unemployment at all.

Nothing could have been stricter than the guilds' regulations. They accounted for a multitude of small workshops turning out an amazing variety of products and selling directly to the clients. The multipurpose store was firmly banned. The size of each workshop, the number of its employees, the methods to be followed, all were strictly fixed. Milliners could make a robe or a skirt, never a whole dress: that was up to the tailors, who in turn were forbidden to make buttons of the same material they were cutting. Workers must live where they worked; families, toiling for centuries at the same task, displayed a high degree of cohesion. When like married like, as was nearly always the case, everybody contributed to the wedding. And since each trade had its own neighborhood, no cousin ever wandered farther than a few houses away. The result was an extremely cohesive urban fabric, largely free of slums, where all classes lived together in the same areas and neighborhoods changed very, very slowly. Just as much as the palaces and great town houses, these well-organized, strictly localized, infinitely numerous stores gave Paris its physiognomy, one which lasted well beyond the abolition of both the guilds and their regulations in 1790, one which, indeed, survives to this very day.

This very stable framework gave way altogether several times a year when great fairs were held in and around the city: the Foire Saint-Germain in the Rue de Tournon in February, the Foire Saint-Laurent in July, the Foire de Saint-Cloud in August, among others, where everything was sold, gypsies told fortunes and traveling comedians entertained the crowds. All the city met at these fairs, as it did in September to watch the King review his troops on the Plaine des Sablons, or to dance at the public balls given on great occasions: the birth of the Dauphin in 1781 or the Peace of Paris in 1783, for instance. And, more modestly but more frequently, workers and small shopkeepers could board a barge that went down the Seine to Saint-Cloud, there to wander in the palace park and eat fried fish in little restaurants. Or they could indulge in another Sunday excursion that led them to the country just outside the new walls where they sat under the trees, heard the birds and fancied themselves in some faraway land. All these trips, planned and anticipated for many weeks, were probably enjoyed far more intensely than our modern continent hopping.

All these people made the city what it was, but they were soon forgotten by visitors and Parisians alike, whose eyes were caught by the glitter and dash of the fashionable life, the smart shops, the gilded carriages and the elegant new town houses.

Then there was the wit of Paris, which seemed to belong to the city quite as much as its monuments. Foreigners came, listened, and went away dazzled. "[At supper] there were some ingenious men present with a mixture of agreeable women who remained to the last and joined in the conversation even when it turned on subjects of literature . . . those who understood anything on the subject delivered their sentiment with great precision and more grace than the men; those who knew nothing of the subject rallied their own ignorance in such a sprightly manner as convinced everybody that knowledge is not necessary to render a woman exceedingly agreeable in society," an English traveler wrote—and he is one of a thousand witnesses. There were great and influential salons (see Chapter Ten) to which relatively few people had access; but this pleasant wit, this art of cheerful yet intelligent conversation, was everywhere, every day, typically Parisian and universally famous.

Yet something was missing: Paris was a capital without a court. Louis XIV had removed the monarchy to Versailles a hundred years earlier, and since then the King had traveled only to other country châteaux, Marly, Fontainebleau, Compiègne. The Louvre had become a public building, housing the royal collections, artists and favored officials. Catherine de Médicis' old palace of the Tuileries, where Marie Antoinette sometimes stayed rather than drive back to Versailles at dawn, was almost completely given over to grace-and-favor lodgings for impoverished courtiers. But now the great hive at Versailles began to come over to Paris. The court was, if anything, more splendid, more hieratic than in the time of Louis XIV; the aristocracy still flocked to it; but courtiers with rooms in the palace and houses in the town remembered they also owned houses in Paris, and they spent half their time there, attracted, just like other foreigners, by its fashion, its bustle and its wit. And as they came back they brought with them both the manners and the luxury of the court.

The King and Queen ignored it all at their very great cost. The Revolution was born in Paris, fed by its intellectuals and its lawyers, nurtured until it had grown strong enough to lead the entire nation. On October 3 and 4, 1789, the city marched to Versailles and came back with court and government, its supremacy finally established. For almost a century after that, Paris, frivolous and powerful, reigned unchallenged, making and unmaking fashions and governments as it ruled France and sometimes the world.

Chapter Two

THE COURT:
ANOTHER COUNTRY

There was much to be reformed, in May of 1789. From all over the country deputies came to the Estates-General, intent on reducing the deficit, pruning the budget and throwing out the Queen's favorites. They carried long lists of grievances with them to this the first meeting of the three orders of the realm since 1614: it was a great moment. Still, most of the provincial deputies suffered an overriding anxiety: before the sessions began, they must first see the fabled palace of Versailles and most especially the room built for the spendthrift Marie Antoinette in Trianon—the one with a décor of diamonds heightened by serpentine columns of sapphires and rubies. When they couldn't find it, they insisted they were being tricked; it was there somewhere, everybody knew it. This demand puzzled the court, since of course there was no such room, until Louis XVI finally remembered having seen a theater set made of paste diamonds, sometime in the late sixties, in the reign of his grandfather Louis XV.

Those deputies weren't so entirely mistaken, though: ever since Louis XIV had built his great palace a hundred years before, Versailles and its inhabitants had been a show of unequaled splendor, a parade of gold and brocade and precious stones, a gathering of the highborn around a resplendent monarch, with its own laws, its own language, its own customs. There was really no telling what might be going on there: it was another country.

Its denizens knew it, too: *ce pays-ci* (this country), they called it, and it was a place where different rules prevailed. Ministers rose and fell at the whim of the King—or his mistress, or his wife. Competence generally had little to do with it. Precedence meant everything. When Louis XV gave a ball to celebrate the wedding of his grandson with the Austrian Archduchess Marie Antoinette in 1770, he allowed the Princesses of Lorraine, who were cousins of the bride, to dance before the duchesses. First there was a horrified gasp; then the dukes got together and produced a letter to the King. Rather than allow themselves to be so degraded, they wrote, they would be forced to stay away. It was a tense situation. Finally, after much worry, a compromise was reached: the Princesses of Lorraine did dance first, but on that occasion only.

The court was highly exclusive. Only people whose families had been noble before 1400, and those whose forebears had been ministers, ambassadors or marshals of France could be presented to the King. It was also highly greedy: all this splendor cost a lot of money.

Attendance on the King was compulsory and constant, either because of a court position (and there were many) or simply because His Majesty was the source of all good things, especially advancement: military, if you served in the army during the wars, or political, if you hoped to become part of the Council of State. Most important, there was no hope for a lavish yearly pension from the Royal Treasury unless the King liked you—and the King only liked the people who were constantly near him. It was unthinkable not to be at court, if you were noble, but court life was hideously expensive.

We have lost all notion of what really luxurious clothes were like. Then, they were made of silk, satin, brocade, velvet, lace and fur, all heavily embroidered in gold (*real* gold) and silver. A court dress or suit could cost more than ten thousand livres. Then there were servants, and carriages, and a house in Versailles, since apartments in the palace were cramped. On top of that, no one had the time or the inclination to visit his country estates, which provided the income for all this expenditure. Often, less money came in than had been expected. There was no help for it but to seek the King's preferment; and so the palace was always filled with a dazzling crowd.

The King and court traveled to other palaces, but they lived in Versailles. That great majestic pile had been built by Louis XIV for a number of reasons: he wanted to get away from rebellious Paris; he liked the country and the hunt; but most of all the huge, sumptuous palace was to reflect the power of the Sun King and provide a suitable framework for unceasing display. It also neatly solved a severe political problem. The French aristocracy, if left to itself, had an unpleasant habit of starting civil wars. The best way to keep them quiet, as Louis XIV had discovered, was to provide a court setting so splendid and so entertaining that all would want to attend, and so expensive that none could do so without his financial help; then he created endless functions about his person which he invested with a high degree of glamor, so that dukes would scheme and plot for years in order to become First Gentleman of the Bedchamber or Captain of the Guard. And since he apparently felt no need for privacy at all, he made ceremonies of his every gesture: he rose and went to bed in public, he ate, walked, danced and hunted in front of admiring crowds.

The palace itself was the wonder of Europe. Its Hall of Mirrors, its gilded and painted walls and ceilings, its windows, wide open to the perspective of the great park, all are still there, but only as ghosts of their former splendor. In 1770, when Marie Antoinette first walked on its parqueted and inlaid floors, it was lavishly furnished, not just with chairs and tables and chests and objects of the most exquisite craftsmanship but with hangings made of brocade and cut velvet, silver and crystal chandeliers and, perhaps most important of all, a crowd just as spectacular as its setting.

All around the palace was a huge formal park, with geometrically drawn alleys and flower parterres bordered by huge trees and enriched with sculpture and water, which flowed from bronze and marble into round basins, down cascades, and in a mile-long canal; at the end of the park, miles from the palace, was a forest in which the King hunted. Far away, toward one end of the park, Louis XV had built a relatively small, dignified but simple house, the Petit Trianon. It was Louis XVI's first act as a new monarch to give it to the Queen. Quickly, an English garden took shape, with hills and streams, a grotto and a temple of Love, through which Marie Antoinette could wander freely, away from court formality. It was enclosed with walls and, when the Queen was there, open only to her guests and servants, free from the constant stare of the courtiers.

It was no wonder that the Queen felt the need for privacy. When she came to the throne in 1774, etiquette was still just the way Louis XIV had first created it: all-encompassing from morning to night. "When I write the word etiquette," Madame Campan[1] commented, "I do not mean that majestic order obtaining at every court on days of ceremony: I mean those minutely detailed rules which pursued our kings into their most secret retreats, through their hours of suffering or pleasure, and surrounded their most repulsive infirmities." The courtiers held court offices which carried "rights" with them—to give the King his shirt or the Queen her fan; to be present first thing in the morning or last thing at night; to order the royal meals or serve them; to organize balls and to dance at them. These offices were legion; yet their owners (for that is how they thought of themselves) viewed every detail of their useless functions as a distinction. Any attempt to simplify these in the slightest met with stony and loud indignation. All this, of course, was enormously expensive since the noble domestics were paid huge salaries and given endless perquisites of office as well. In 1787, finally, when the state was in dire financial straits, a few of the more useless of these offices were abolished, prompting one of the Queen's courtiers to tell her, with heartfelt anger: "How very dreadful to live in a country where you can have no certainty of still owning tomorrow what you had yesterday. It is quite as bad as in Turkey!"

[1] She was a Woman of the Bedchamber to the Queen.

1. *Moreau le Jeune, The Royal Banquet. The city of Paris is feasting the King and Queen to celebrate the birth of a crown prince. Crowds pressing around the luxuriously decorated table include both courtiers and berobed members of the Parlement. The room has been completely redecorated in the current antique style. Louis XVI and Marie Antoinette sit with their backs to us at the head of the table; even here they are attended by the First Gentleman of the Bedchamber and the dame d'honneur.*

This kind of proprietary spirit made for endless quarrels. Even after a century there were still uncertain zones. Was the First Gentleman of the Bedchamber or the *intendant des menus plaisirs*[2] to order the fireworks? The resulting row was fearful. Then there was the delicate question of *survivances* or reversions. The Queen incurred the lasting enmity of the powerful Noailles family when she announced she was appointing the duc de Polignac to be the *survivancier* of her First Equerry, the comte de Tessé. Of course, the comte de Tessé first had to die before anyone could succeed him —and he was in his forties. Still, the Noailles had understood the *survivance* was to go to one of them and they neither forgot nor forgave. It was no wonder, they said, when this was actually the *second* affront they had had to bear. A few years earlier the Queen had chosen to revive the extinct office of *Surintendante de la Maison de la Reine*[3] in order to confer it on her dear friend, the princesse de Lamballe (along with a salary of two hundred thousand livres a year). Unfortunately, the highest-ranking lady in the Queen's Household until then had been her *dame d'honneur*, the comtesse de Noailles. In her rage at finding herself suddenly outranked and outpreceded, that lady promptly resigned, much to Marie Antoinette's relief. Having thus removed herself, the comtesse resorted to that last resource of the disappointed courtier, the nasty pamphlet. She financed not one but many, blithely unaware that, in attacking the Queen, she was contributing to the downfall of the social structure on which her own wealth and privileges depended.

Marie Antoinette hated all this. There had been nothing like it in her native Austria, where Their Apostolic Imperial Majesties led quite simple lives on non-ceremonial days. Almost without exception, all her courtiers, even those who were completely devoted to her, thought the Revolution was brought on in good part by her taste for simplicity, because it helped to destroy the awe with which a monarch should be regarded. Who, then, was this dangerous anarchist?

Marie Antoinette, Archduchess of Austria and Dauphine of France, was barely fifteen when she came to her adopted country. She knew some French, some Italian, how to play the harp, how to dance, and not much else. Like many children, she saw the world as sharply divided between good and evil: her mother, the great Maria Theresa, was good, along with everything Austrian; so were her grandfather-in-law Louis XV, his daughters, the ex-Prime Minister, the duc de Choiseul, who had brought about the Franco-Austrian alliance, any friends she happened to make and all who agreed with her. The King's mistress, Madame du Barry, her coterie, the new ministers (who had replaced Choiseul) and people who bored or bothered

[2] Literally, the Supervisor of Minor Pleasures; in fact, the man in charge of court festivities.

[3] Superintendent of the Queen's Household.

her were evil. This simplified way of looking at life never changed much; only the Revolution taught the Queen how to hide some of her feelings, and imperfectly at that.

None of this would have mattered very much if the archduchess had married some German princeling with a large *Schloss* and a tiny court; at Versailles it proved disastrous. Between her arrival in 1770 and the onset of the Revolution in 1789, Marie Antoinette, first as Dauphine, then as Queen, managed to alienate just about everyone outside of her immediate circle. She opposed reform and spent hugely, yet her hatred of etiquette turned most of the court—people who shared her political views—against her. In person, she was kind and considerate, had a genuinely charitable streak and felt real pity at the distress of the poor, whom she often tried to help. She wanted to be loved, and cried bitterly when she was received with hostility on a visit to Paris; but that didn't make her change her behavior in any way or stop her from supporting reactionary policies simply because they would stop financial reforms.

The Queen had enormous charm—all her visitors went away singing her praises, and even Horace Walpole, that cold fish, wrote that seeing her dance was so magical that if she failed to keep time it was the music's fault, not hers. As late as 1793 her jailers, the toughest revolutionaries, fell for her and tried to help her escape. This overwhelming charm, somewhat akin to that of Mary Queen of Scots, has continued to fascinate just about every historian who has written about her. But she remains known, universally and wrongly (the anecdote is purely apocryphal), for having said "Let them eat cake," and was loathed by millions of her contemporaries—courtiers, because she simplified etiquette and deprived them of their "rights" and because she had favorites who became all-powerful to the exclusion of everyone else; and the French people, because she was seen (rightly) as supporting Austrian policies to the detriment of her adopted country, because the King was a mere puppet in her hands, because she spent so much money, because she was so haughty.

Here we come to another contradiction. To all the people she knew and liked, Marie Antoinette could be kindness and consideration personified. Madame Vigée-Lebrun, who painted many portraits of the Queen, once missed an appointment and kept her subject waiting an entire afternoon. When she appeared the next day, expecting the worst, and explained that she had been sick because of her pregnancy, the Queen canceled all her appointments and posed for her, so that she might not have come to Versailles in vain. More extraordinary, when Madame Vigée-Lebrun spilled her paints, the Queen, whose handkerchief was handed to her on a gold plate by a curtsying lady, promptly bent down and picked them all up, telling the painter she knew what it was like to be pregnant. Of course, she also won her lifelong devotion. Yet on another occasion, Madame Vigée-Lebrun tells us, "I made so bold as to tell the Queen how greatly the way she carried her head added to the majesty of her demeanor. She answered in an ironical tone, 'If I were not Queen, people would say I look insolent, wouldn't they?'" People said it anyway, and with increasing hatred.

Marie Antoinette was fairly tall, well built and somewhat buxom. "Her arms were superb, her hands small, perfectly shaped, and her feet charming. Of all women, she was the one who best knew how to walk, carrying her head high, with a majesty which made her instantly recognizable in the midst of a large court. . . . She had two kinds of walk, one firm and a little hurried, the other softer and more sinuous, I might say almost caressing, but without causing one to forget the respect which was her due. . . . Her features were irregular. She had inherited from her family a long, oval face. . . . Her eyes were not large, their color was almost blue; her glance was both witty and kind, her nose fine and pretty, her mouth just big enough, although her lips were a little too thick. But the most remarkable thing about her face was her dazzling complexion; I never saw a better one. . . . Her skin was so transparent it reflected no shadows. . . . No one ever curtsied more gracefully, acknowledging ten people with a single bow and, with a glance or a slight movement of the head, giving every person his due. . . . In a word, just as one brings other women a chair, one would have liked to bring her a throne."

This charming, attractive woman was also a leader of fashion. She spent hours every day deciding on dresses and coiffures and was the first to wear the tallest plume and the largest hoop. Her clothes were, in truth, as dazzling as they were numerous. Every morning her *dame d'atours* (Mistress of the Robes) brought her a thick book in which were pinned samples of every dress, along with its description, so she could choose a morning dress, a court dress and whatever else she would wear that day. Her interest in fashion soon appeared excessive; the truth was that she cared about very little else: she had not a single intellectual interest and was never known to open a book. She liked acting, and did so, privately, in a theater built expressly for her in Trianon. She liked dancing, she liked gossip, she liked being among that small circle of friends with whom alone she felt she could be herself.

This need for close friends created a double problem: in France the King could have official mistresses (indeed, he was expected to) but the Queen was not supposed to have favorites. When those favorites ruled the Queen, who in turn ruled the King, a doubly dangerous situation arose. First, the Queen was blamed for whatever went wrong in government; second, the unscrupulous favorite might, and did, demand an endless stream of favors which proved costly in both money and political mistakes.

The Queen's first friend was the princesse de Lamballe, an enchanting, sweet, sentimental and excessively stupid young woman of very high birth (she was a relative of the King of Sardinia) whose husband had just died of syphilis. Since she was also very rich indeed, she really didn't ask for much. The Queen made her Superintendent of the Household, as we have seen, and that was that. Luckily, she did not have any politics: they were alto-gether beyond her intellectual reach. Soon, however, Marie Antoinette met another charming young woman, the comtesse Jules de Polignac. She had every quality, it seems, looks, intelligence, sensitivity, and a complete lack of greed. She refused several official positions the Queen offered her. "No," she said, "I just want to be your friend, all I need is Your Majesty's affection." It was all true; the Queen was thrilled. Soon she was ending every evening in the countess' salon, right near her own apartments in the palace.

The trouble was that the countess had a family—and they weren't quite so disinterested. Madame de Polignac went on saying she wanted nothing for herself; but her poor husband was created a duke, then appointed an officer of the household (that tricky *survivance*) at a salary of eighty thou-sand livres plus perks, and her lover was given a pension; then her sister and sister-in-law both received official positions near the King's sister and sister-in-law (at handsome salaries); and a marriage was arranged between the new duchesse's fifteen-year-old daughter and the son of the duc de Gramont, who was created duc de Guiche for the occasion, with the King supplying the unheard-of dowry of eight hundred thousand livres. Then, in 1783, the *Gouvernante des Enfants de France*,[4] the princesse de Guéménée, had to re-sign her post because of her husband's sudden, scandalous bankruptcy—to everyone's amazement, he had managed to accumulate debts totaling thirty million livres. No one would do to replace her but the duchesse Jules, who after many tearful refusals finally felt compelled to accept ("I want my best friend to raise my children," the Queen said firmly) and, at one blow, gained precedence over all the other duchesses as well as a large salary.

There was still worse. The duchesse's entourage had political ambitions and soon her protégés came into positions of power. Just how this was done we shall see a little later; but the net result was the appointment of a new set of ministers headed by a new Controller General of Finance, in effect, a Prime Minister: Monsieur de Calonne, whose one idea was as simple as it was disastrous. Since the Treasury was already running a large yearly deficit, it had to borrow. It would obviously be easy to borrow if it seemed that the King really didn't need the money. He therefore proceeded to spend at an unprecedented rate. The consequence, in short order, was the complete ruin of the Treasury, which made it necessary to call the Estates-General. Calonne thus became one of the three or four people most directly responsible for the coming Revolution; and his depredations were held not just against the Polignac coterie but against the Queen herself, who was promptly nick-named *Madame Déficit*.

Curiously enough, this little group, whose every wish the Queen granted, still didn't like her much. Here is what one of its charter members, the baron de Besenval, wrote about the woman to whom he owed everything: "A great taste for pleasure, much coquetry and frivolity, a scarcity of natural gaiety

4 Governess of the Children of France, i.e., the royal children.

prevented her from being as popular in society [i.e., the Polignac set] as her inner qualities and her appearance would have led one to expect. She never quite knew what she thought. Her familiar manner detracted from the respect due her; and the attitude which advice and circumstances often forced on her seemed shocking in an amiable woman: for that is how one is all too used to think of her. Because of this, there wasn't one person but was sometimes annoyed, and one often spoke ill of her while being surprised to find oneself doing it." The Queen, it seems, was not very good at choosing her friends.

None of this would have mattered quite so much if she had not been so powerful, but it was well known she had absolute control over the King. The reasons for this were equally plain.

Louis XVI was certainly a good, even virtuous monarch; his intentions were the very best. He cared about the people and wanted to improve their lot. Unfortunately he was weakness itself, and spent his life doing what he was told—first by his father, who died in 1765, then by his grandfather, the King, then by his chief minister, the aged and cynical comte de Maurepas, and finally by his wife. This was an accepted and public fact of life, and it is reflected in the following anecdote, told us by Tilly.

"The Duke of Manchester, then a young man, was travelling in France. He was having dinner with M. de Maurepas, and sitting next to him. 'M. le comte,' he asked, 'who is this gentleman (it was M. de Pezay), in a pale green suit, pink vest and borders, and silver embroidery sitting over there across the table?'

" 'He is the King, my Lord.'

" 'What?'

" 'I tell you, Monsieur, he is the King.'

"The conversation stopped there. After dinner:

" 'M. le comte,' the Duke said, 'how did I deserve the mockery with which you answered my question about this gentleman who looks so self-satisfied, so thoughtful, and to whom, in your very salon, everyone is paying court?'

" 'My Lord, I never mock. This is no gentleman, I tell you, but the King. I see you want proof: I will give it to you. He sleeps with a cousin of mine, Mme. de Montbarey, who rules Mme. de Maurepas, who does anything she likes with me; I rule the King, so now you see that it is this gentleman who reigns.'"

It is clear from this story that Madame de Maurepas ruled her husband just as the Queen was shortly to rule the King; the reason in both cases was the same: the two men were equally impotent. The consequences, of course, were vastly different. Madame de Maurepas had lovers, and that was that; but a king without direct heirs is in a very unpleasant position.

First, Marie Antoinette was mortified, all the more since her mother kept writing and urging her to encourage the King. She tried but got nowhere.

We know exactly what was happening in the royal bed thanks to a visit the Emperor Joseph II, the Queen's brother, paid to Versailles in 1777, and to a letter he then wrote another brother, Leopold, Grand Duke of Tuscany. Louis XVI suffered from phimosis. In spite of repeated instruction in the form of obscene prints and paintings (the long corridor leading to the nuptial chamber was lined with them), he also conceived of sexual intercourse as an activity requiring no movement after conjunction; so, patiently, he would wait for a minute or two and withdraw. It must have been a highly frustrating way of making love for a normal young woman; in short order, Marie Antoinette was coming in so late at night that Louis XVI, who liked his sleep, moved out of her bedroom; and she compensated for her lack of satisfaction by a frenzied search for other pleasures. The problem was finally solved by a simple surgical intervention, akin to circumcision, which the King finally endured at the Emperor's urging.

Unfortunately, gambling was the chief pleasure of the Queen. A new card game, called pharaon, and probably not unlike chemin de fer, had just come into fashion. Its main attraction was that it was possible to win—or lose— huge sums in a very short time. The duc de Chartres, for instance, once came away from a night's play the poorer by 800,000 livres; and even the Queen managed to accumulate debts of 487,272 livres (about $1,500,000) for the year 1777. The King paid up, of course, but it did not make either of them more popular.

The Queen's insatiable thirst for pleasure also led to other incidents which were immediately publicized and helped establish the image of an irresponsible Queen controlling an idiot King. There was the time when Marie Antoinette convinced her husband to allow pharaon to be played at court for just one evening after it had been formally made illegal. The evening turned into thirty-six hours and the Queen went around saying, laughingly, well, he hadn't said how long an evening. Another time, anxious to be rid of the King's repressive presence, she pushed the clock forward an hour. The King left when he thought it was eleven but reached his apartments to find them empty of his usual attendants. Then, too, it didn't help when the Queen made a habit of referring to her husband as "the poor man." Soon a handbill was going the rounds, citing this and adding, "The Queen says so without thinking, we all think so without saying."

Curiously enough, when at last the King was able to consummate his marriage, and then became a father, the Queen's influence on him became even greater—possibly because Maurepas, the chief minister, had finally died of old age. Right up until 1789 the King, supposedly an absolute monarch, was seen by all as his wife's plaything: it did not help the cause of monarchy.

Even Louis XVI's appearance worked against him. He was extremely shortsighted and thought it beneath his dignity to wear glasses. As a result, he walked around in a permanent haze. All the contemporary descriptions agree: "Louis XVI had rather noble features, but with a melancholy cast; his walk was heavy and awkward; his personal appearance always messy; his hair, no matter how talented his coiffeur, was always disordered because of the little care he took of himself; his voice, while not really harsh, was not pleasant, either; and if he became excited, it went from medium to high, shrill tones." "He was a fat man, five foot six to seven inches tall, and looked like a peasant trotting after his plow; there was nothing regal about him. He kept catching his legs on his sword and didn't know what to do with his hat. His clothes were always rich and adorned, not that he cared much, for he wore whatever he was given." "The King was unfortunately much too fond of the mechanical arts. He liked carpentry and lockmaking to such a degree that he allowed a locksmith into his private rooms, and, together, they made locks and keys. His hands, blackened by this work, were several times . . . the subject . . . of rather strong remonstrances from the Queen."

With all this, Louis XVI was quite cultivated. He understood nothing of the arts or literature but was a competent historian and geographer. He also spoke English quite fluently, at a time when this was a rarity indeed. In another, more peaceful era (though one wonders if any era is really peaceful) he might have made an adequate monarch, though his appearance alone would have debarred him from being highly respected. Unfortunately his sense of humor was completely undignified: his favorite jokes consisted in tickling an old valet until he fell to the floor, raising people up in the air (he was extremely strong) or bombarding his attendants, the noblest people in the kingdom, with little pellets he made by rolling together the dirt on his feet: obviously, unlike the Queen and most of his subjects, he had no great taste for personal cleanliness.

Despite all this, the royal pair's worst shortcoming was their total unawareness of what constituted appropriate behavior. The King never minded looking the fool he really wasn't, and his lack of convincing authority was certainly one of the causes of the Revolution. As for the Queen, she sometimes seemed to be living in another world. One incident among many attests to this. All through the eighteenth century a yearly masked ball was given at the Opera. One year the Queen asked her husband for permission to go; he promptly gave it. Here was a first mistake: it was highly undignified, and suspicious—whom was she secretly meeting?—for the Queen to attend a masked ball famous for its easy pickups.

Since she would hardly have remained incognito if she had arrived in a carriage bearing the royal arms, Marie Antoinette had arranged to go to the house of a friend, the duc de Coigny, and there get into an escutcheonless old coach. All proceeded according to plan until the old coach broke down on its way to the Opera. A hansom cab came by, she got in, and, having finally arrived at the ball, she told everyone, laughing, "Me, in a hansom cab, can you imagine anything funnier!" The story spread right through Paris, becoming distorted in the process and prompting people to wonder what the Queen of France was doing, alone, at night, in a hansom cab. The answer was obvious: she had been meeting her lover. It was typical of the daily slanders gaining currency. Marie Antoinette, careless but perfectly innocent, had given all the appearances of sin. Here again, a vast reservoir of hate was filling up. It was to disgorge within a very few years.

--❧ ❧--

Life at the palace answered to a strict timetable. Every day the King's *lever* gathered the same courtiers at the same time; certain ceremonies came, every year, on the same day; and all were ruled by etiquette. The discomfort this implied is hard to believe. It was the "right" of one group of attendants to make the Queen's bed in the morning, that of another to straighten it out if she used it during the day. If Her Majesty wanted a glass of water the order had to reach some dozen people before anything happened. She was not even allowed to dress in peace. "The way the Queen was dressed," Madame Campan noted, "was a masterpiece of etiquette: everything was regulated. The *dame d'honneur*[5] and the *dame d'atours*, together if they were both there, helped by the First Woman of the Bedchamber and two Women in Ordinary, carried out the main service; but there were distinctions that separated them. The *dame d'atours* would put the petticoats on and hold out the dress. The *dame d'honneur* poured out the water to wash the Queen's hands and put on her chemise. When a princess of the immediate royal family was present, the *dame d'honneur* would leave her this function but would not hand the chemise directly to a Princess of the Blood Royal.[6] In that case, the *dame d'honneur* would give the chemise to the First Woman, who would hand it to the Princess of the Blood. Every one of the ladies would scrupulously observe these rules since they pertained to their rights. One winter day, the Queen was already fully undressed and about to put on her chemise; I was holding it ready. A scratch at the door, it opened: it was Madame la duchesse d'Orléans.[7] She took off her gloves and came forward to be given the chemise but the *dame d'honneur* could not hand it to her; she gave it back to me, I presented it back to the princess. There was another scratch: it was *Madame*, the comtesse de Provence;[8] the duchesse d'Orléans held the chemise out to her. The Queen was keeping her arms crossed on her chest and looked cold. *Madame* saw how uncomfortable she seemed and, just dropping her handkerchief, kept her gloves on, and, as she slipped on the

[5] The Queen's attendants were headed by a single *dame d'honneur* (under the *surintendante*). The *dame d'atours* was in charge of her clothes. The twelve *dames du palais* were ladies in waiting.
[6] The royal family consisted only of the King, his wife, children, grandchildren (if any), brothers and sisters. Cousins of whatever degree were merely Princes of the Blood Royal.
[7] The wife of the King's distant cousin and First Prince of the Blood.
[8] The wife of the King's next brother, whose official title was simply *Madame*.

chemise, messed up the Queen's coiffure who started to laugh so as to hide her impatience but muttered several times: 'How odious! What a nuisance!' "

It seems intolerable to us; it did to Marie Antoinette as well, but her entourage considered all this absolutely normal. "All these customs were, in fact, awkward," Madame Campan goes on to say, "but they answered to a necessity: that of showing the French everything which could command their respect, and especially that of protecting a young Queen from the mortal shafts of calumny by always surrounding her with an imposing entourage."

Marie Antoinette was severely blamed for wanting to simplify Louis XIV's etiquette. She often failed in her attempts. When that glass of water mentioned earlier finally arrived, the footman would hand the First Woman a silver-gilt plate bearing a covered gold cup and a small carafe; but if the *dame d'honneur* came in the plate must be handed to her, and if the comtesse d'Artois[9] then walked in, she must in turn take it and give it to the Queen.

All these endless rules and regulations, governing every gesture and action and defining precedence, helped to create a world apart. By the middle of the century the people at court walked differently, gliding (or shuffling) without raising the feet from the floor; bowed differently, more gracefully and with infinitely subtle degrees; spoke differently, using a separate vocabulary in a different accent so you knew, as soon as they opened their mouths, whether or not the people you were conversing with belonged to the court. They even responded to a separate reality. It really didn't matter if a war was going on or not, and still less whether it was being won or lost; whether it was a time of famine, whether trade was prospering or the reverse; or at least it mattered only inasmuch as it could be used as a lever to unseat a minister or a favorite. It was obviously better to have the army lose a major battle if that entailed your replacing the general-in-chief; better to have a dramatic diplomatic reverse if you could, at last, get rid of a Foreign Minister who belonged to an opposite coterie. Curiously, this attitude, limited in the eighteenth century to the court, became a deeply ingrained feature of French life. It found its fullest expression in the rejoicing candidly expressed by a large section of the French upper class when Nazi forces occupied the country in 1940: they considered this a neat revenge for the 1936 victory of the Popular Front.

The nobles who spent their whole lives at Versailles felt, of course, the greatest scorn for the rest of the world. Any Parisian, any provincial noble who, through unusual circumstances, found himself at court was constantly made fun of and rejected. In any case, such people tended not to last very long since they had to move on a terrain where every inch of ground was mined and those who professed to be their friends would induce them to make the most devastating mistakes.

[9] The wife of the King's youngest brother.

There were good reasons for all this: since the King was the source of all wealth and power, you had to gain, and keep, his favor. Obviously it wouldn't do to walk up to him and say: "I wish Your Majesty would make me a duke, or a minister, or a marshal of France, and give me half a million." In fact, you were likely to find yourself in the deepest disgrace, in which case even your best friends suddenly stopped remembering they had ever met you. You might even find yourself exiled—and nothing, it was generally agreed, was worse than exile; it was only a step better than being dead because at least there was always a faint hope that you might one day be recalled.

Being exiled meant that an ex-friend or an old enemy, wearing an expression of hypocritical sympathy, would hand you a *lettre de cachet* signed by the King and ordering you away from court. In mild cases, you might only be forbidden the royal palaces and you could still live in Paris; but more often you were sent to a château you owned, far away somewhere in the provinces, where you would die of boredom and lack of fashion. This was the automatic fate of every dismissed minister and was meant to spare the King's feelings by removing reproachful figures; more important, it also prevented these fallen worthies from intriguing to regain power.

It may seem strange today that people should have so dreaded what appears to most of us as a very enviable life style: we would not refuse to live in a beautiful castle surrounded by a park and large estate, with an excellent income and a vast retinue of servants. All the pleasures of life were there if you wanted them, from delicious food to the hunt, from good books and private theatricals to the pursuit of pretty country girls; yet to an eighteenth-century courtier the only life was that of the court. Away from its display and intrigues, everything just melted away into a boring, drab wasteland, to be endured but never enjoyed.

Life at court was, of course, a series of magnificent pageants—a great distraction for idle, often uneducated people. Balls and ceremonies gave courtiers a chance to display their splendid new clothes in an enchanted setting; even an ordinary Sunday provided a chance to be admired. The marquise de la Tour du Pin, an intelligent woman who wrote her memoirs well after the Revolution, and who thoroughly adapted to the changed circumstances of her life, is thus an especially trustworthy witness. As a bride of eighteen she was presented to Marie Antoinette, whose *dame du palais* she was slated to be when she reached the age of twenty-one. On the day, she tells us, "I wore a *grand corps*, that is, a specially made bodice, without epaulets, laced in the back, but so narrow that the lacing, about four inches wide at the bottom, showed a chemise of the finest batiste through which one could easily have noticed an insufficiently white skin. This chemise had sleeves that were only three inches high, without an epaulet so as to leave the shoulder bare. The top of the arm was covered with three or four rows of lace which fell to the

2. *Saint-Aubin, An Elegant Ball. The young women are dressed in the height of fashion wearing the new shorter skirts, unlike the older lady (a "dragger") coming in on*

the left. The brilliantly lit room, while decorated in the sober Louis XVI style, is still furnished with Louis XV chairs. The scene takes place in 1774.

elbow. The chest was entirely exposed. Seven or eight rows of large diamonds which the Queen had decided to lend me hid mine in part. The front
of the bodice was interlaced with rows of diamonds. I also wore a great
quantity of them on my head, set either straight or in an aigrette. . . . My
white skirt [over a very large hoop] was embroidered all over with pearls and
silver threads. . . .

"[On Sundays] the ladies went, a little before noon, into the salon which
came before the Queen's bedroom. No one sat, except for older ladies, then
greatly respected, and young ladies thought to be pregnant. There were always at least forty persons, and often a great many more. We were sometimes squeezed against one another because of our huge skirts, which took
up so much room. Usually, Madame la princesse de Lamballe, *surintendante*
of the household, arrived and immediately went into the bedroom where the
Queen was being dressed; most of the time she had arrived before Her Majesty even began. Madame la princesse de Chimay, a sister-in-law of my Aunt
d'Hénin, and Madame la comtesse d'Ossun, the one *dame d'honneur*, the
other *dame d'atours*, had also gone into the bedroom. After a few minutes an
usher would walk to the door of the bedchamber and call out in a loud
voice: 'The service!' Then the week's four *dames du palais*, those who had
come to pay court to the Queen even though it wasn't their week, which was
a well-established custom, and the younger ladies who would later be part of
the royal service, like the comtesse de Maillé, née Fitz-James, the comtesse
Mathieu de Montmorency and myself, also went in. As soon as the Queen
had greeted us individually, the door was opened and everybody was allowed
in. We would line up on the right and left of the room so as to leave the
doorway clear and the middle of the room empty. Quite often, when there
were many ladies, there would be two or three lines of us; but the first to arrive would adroitly move to the door of the gaming salon which the Queen
had to cross to go to mass. In that salon, a few, privileged men were admitted, either because they had been granted an earlier private audience or because they were introducing foreigners. . . . At twelve-forty the door would
open and the usher announce: 'The King!' The Queen, always wearing
court dress, walked towards him with a charming, welcoming and respectful
look. The King would nod to the right and left and speak to a few ladies he
knew, but never to the younger ones. He was so nearsighted that he
couldn't recognize people from three feet away. . . .

"At one fifteen we all moved off to mass. The First Gentleman of the Bedchamber of the year,[10] the Captain of the Guard of the quarter, and several
other guard and household officers went first, with the Captain of the Guard
closest to the King. Then came the King and Queen, walking side by side
and slowly enough to say a word in passing to the numerous courtiers lined
up along the Hall of Mirrors. Often, the Queen would speak to foreign la-

[10] There were four First Gentlemen, each of whom served a year in rotation, and four
Captains of the Guard, each of whom served for three months.

dies who had been privately introduced to her, to artists or men of letters. Nods and gracious smiles were distributed with discernment. Behind came the ladies according to their rank. The younger ones tried to walk on the wings of the battalion: we were four or five across, and those who were said to be in fashion, and to whom I had the honor of belonging, took great care to walk near enough the lined-up courtiers to hear the pretty things that were whispered as they passed by.

"It was a great art, knowing how to walk through these vast apartments without stepping on the long train of the lady in front. You could never raise your feet but had to glide along the parquet floor, which was always kept very shiny, until the Salon d'Hercule had been crossed. Then we would throw our trains on one side of our hooped skirts and, after having been noticed by one's footman, who was waiting with a big red velvet bag adorned with gold tassels, we would rush into the rows on the right and left of the chapel so as to be as close as possible to the balcony where the King and Queen and princes who had joined them . . . were gathered. Your footman would put your bag in front of you; you would take out your book, which you hardly used since, by the time you had arranged your train and looked through the huge bag, the mass had already reached the Gospel.

"As soon as it was over, the Queen curtsied deeply to the King and we would return still in the same order as before; only the King and Queen would then stop longer to speak to a few people. We would go back to the Queen's bedroom, and people in the know stayed in the gaming salon, waiting for the dinner which was served after the King and Queen had spent a quarter of an hour talking to the ladies who had come from Paris. As for us, with the impertinence of youth, we called them 'draggers' because they wore the skirts of their court dresses so long that one couldn't see their ankles.

"The dinner was served in the first salon where a small rectangular table with two settings had been placed. . . . The Queen sat on the King's left; ten feet in front of them, there was a circular row of stools on which sat the duchesses, princesses and Ladies of the Household who were entitled to that privilege; behind them stood all the other ladies, turned toward the King and Queen. The King ate with a hearty appetite, but the Queen did not even unfold her napkin or take off her gloves. . . . After the King had drunk, we curtsied and left. . . .

"Then we started a real race to go and pay court to the princes and princesses of the royal family, who ate their dinner much later; everyone tried to be the first to get to them. We went to Monsieur le comte d'Artois, to Madame Élisabeth,[11] to *Mesdames Tantes du Roi*, and even to the little Dauphin. . . . These visits lasted only for three or four minutes each."

Madame de la Tour du Pin belonged to a group of chic young women, but she was far too young to be involved in the constant power plays hidden

[11] Madame Élisabeth was the King's sister; *Mesdames Tantes* were his three maiden aunts; the Dauphin, then four years old, was the heir apparent.

beneath the stately course of the etiquette. At the time she describes, the court was bitterly split among several factions. First there was the powerful Polignac coterie, solidly installed at the posts of power but beginning to slip: the duchesse Jules cared more for her friends and lovers than for the Queen, who was beginning to be miffed. Still, Marie Antoinette and the Polignacs agreed on some basic principles: nothing needed to be changed, the court was really not spending too much money, privileges must never be touched or the King's powers limited, and any unrest should be put down by force.

At the opposite pole there was a large group of young, liberal aristocrats, Mathieu de Montmorency, the vicomte de Noailles, the marquis de La Fayette. They had all been involved in the American war, understood, or thought they did, the English constitution, and favored a reform of the system that would produce a limited monarchy: the King would rule with the help of a Parliament, special privileges would be abolished and the court reformed. This faction looked for leadership to the duc d'Orléans, the King's distant cousin and a great Anglophile, who plotted to bring about a limited revolution patterned after that of 1688. He hoped to play William III to Louis XVI's King James, and end up on the throne. This was quite a powerful faction: the duc d'Orléans was immensely rich and quite willing to subsidize pamphlets, books and politicians; he counted on the Queen's unpopularity and the King's incompetence, and made sure everyone knew about them.

There was also a large group of reactionary courtiers whose ideal was an aristocratic government in which the great families would rule the country for a figurehead King. They deplored the absolutism of Louis XIV, despised all middle-class ministers and gathered around the King's youngest brother, the comte d'Artois. It was a symbolic choice: he was as empty-headed and foolish as their policies. The only sign of their influence was the new law stating that only noblemen could be given commissions in the army. They did, however, contribute heavily to the coming Revolution by combing their archives for long-forgotten feudal rights, which they now proceeded to reassert. It was thus not very surprising that the first thing the peasants did in the spring of 1789 was to burn every old parchment in sight.

Less influential still were a number of subgroups. One of these gathered around the comte de Provence, who thought, rightly, that he was a great deal smarter than his brother, the King, and whose devouring ambition was to replace him on the throne. So he tried to create his own party, without much success, however, partly because of his generally unpleasant manner, partly because he was known to be impotent, and therefore an object of ridicule. Another party still consisted of the remains of the reformers who had lost their posts when Turgot was dismissed in 1777; alone, perhaps, this party might have saved the monarchy, but it was never able to overcome the Queen's hostility. Then there was a party of assorted malcontents: the

Noailles, who were numerous, loud and vigorous because they resented the favor shown the Polignacs; the Richelieu-d'Aiguillon coterie who had been in power during the last years of Louis XV's reign thanks to their friendship with the King's last mistress, Madame du Barry, and who vainly hoped to recoup their fortunes. Finally, there were isolated courtiers desperately trying to succeed, and Princes of the Blood, the prince de Condé especially, who felt they were being ignored. All this made for a great deal of confusion, intrigues and counterintrigues, shifts, movements, all becoming ever more unpredictable because of the King's weakness.

All these factions claimed, with equal stridency, to be working for the greater good of the country. The baron de Besenval, who was the chief planner of the Polignac coterie, left a curious book of memoirs; in it, he never stops claiming the most complete selflessness and reminding the reader that his only object is the greater glory of France; yet that glory depended on the triumph of his own friends through the duchesse Jules, whose only fault, he asserts repeatedly, was her utter lack of ambition and greed. Yet we find him, time after time, engaged in deep plots simply to achieve another pension or honor. A case in point is the dismissal of the War Minister, the prince de Montbarey, in 1780. That luckless gentleman had forgotten to promote Besenval to the rank of major general. With tireless industry, Besenval worked for his downfall, helped by the duchesse Jules, who wanted her lover, Monsieur d'Adhémar, to become assistant minister.

"The duchesse de Polignac," Besenval writes, "who was the recipient of the Queen's most secret thoughts and enjoyed her full confidence, was able to lead her anywhere she pleased, not so much in her everyday life as in major enterprises, and was able to dispose of the immense influence that princess had over the King. . . . It was through her I thought I would make Monsieur de Ségur the War Minister."

Monsieur de Besenval went to work. First he convinced Madame de Polignac to push for the current minister's expulsion; then he organized a campaign of pamphlets and rumors to spread the idea of Monsieur de Montbarey's incompetence through the court and public. After that he put his own candidate forward. It then took a little while to convince the duchess, but she agreed to talk to the Queen. In her turn, Marie Antoinette soon gave in and promised she would push Monsieur de Ségur. "This was only the first step, and by far the least difficult. The King was no great problem, either; but there was Madame de Maurepas, who had pushed Monsieur de Montbarey to that success he had finally reached. . . .

"Several months passed. I constantly, throughout that time, went on pushing Madame de Polignac to keep the heat on the Queen, who would answer that she was continuing in her purpose but was afraid of rushing things. Monsieur d'Adhémar, who grew impatient of these delays, was blaming Madame de Polignac; I treated her with more kindness."

Then fate helped the plot. The Minister of the Navy, Monsieur de Sartines, was discovered to have spent twenty million livres over the sum allotted to his department. He had to resign, and the Queen convinced her husband to appoint Monsieur de Castries, one of her protégés, as his replacement.

"I took advantage of Monsieur de Castries' appointment," Besenval continues, "to ask Madame de Polignac whether the Queen would stop there or whether, since she had enough influence to make a Minister of the Navy, she would not want to make a War Minister as well." Then, suddenly, it seemed as if all these efforts would be in vain. First Monsieur de Ségur told the coterie he refused even to consider Monsieur d'Adhémar as his deputy, and it took some fast and persistent work on Besenval's part to keep Madame de Polignac in line. Worse still, Maurepas, who got wind of the intrigue, started pushing the King the other way. Finally Monsieur de Ségur appeared at court on a day when he was having a severe attack of gout. As a result, he looked like a dying man, and Maurepas pointed out to the King that Ségur was obviously in no state to run anything. "He [Maurepas] even apparently managed, through the King, to convince the Queen that she had been deceived and that Madame de Polignac had taken advantage of her friendship.

"That princess, in the first moment of her anger, sent for Madame de Polignac and reproached her in the bitterest and most offensive way. . . . Mastering the fury [sic] that she felt at hearing the Queen, Madame de Polignac rose and answered that, as long as the Queen was so bold [sic] as to harbor the opinion of herself which she had just expressed, she [Madame de Polignac] could no longer do herself justice and retain her friendship for the Queen at the same time, and that she would leave the court immediately and forever. . . .

"The Queen, surprised by Madame de Polignac's speech, and apparently realizing the loss she was about to incur, felt her friendship coming back to life, and remembered they were bound by all the ties which a boundless confidence had created. She promptly calmed down and tried to repair the damage she had just done, but it was all in vain. Madame de Polignac could not be budged. . . .

"In this terrible situation, the tears poured out of the Queen's eyes; she finally threw herself at Madame de Polignac's knees and begged her for forgiveness [sic]."

At that point Monsieur de Montbarey finally resigned, but did so in such a way that, for a day, nobody knew about it. The King, wholly surprised, appointed Vergennes, the Foreign Minister, as acting Minister of War. The enraged Madame de Polignac then promptly went to the Queen and pointed out that here was an intolerable humiliation: since all the court knew that the Queen was backing Ségur, she would be universally laughed at. Marie Antoinette saw her point. The very next morning, at seven o'clock, she assaulted the King in his bedroom. "The King, more, I think, to please his wife than because he found her reasons convincing, finally agreed to Monsieur de Ségur; and the Queen, in the flush of her success, [sent for] Monsieur de Maurepas and told him: 'Monsieur, you hear the King's decision; you will ask Monsieur de Ségur to come and tell him this news immediately.'"

Monsieur de Besenval had triumphed and was promoted. The Queen, once again, had proved her power over the King, and Madame de Polignac hers over the Queen. As it turned out, Monsieur de Ségur was fairly competent—not that it really mattered one way or the other.

—◁ ▷—

The Revolution, when it came, turned out to be a considerable surprise; yet, at the very center of monarchical power, many premonitory signs appeared all through the eighties.

Every day, almost, pamphlets were published at the instigation of the very courtiers who filled Versailles. They reviled the King and Queen with a violence not seen since the civil war of the 1580s. The imbecile, the impotent fat pig and his whore, as the royal couple were described, were pictured, she as a frantic nymphomaniac, attacking both men and women, whose children were not her husband's, and whose only object in life was to satisfy her lusts and greeds, he as an idiot cuckold dazed by gluttony, drunkenness and weakness.

Their most innocent actions were transformed and traduced. After he had spent the day hunting, Louis XVI often fell asleep in the carriage taking him home. When he got back to Versailles he sometimes staggered for a few steps before awakening fully: it was very simple, he was drunk every night. During the hot summer of 1777, Marie Antoinette would go for walks at night on the terrace outside the palace, with her sisters-in-law, but without guards: obviously, she was picking out the lovers who would participate in revolting orgies. By the middle eighties, people were thoroughly convinced, so much so that, later, many revolutionaries were astounded when they finally met the royal family face to face. Where were the idiot and his Messalina? they asked.

At the same time the obviously mismanaged finances of the monarchy provided yet another handle for the Orléans faction. At various times Louis XVI tried to reduce expenses: his stables shrank from over three thousand horses to some sixteen hundred; the privileged regiments of the King's Guard were dismissed; a few offices were abolished. Still, no one was going to touch the Queen or her friends; she remained *Madame Déficit*. In 1785 the Necklace Affair (see Chapter Four) put an end to what little popularity she may still have had; she avoided the public as much as possible, since she was greeted by jeers or a frigid silence. The applause of her youth was long gone.

At the same time the court was losing its glamor. There was little point in attending a King who was completely controlled, year after year, by the Polignac coterie. The Queen disliked etiquette and display; she retreated more and more to the privacy of Trianon. By the middle eighties, except on some ceremonial days and Sundays, the great palace was half empty and the courtiers were in Paris. Slowly, steadily, Versailles lost the primacy it had enjoyed for a hundred years. Even members of the Household groaned when they had to leave their comfortable Paris salons to go and stand all day, waiting on Their Majesties. It was still chic to attend the great court functions, but little by little Versailles ceased to be *ce pays-ci*. When, on October 3, 1789, the people of Paris rose, marched to the palace and came back with *le boulanger, la boulangère et le petit mitron* (the breadmaker, the breadmaker's wife and the little apprentice), an age and an institution were seen to end; but they were already more than half dead. There had been no real court without a masterful, all-powerful King, and, as Versailles emptied, it died, never to be reborn.

Chapter Three

PALACE, HOUSE AND HOME

Travelers who visit the great English country houses may notice, now and again, an especially dazzling chair, or desk, or bed. When they consult their little booklets, they will probably find that it was made by Jacob, or Riesener, or Weisweiler, and that it came from Versailles.[1] These pieces of furniture are not only great works of art; they are also witness to a quality shared by English aristocrats and French revolutionaries alike: a lively appreciation for decoration and furniture.

Never more, perhaps, than in the twenty years preceding the Revolution have people cared about what their houses or apartments looked like. Like architecture (see Chapter Seven), interior decoration was influenced by the newly excavated Roman cities of Pompeii and Herculaneum. A new sense of restraint, of simplicity, in forms if not in details, a feeling for comfort all came together with a desire for light and openness. At the same time the quality of the work produced by architects, painters, cabinetmakers, wood carvers and fabric designers reached a new high.

All through this period French taste reigned supreme from St. Petersburg to Naples. People read French books, ordered French porcelain, wore French clothes and bought French furniture. More startling, perhaps, cabinetmakers everywhere copied the great French masters; and when in the late sixties they gave up the convolutions of the rococo for straight lines and simple shapes, the rest of Europe promptly followed. If one is familiar with the pe-

[1] All the furniture in Versailles was sold at auction by the Revolutionary government. Much of it went to English buyers; some of it, in the fullness of time, made its way to the United States and can be seen, for instance, in The Metropolitan Museum of Art in New York.

riod it is still possible to tell whether a piece is French by the perfection of its details and the harmony of its proportions.

The interiors created in the Louis XVI style also reflect a cooperation between patron and artists. No one would have thought of leaving the work to a decorator: Marie Antoinette, at Compiègne or Trianon, just like the nobleman in his new town house on the Rue de Varenne or the simple bourgeois in his little apartment, worked together with the artists and artisans to make sure their environments were just what they wanted. They stared at plans, pored over watercolor renderings, fingered swatches of materials, praised, criticized, demanded. It was all well worth it.

-◄ ►-

"When a house is finished building," Mercier wrote, "nothing is done yet; one hasn't even reached a quarter of the total cost. Then come the carpenter, the upholsterer, the painter, the gilder, the sculptor, the cabinetmaker, etc. And you still need mirrors, and bells must be installed everywhere. The inside of a house takes three times longer to do than the outside. . . .

"Furnishings have been given excessive and disproportionate magnificence. A superb bed which looks like a throne, a sparkling dining room, andirons worked as finely as jewels, a dressing table of gold and lace . . . the nation's splendor is all inside its houses."

Mercier's complaint was linked to his ever recurrent plea for magnificent public monuments; but his point is somewhat weakened because these private houses could be visited by the public just like the King's palaces.

We are accustomed to well-guarded public officials, isolated in their residences. No one today goes into Buckingham Palace, or the Élysée, unless invited by the Queen or the President; only the American White House still maintains, in part, the old tradition of accessibility. In the eighteenth century anyone could visit Versailles if he or she was decently dressed; you could even rent a hat or sword from the palace's concierge, so that, in a very real sense, these magnificent buildings belonged to the people as well.

Of the royal couple, only the Queen cared about the décor of their lives; Louis XVI gave it as little thought as he did to his clothes. Luckily, Marie Antoinette amply made up for her husband. She constantly encouraged the great cabinetmakers and kept them well supplied with orders. She looked at the new style with a discriminating eye and purchased its finest examples. More, she loved to achieve a completely integrated look. This was seldom possible in Versailles: she could hardly tear out the Hall of Mirrors. She did have her state bedroom redecorated; thanks to American gifts and French research, it can be seen today just as it was when she lived in it.

But it was in the new palace of Compiègne that Marie Antoinette was really able to do what she wanted. The new southwest wing, scheduled to hold the Queen's apartments, was finally completed early in the reign; and

Le Dreux, who succeeded the great Jacques-Ange Gabriel, promptly produced plans for its interior décor, showing not only the shape of the rooms but their paneling and ornamentation as well. He suggested white boiseries[2] with grisaille[3] paintings; he designed all the new sculpture for panels and doors and ceiling cornices, which were to consist of figures of children, genies, initials and emblems. Above all, he wrote, he would aim for simplicity: there would be a lot of white. He meant, of course, a lot of white carved or sculpted boiserie, not bare plaster. The gilding was to be restricted to the tapestry and mirror frames, and to the balustrade along the bed: it was to be a look of elegance rather than splendor.

A painter, Pierre Sauvage, was engaged, along with several sculptors, and the work was begun. It can still be seen today. Compiègne is only two hours away from Paris, and well worth the trip.

The Queen's state apartments (as distinct from her private apartments) consisted of four very large main rooms: a first antechamber where she would eat in public; a second antechamber where the courtiers waited; a gaming room; and, finally, the bedroom. This apartment was followed by an antechamber and a bedroom each for the Queen's two eldest children, the Dauphin and Madame Royale. Behind this suite, which ran along the new wing's garden façade, were two bathrooms, one with two bathtubs, three other general-purpose rooms and two dressing rooms lined with closets.

Let us imagine, for a moment, that we have been transported to Compiègne in 1788, say, or 1789, and have asked to see the new wing. We have walked up the wide stone staircase with its sculpted banister and reached the door to the Queen's first antechamber.

As we stand in the middle of this large room we see, opposite the windows, a tall white marble mantelpiece framed with a gilded, sculpted double border of leaves and surmounted by one of Sauvage's paintings showing Anacreon, served by a charming young nymph, near a smoking tripod incense burner. A little Cupid shyly offers him a crown while another, holding a torch, flies through the air.

Eighteen white engaged pilasters topped with Ionic capitals decorate the walls and lead the eye up to a gilded cornice carved with leaves and geometric patterns. Above the doors, grisailles the color of stone represent more cupids and young fauns, near antique altars and baskets full of fruit and game, drinking from gold vases. The door and window handles are made of sculpted, gilded bronze; the floor is inlaid and parqueted.

Let us now go a little farther, through the second antechamber and into the gaming room. There the white-veined marble chimney made by Thomas is topped by a painted oval of lapis-colored stucco adorned with figures of women and children painted to look like white marble. The wall panels are

2 A boiserie is a carved, sculpted wood panel that covers an entire wall.
3 A painting done entirely in different shades of gray.

carved with lyres and thyrsi from which fall leaves intertwined with ribbons, surrounded by draped vases with twisting handles on a ground of vine leaves, and framed with richly sculpted borders. Above each panel the painted ovals are surrounded by thick garlands of fruit and flowers.

As for the doors, they are adorned with bas-relief lunettes—Mercury's winged hat resting on crossed trumpets laced with laurel branches surmounting oval vases from which cascade garlanded acanthus-leaf decorative motifs.

Between the windows there are mirrors framed with flowering vases and cups of fruit in front of which Cupids kneel. On the facing wall the double eagles of the Austrian Archduchess are topped with laurel-leaf crowns; a lyre with a globe in its center is flanked by flute-playing Cupids who sit with their legs dangling onto the central mirror. All the carving in this room is gilded in varying shades of gold.

Through another door is the bedroom, with its walls and bed covered in blue and silver brocade with thick bouquets of feathers surmounting each of the bed's four columns. The folding stools and sofas are upholstered in blue and white striped silk, and in the four painted ovals are grisaille figures of nymphs and zephyrs on a white-veined stucco ground.

As for the cost of all this splendor, it was surprisingly modest. Each of the carved marble chimneys cost 900 livres; all the sculpture on the doors and boiseries amounted to 22,000 livres, while the paintings came to 4,000 livres each and 8,000 livres for the big panel in the first antechamber. Compiègne was considered a highly countrified palace, but it was an official royal residence and no one thought the money ill spent. It was very different at Trianon.

Louis XIV had built Versailles to be just what it was—a splendid show place—but it was also uncomfortable. The fireplaces smoked, drafts came through the windows, the huge, high-ceilinged rooms were almost impossible to heat. Even the Sun King felt the need for a little more privacy, so he built a pink marble château in the park of Versailles at Trianon.

Louis XV knew his duty and spent much of his life in the palace his great-grandfather had built, but he shared his contemporaries' taste for small, cozy rooms; even Trianon was too grand, too showy, too uncomfortable. So he commissioned Gabriel to build him a small, simple stone house.

The Petit Trianon, as it came to be known, was a square house with four columns adorning the front and chastely bracketed windows. It is also its architect's masterpiece and the best example of that classical, restrained style for which the French were so famous. Its whole effect depends on perfect proportions, grace and harmony. Nothing could be less showy or bombastic, nothing more unpretentiously perfect. Around the Petit Trianon the King had ordered the planting of a garden full of rare, exotic trees and flowers and, at the end of a long green lawn, the building of a charming octagonal stone pavilion.

The Petit Trianon, like the rest of Versailles, was open to the public, but only when the King was elsewhere. Its gardens were walled and you had to apply for entrance to the concierge at the gate. Since there were less than half a dozen master bedrooms, the court was excluded.

The dining room was designed for the King's private suppers. The table would, at the touch of a button, vanish downstairs through an opening in the floor, then come back up fully served and laden with food, thus making the presence of the usual servants unnecessary. As for the décor, it was charming but simple. There were no state apartments, just pleasant rooms where the King could pretend he was a simple—if rather well-off—country gentleman.

Trianon was also just what Marie Antoinette wanted. She had spent most of her childhood in Schoenbrunn, playing in the park and enjoying an etiquette-free family life. During her years as Dauphine she was forced to stay in the great royal palaces and yearned for a country retreat. As soon as he came to the throne Louis XVI gave her the Petit Trianon.

There was nothing really scandalous in that gift; still, it had not been the custom for Queens of France to have private houses, largely because the last two Queens had been too lethargic to think of wanting one, and so people were shocked when a new set of regulations went up on the gate to Trianon bearing the words "De par la Reine [On the Queen's orders]."

People's apprehensions were quickly confirmed when they realized what was actually going on. For one thing, the servants at Trianon now wore the Queen's livery of red and silver; then, as in all royal country residences, a few privileged courtiers were allowed to wear a special scarlet and gold uniform, thus infuriating all those who were rejected. At Trianon Marie Antoinette considered herself a private person, not a Queen, so she invited only people she liked instead of people whose position at court gave them the "right" to wait on her, and thus turned them into bitter enemies.

Worse was yet to come. Since Marie Antoinette enjoyed Trianon so much, she spent more and more time there: after all, she could be free of the hated etiquette while enjoying the company of the Polignac coterie. But a Queen of France was supposed to be visible, and people of all ranks and categories who came to Versailles to pay court to the Queen or watch her eat her supper, only to find that she was hiding behind the walls of Trianon, were justifiably angry. And when they read pamphlets describing the Queen's hidden orgies, of course they believed them.

Now and again people complained to the King. Her Majesty was supposed to receive foreign ambassadors every Wednesday, a minister protested, but she had been at the palace only one Wednesday that month. Louis XVI went straight to his wife, who exclaimed in astonishment. She had received the ambassadors already just two weeks before, she said: surely she couldn't be expected to come back from Trianon just to have her hand kissed by some tiresome envoy. The King saw her point immediately. Of course she must stay in Trianon, he said. Once again Marie Antoinette had had her way; once again she had failed in her duty.

All this would have been bad enough if it hadn't cost anything; unfortunately (though luckily for us), the Queen felt she had to remodel the gardens. Nothing could be duller, she said, than the formal, geometric French gardens. Louis XIV might have liked them; she certainly didn't. After all, she was nothing if not a fashionable woman, and there was a new fashion in gardens, just then, the English garden.

Many people, in fact, would have agreed with her. Formal gardens were suddenly considered dull, unnatural. The great thing now was to have a (carefully designed) *natural* landscape, with hills and little woods and meandering streams and waterfalls and, perhaps, a ruin or a few cottages. In this most polished of societies, thanks, in part, to the influence of Jean-Jacques Rousseau, it was suddenly smart to like nature.

So Marie Antoinette gave her instructions. Mique, her architect, made up plans. They were scrutinized, modified, checked again. Artificial ruins came and went. The final result was very much what we see today—one of the most attractive gardens in France.

It took some two years to finish, an eternity, thought the Queen. When she asked why the work wasn't progressing faster, she was told it was because the bills hadn't been paid; so she turned on Turgot and demanded to know the reason why. His answer that there was no money in the Treasury left her quite cold; find some, she said. In the end, money went on being due for many years; but, after spending over a million livres (magnified by rumor to at least ten), the Queen had her garden.

A lake was dug out between two hills; at one end rose a great rock from which a spring flowed. At the other, a river ran out sinuously, formed an elegant curve to the north of the garden, then returned to its center, widened so as to accommodate an island and ended in two separate streams on the lawn before the house. Along the way was another rock, complete with cascades, reached through curving alleys and little woods planted with all different kinds of trees.

It would never have done to leave the island bare, so in the center Mique placed a Temple of Love. It was made of an open circular white marble colonnade which held up an entablature decorated with flowered, curving branches and a stone cupola. On the pavement white marble squares were outlined in red, and in the center of the temple an earlier statue by Bouchardon, showing Cupid carving his bow out of Hercules' staff, had been placed. At the top of the cupola was a big trophy framed by flowers and composed of Cupid's attributes—arrow holders, arrows tied with ribbons, garlands and torches—all crowned with roses. You reached the island over a wooden bridge lined with flower boxes. The temple itself, which was inaugurated in

September 1778, was surrounded with rosebushes and odoriferous shrubs. Altogether, it was a lovely place to sit in.

Still, what is a garden without a grotto? So of course there had to be one. Next to the entrance and its little cascade Mique had planned a mossy bench from which an opening into the rock gave a view onto the path and any people who might be coming; a little stone stairway going through the rock made for quick and discreet getaways.

Then there were those two hills which framed the lake. They looked unfinished, somehow, until a belvedere was built on top of the tallest. It was a little octagonal stone pavilion raised on a few steps flanked by four couples of stone sphinxes, each with a different woman's face, coiffure and drapery. Carved into the pediment over the door were gardener's tools, braided roses framed in branches of laurel and oak, trophies of game and a duck hunt; above the windows, allegories of the four seasons had been carved.

When you walked in, you saw a mosaic pavement of red-, blue-, green- and white-veined marble. On the dome a sky had been painted; there Cupids played with flowers among light clouds. The stucco walls were also painted. There were three-legged incense burners, and tables bearing cups. Here a squirrel was gnawing at some fruit; there a monkey tried to reach goldfish swimming in a crystal cup, and at the top were more trophies and emblems. This pavilion was also furnished—probably with a sofa or two, some chairs and tables.

Even then, Trianon was not complete. Marie Antoinette was a dedicated actress, so a little theater had to be built in which she could perform herself or watch professionals. For a cost of 141,200 livres she got a blue and gold interior of watered silk and velvet, with boiseries painted to look like lavender marble and a proscenium in trompe-l'oeil white marble. The moldings and sculpted figures were heightened with yellow or green gold. All around the stage was a riot of papier-mâché figures: lions' heads, children playing with garlands of flowers and fruit, etc., with, on either side, a life-size figure of a woman holding a torch; on the ceiling Apollo and the Muses were surrounded with Cupids and Graces.

All this was where the money went. The Queen left the house itself pretty well alone, except for one small room where mirrors rose to hide the windows at the touch of a button. On the walls the Queen's initials were carved amid lyres, rose branches, doves, arrows and incense burners—altogether a very pretty room.

A good garden, of course, seems to grow by itself; so when in 1789 those deputies to the States-General came looking, they couldn't understand why Trianon had been so expensive. The house itself, apart from that one room, had hardly been touched. No wonder they were puzzled when they saw those sun-faded curtains.

All those trees and flowers, those pavilions and grottoes were enchanting to look at, but in spite of it all nature had a way of being dull: entertainment was needed. Gossip helped, of course, and so did the theater. But there was also a Chinese merry-go-round where the men, mounted on dragons, and the ladies, seated on peacocks, tried to reach an elusively hung brass ring with long wands. And there were the parties.

A great fete was given, for instance, to celebrate the completion of the Temple of Love. It lasted all day—September 3, 1777—and all night. Imitations, in painted cardboard and canvas, of Paris shops, set up all along the alleys and fully stocked, had all the Queen's friends for their merchants. There was also a country inn, made of twenty-one leafy trellises, and a Cabinet of Comus, where magic tricks were performed, and a fair, and a parade all through the garden. Then, when night fell, the illuminations came up. There were candles in colored glasses all over the trees and on the ground, and there were torches. A large moat had been dug and filled with brightly burning wood: it looked like the day in the middle of the night and was, eyewitnesses tell us, dazzlingly beautiful. Throughout the evening music could be heard wafting over the crowd; it came from a Chinese amphitheater where musicians from a Guards regiment, dressed like Chinamen, were playing away. All in all, it was a great success—for everyone except the Finance Minister, Monsieur Necker, who blanched when he got a bill for four hundred thousand livres. He complained and paid up in the end; and the Queen's reputation as a spendthrift was even more firmly established.

Perhaps because the life of society in the seventies and eighties was so polished, so refined, so unnatural, really, almost everyone seemed to have a compensatory taste for simplicity. Great ladies in their hoop skirts, their diamonds, their towering, feathered coiffures, sighed for the simple pleasures of the farm. Noblemen in swords and brocades dreamed of being just peasants. Of course reality was never allowed to intrude its unpleasant face into this charming fantasy. It would never do to go to a real farm (much too dirty), but a life-size toy farm, built just for the fun of it—now there was the right kind of simplicity.

Marie Antoinette was not the woman to overlook this kind of trend. Suddenly she was wearing only white linen during her stays at Trianon. She even had her portrait painted in one of these new dresses and allowed it to be shown at the yearly Salon. It was not a wise move. Why was she having herself painted in a nightgown? people asked nastily, and quickly answered that it was another one of her anti-French tricks. Obviously she was trying to ruin the Lyon silk industry by thus patronizing English linen.

The white dresses were only a first step. Trianon now looked sadly deficient: it needed a hamlet, a little village with cottages and a farm. Of course it soon had one, a very clean and charming one, which has lost none of its attractions today.

Quickly, the thatched-roof houses went up, their windows made of tiny panes, their walls covered with plaster made to look like old, cracked brick. There were outside wood staircases, and ivy-covered cottages, and white fa-ïence pots full of growing flowers, and little vegetable gardens.

What's a village without an old, picturesque tower? So there was a tower, and a pond, of course, stocked with pike and carp so you could go fishing (so delightfully primitive!).

Then there were cows—well, not visible cows, perhaps, but they were there somewhere, and they provided milk for the model dairy, with its white marble tables and walls and a little open pipe full of running water to keep it all cool. The white and gold porcelain pots, in which the cream was allowed to rise, all bore the Queen's initials. Rumor even had it (could it be true?) that there were drinking cups shaped like a woman's—a queen's—breast.

Then there was a real farm with a real farmer and his wife, and real chickens, and a dovecote full of real doves. There was a smithy, and a mill, and the Queen's own house, built to look like all the others, only a little larger, with simple furniture and cotton curtains. It was all a dream of simplicity come true.

More and more, as the times became rougher and more unpleasant, Marie Antoinette retreated to her little make-believe world. There nothing changed. The doves still cooed, the cows still provided milk, the mill still turned lazily. Nothing would disturb an increasingly unhappy Queen. Then, on the afternoon of October 3, 1789, a page came running to the hamlet. "Madame," he said, "Your Majesty must come back to the palace at once," and Marie Antoinette hurried away, away from the hamlet and Trianon to her room at the palace where she was to spend just one more night. The next day the royal family was bundled into a carriage and taken to Paris by a screaming, triumphant mob. The Queen never saw Trianon again.

—◦{ }◦—

Marie Antoinette had her way at Trianon; but Louis XVI was planning to do things on a grander scale. By the 1780s, Versailles was a hundred years old. Its measured, majestic architecture no longer suited the mood of the times—and, besides, the need for major repairs was becoming urgent. So the King decided to leave everything as it was for a while; he had conferred with his architects and realized a whole new palace was the answer, with a different façade, much more massive than the old. Since this was obviously going to be a major enterprise, and an expensive one, too, it would, he said, be spread out over ten years—the last ten years of the century. The rebuilding of Versailles was thus scheduled to start in 1790 and be completed in 1800, but, like many another project, it was canceled by the Revolution. Versailles stayed as it was.

Even the King's private rooms were kept much as they had been in his grandfather's time. "It is an assemblage," Mercier wrote, "of rooms which open one into the other. In order to build them, they have had to hollow out walls or break through them, interrupt staircases to create new ones, so that one has to go up or down constantly in order to follow the continuity of the numerous rooms. . . .

"The King has three rooms full of books . . . where twelve to fifteen thousand volumes may be found. One sees all the best works of the English poets on the shelves. One very used-looking book in that library is Boyer's English dictionary . . . along with the Gazette de France . . . because of its accounts of presentations. It is a monument of etiquette for weddings and ceremonies of all kinds. . . .

"In other rooms, one sees many scientific instruments used in physics and very few paintings. . . . The attendants open big drawers full of gold spoons, gold forks, gold salt cellars and egg cups which are never used; one also sees gold candlesticks and Louis XIV's cane." It all sounds rather uncomfortable at a time when comfort was greatly in demand.

Specialization was the keynote in non-royal houses. Only the King now ate in a salon: elsewhere, the dining room had come into being. All through the seventeenth century, rooms—except the bedrooms: beds were too heavy to move—were interchangeable. Now, finally, each room had its function, and it made for an easier, more comfortable life. You were also less likely to have grease spots on the bedroom carpet.

One of the drawbacks of peripatetic dining had been that the food was generally stone cold by the time it reached you. Now the new, permanent dining room, with its handsome table and comfortable chairs, was backed by another room where food was warmed up before it was served; the kitchens were still generally placed in a wing outside the main house.

Another great progress was the appearance of the toilet. Until the 1770s the grandest people, even the Sun King, had used the chaise percée, a chair with a removable seat which concealed a chamber pot. The effect of this instrument's use in a bedroom need hardly be described. Now a special room, usually paved with marble (easy to wash), was reserved, and it even contained, in the more luxurious houses, real English flush toilets. This was a great novelty: at Versailles, always a little behind the times, only the King and Queen had them.

Even if you didn't have English toilets, there was a new, improved kind of chaise percée with a tank behind it for water and a sort of flush—though the removable seat and chamber pot remained unchanged. Since central heating had yet to be invented and houses could get very cold at night, there was no bedroom without a chamber pot concealed somewhere near the bed.

Bathrooms were another great innovation. No modern house could be without one. Marie Antoinette, who was considered a bit of a fanatic, bathed as often as three times a week. Still, weekly or biweekly baths were now in order, and no bathroom worthy of the name had less than two bathtubs, one for hot, one for cold water. Of course, you didn't just turn on the faucet when you wanted to take a bath. While running cold water was not infrequent—it came from a tank filled slowly by the pailful—hot water had to come up in big pails from the kitchen. And of course it eventually went back down in those very same pails.

Not everyone had a bathtub. If you liked being clean but couldn't have a tub installed, you could rent a boot-shaped copper bathtub for an hour or so; it arrived complete with hot water for a modest fee. And if you were too poor, or too cheap, even for that, you could always go to one of the numerous bathhouses distributed all over the city and have a good soak for just a few sous.

Since they were usually brand new, bathrooms were also often luxurious. Marble walls and floors were the norm. The tubs, often made of copper but sometimes of marble, generally four feet square and quite deep, were placed in an alcove enclosed by curtains on swinging rods so you could open them with one push. You closed them while bathing so as to stay nice and warm, since you were unlikely to get any more hot water.

Some people did things in a grander way. The Baron de Besenval, Madame de Polignac's friend, had a bathroom which measured thirty by eighteen feet. "A mysterious light comes in from above and shows up the twelve columns with their Tuscan capitals which hold up the vault; the Greek vases stand between the columns along with an urn held by a larger-than-life reclining naiad." And a full indoor swimming pool framed by a colonnade could be found in one of the "little houses" outside Paris.

These little houses, too, were an innovation. Smaller than the formal town houses but no less luxurious, and usually surrounded by a high wall, they afforded complete privacy and were the ideal place to meet someone, like a dancer, you might not want to be seen with in your proper house.

Just as rooms were now specialized, so was furniture. There were sewing tables and writing tables and little round tables you could wheel about, and even tables with tin-lined tanks so you could have enormous bouquets of cut flowers or large plants growing right out of them.

Comfort and convenience were important—just as in the late nineteenth century or in our own day; but the main, the shining quality of Louis XVI interiors is their great beauty. Never again has there been such a combination of great cabinetmakers, textile designers and weavers and artisans of all kinds—carpenters, upholsterers, bronze sculptors, gilders, frame makers, carpet weavers, parquet makers, marble cutters—together with architects who had a real sense of decoration.

Any good piece of Louis XVI furniture, or silver, or porcelain, any boiserie, any carpet, any bolt of cloth is beautiful—and also something more.

It embodies a general sense of harmony, an unconscious demand for perfection, a balance, ever achieved anew, between richness and restraint.

The "decorative arts," a phrase now so often spoken with contempt (the worst thing you can say today about a painting is that it's decorative), were then considered, rightly, to be art, period. The modern split between the intellectually challenging and the merely pleasing was still far in the future. A whole society of rich, idle but immensely discriminating patrons cared passionately about things like dinner plates and armchairs.

It would not now occur to an art critic that he ought to review the latest furniture or style of interiors—and most likely he would be right. But in those twenty years before the Revolution the latest set of Jacob chairs, the latest Riesener table, the latest salon, with its boiseries and mirrors, curtains and vases, mantelpiece and furniture, represented not just a trend, not just a pleasant look, but an artistic triumph. In a very real sense the great cabinetmakers were just as truly sculptors as a man like Houdon.

Most of the Louis XVI pieces that we see today are fragments, mere indications of a vanished whole. That is not to say that the chairs are broken and pieced together: luckily, many of them are still in excellent condition; sometimes we even come across a whole set of four or six chairs and a sofa. Again, we can still find unfaded bolts of those wonderful Lyon silks. A number of Sèvres porcelain services have survived the breakages of two centuries. Louis XVI tapestries are sold every year at auction. There are magnificent tables and clocks and fire screens, sometimes in museums, sometimes in private collections; but all have been torn from their original settings.

Today people rent an apartment and move into ready-made rooms; then they go out and buy ready-made furniture, ready-made porcelain, ready-made silver or stainless steel. If they want some paintings on those flat plaster walls they purchase them (ready-made) from a gallery; depending on their degree of boldness and sophistication, that work of art may or may not match the couch and the rug. But in the 1770s and 1780s people asked an architect to help them design a room; even when they rented an apartment (as opposed to building a house), the rooms were often reshaped. The walls disappeared behind carved, painted, often gilded boiseries designed specifically for that one room. Furniture was commissioned, not bought; models or renderings would be made, discussed, modified and had, in any event, been invented specifically for that setting, just like the design of the curtains and carpets. When panels were reserved for paintings, the artists, yes, the greatest of them, painted a work specifically to fit into the space and with the theme of the room. Every detail mattered, doorknobs and andirons, ceiling cornices, and the ceiling itself, almost never white, but painted to look like a sky or in a soft color that went with that of the room. Even after the specially ordered chairs and sofas and tables were ready, they must still be upholstered with a specially ordered brocade, or silk, or velvet. In a good Louis XVI room each

3. *Lavréince, The Little Favorite. This engraving, while full of the slightly ambiguous eroticism so often seen in this period, is also a perfect depiction of a Louis XVI bedroom, with its draped and feathered bed, the straight, graceful lines of the bed table and the softly upholstered armchair.*

individual piece played its part in the composition of a complete, harmonious whole.

We can rarely see Louis XVI rooms just as they were. More often—the Wrightsman rooms in The Metropolitan Museum of Art in New York are all too typical of this deplorable habit—we see a curious assemblage of boiseries from one house and tapestries from another; one table from here, a chair from there, a porcelain from elsewhere still; and even worse, the boiseries are sometimes "augmented" by one or more new panels to make them fit their new setting, without, apparently, anyone realizing that when you change the size of a room you also distort its proportions. If you add a glaring white ceiling to this betrayal, and carefully place barriers so as to prevent the public from entering the room, incidentally making all details invisible because of sheer distance, then you create the very opposite of what a Louis XVI room actually was. It would really have been better to show the individual pieces alone, especially since they are so very rare and beautiful.

The people from whose houses these fragments have come knew full well it was both time-consuming and costly to achieve that perfect ensemble. The décor of *one* salon, in a house on the Place Vendôme, cost 300,000 livres. Beaumarchais, when prosperity finally came and he built himself a house, spent over 1,600,000 livres. Of course, he had a circular, thirty-foot-high salon topped by a cupola, a billiard room with boxes for the spectators, and a semicircular façade adorned with columns. Part of the money also went for furniture, but not as much as we might think, given the quality of the pieces. Louis XVI paid a mere 7,000 livres for his Riesener desk in Compiègne (today, it would be worth hundreds of thousands of dollars). Still, that was a country residence, and Roentgen charged him the exceptionally high price of 80,000 livres for his desk in Versailles. But you could buy a large armchair from Jacob for 150 livres, a big carved screen for 230 livres, a chair for anything from 60 to 96 livres, a console for 72 livres and a complex, ornate bed for 880 livres. None of these prices included upholstery or the gilding, though, which, in the case of the bed or large armchair might double the cost. The furniture of the Queen's gaming room in St. Cloud cost 8,536 livres and the gilding 12,160. Real gold was used for this, in a subtle, refined juxtaposition of different shades—green, yellow and red golds. Most furniture was not gilded however, but painted and varnished in white or a pale shade of blue, green or lilac with white highlights.

These delicately tinted chairs also give us the key to the colors used throughout the room. Boiseries were almost always painted, often in white or pale gray with gilded moldings. Of course the gray could shade into blue or lilac; and there were pale green or even pale pink rooms. And always, besides the tall, wide windows which abundantly let in the light of day, there were mirrors that multiplied it.

The walls were often covered with boiseries delicately carved with motifs of pearls, ribbons, stepped lines, interlacings, ovals, draperies, garlands, medallions, musical instruments or rams' heads; and a rhythm was established by the use of flat, lined pilasters leading the eye up to the sculptured cornice.

Curiously, most of the forms listed above eschew the use of the straight line, and this may well be one of the reasons why the Louis XVI style is so successful: nothing is more tiring to the eye than perfect conformity. If you were to try to define the Louis XVI look, as opposed to the Louis XV, you would have to say it witnessed the triumph of the straight, angular look inspired, in part, by the houses just dug up at Pompeii—and that would largely be true. Certainly the wild curves of the rococo were gone. Yet within this general trend there is a profusion of details which lend grace, ease and polish to what would otherwise have been too strict and austere. It was just the removal of these touches of fantasy which produced the later heavy-set Empire style.

Sometimes the boiseries left open panels to be covered with tapestries, or silk from Lyon, decorated with flowers or abstract decorative patterns (it cost 60 to 80 livres a yard), or even, in more modest rooms, with that new invention, the wallpaper, which could be bought for only twenty-five to forty-five sous a yard. Nor should another innovation be forgotten: the *toile de Jouy*. Named after the little village, just outside Paris, where it was manufactured, this was a decorative linen printed with monochrome (beige, blue, rust) scenes of country life, or flowers, or landscapes. Its charm was such that it is produced, in the same patterns, to this day.

These fabric panels, like the mirrors, had to have carved frames. Sometimes there was just a plain gilded molding, sometimes you saw palms, garlands of laurel or oak, or a repetition of the motifs used throughout the room.

Along with the relative severity of this style went a strong taste for round or oval rooms, which could be grander, especially if a cupola replaced the flat ceiling, or smaller, more intimate, more graceful than a square room. In the same spirit, there was a fashion for round or oval tables, often on wheels, that could be moved around freely. The copper-gilt open galleries with which they were often surmounted provided a graceful transition between the opacity of the wood and the openness of the space above.

So here we are, in our wood-paneled room, all in light colors, with mirrors, paintings, tapestries. We are stepping on a highly polished parquet floor partly covered with an Aubusson carpet on which a geometric or garlanded border contains a flower motif or an allegory. Still, the most noticeable part of the room, at first glance, is neither boiseries nor furniture but the lushly draped fabrics on windows and sofas alike.

They are also the element of the Louis XVI style we know the least: chairs, tables and boiseries have survived, window drapes have long since rotted away. All windows were lavishly curtained with striped, figured or flowered silk; the edges were a profusion of passementerie, as were the ties which ended in a riot of tassels. And this was not all. The valances were draped with all kinds of complicated hanging effects as were the tied, looped and overlooped curtains. Sometimes they were even topped with bouquets of feathers (always if they were bed curtains). And again, on the sofas, draped fabric was frequently hung below the wooden frame. No matter where you looked, there was a hanging.

This debauchery of fabric must not be confused with the limp, dark brown velvet favored by the Victorians. The fabrics were light and gay, full of decorative motifs, and, far from hanging down, they were arranged so as to provide an array of soft, seductive forms which played very much the same role as those garlands and knots of ribbon on the boiseries. They were also related to the current women's fashions, those masterpieces of draped materials; and, like dresses, they could reach extreme luxury.

This taste for luxurious fabrics was illustrated in the house of Monsieur Bourret, a *fermier général* (tax collector) to whom money was no object. His bedroom had walls covered in pink silk shot with silver over which had been draped an Indian muslin ending in a wide, costly lace border; the window-panes were made of Bohemian crystal, the shutters painted by Vien (see Chapter Seven). As for the furniture, it was such, a witness tells us, that the King himself couldn't have matched it, and in the bathroom solid gold taps enhanced the marble tubs. That solid gold was really not in very good taste: there is such a thing as an excess of showy splendor.

Fixtures were not limited to faucets, golden or otherwise. False fireplaces, for instance, were by no means rare. They were highly functional. Originally invented by the Maréchal de Richelieu, that tireless Don Juan, in the 1750s, to circumvent a jealous husband, they had a trick back which swiveled open. The daring lover simply rented an apartment in the house adjoining that of his beloved, had the hinges put in, and could thus enter the lady's room unseen. This simple device was later perfected: the whole mantelpiece swiveled so you could go from one room to the next without having to crawl. Soon a wide variety of these conveniences appeared in new (or remodeled) houses. There were staircases hidden in the wall and opening (so to speak) into a panel of the boiserie. False closets with removable backs were also popular as were whole walls, with their mirrors and chests of drawers, which, at the touch of a lever, pivoted open and allowed people to come in or out. None of this could have worked, of course, if it hadn't been for the custom according to which husband and wife, when they were well to do, always slept in separate rooms. Even Marie Antoinette, at Compiègne, had a secret passage built which, opening through a concealed door in her alcove, led through the cellar walls to another door hidden in the King's alcove. Her purpose was wholly proper, though: she only wanted the King to visit her at night without having to cross all the public apartments.

Not many of these hidden doors still open today. Boiseries exist, often in museums and French government buildings: many ministries are located in eighteenth-century buildings, as are the residences of the Prime Minister and the President of the Republic; but furniture is more easily seen. We are no longer likely to find a Riesener table or a Jacob chair in the window of an antique shop, though they are collected in museums all across the United States; but even the more modest representatives of the style are marked by its charm, sense of proportion and perfection of detail.

In harmony with the boiseries and ceilings, the furniture was most often carved out of light-colored precious woods: violetwood, lemonwood, rosewood, though oak, pine and walnut were also used; and in the eighties, as a result of the current Anglomania, light mahogany also came into fashion.

Bronze was in constant use, as sculpted corners or cornices, running up the legs of a table, underlining the fluting, as handles, as ornamentation. A typical desk, made of lemonwood, had a cylindrical cover that could be raised or lowered. The narrow top platform, covered with white marble, was outlined by an openwork copper-gilt gallery. Bronze rods and pearls came down the legs and met the bronze feet. Of course, all lines were straight. The joining of the leg with the main body of the piece, be it table, chair or chest, was marked by a sculptured decoration, often a square containing a stylized rose. The upright part of a chair's arm was mostly straight, and the horizontal member bore a little stuffed cushion in the middle; as for the back, it often took on an oval shape.

Here again we note that mixture of grace and severity so characteristic of the Louis XVI style: the lines are straight and sober, but the backs rounded, and the bronze ornamentation very lush. This is what we see when we look at a table with a flat top of inlaid red and white marble. In the center of the drawer, a bronze head crowned with vine leaves is surrounded with wavy laurel branches which reach all the way to both ends of the piece. The legs, narrow at the bottom, wider at the top, are outlined with bronze rods and crowned with bronze Doric capitals supported by acanthus leaves. Each of these, in turn, is topped by a square containing a stylized bronze rose.

Riesener was probably Marie Antoinette's favorite among the great cabinetmakers. And, of course, like Weisweiler and several other cabinetmakers, he was a German who, dazzled by French superiority, moved to Paris, learned his trade and became one of its great masters. He made frequent use of bronze ornaments, often sculpted by Gouthière; he was also fond of Sèvres porcelain plaques set right into the wood, usually on the sides of a little table. Jacob, on the other hand, who preferred carved wood and made less use of bronze, tended to specialize in chairs, sofas and beds which required much less of that kind of ornamentation.

New forms were much in evidence, especially for chairs. They had backs shaped like medallions, lyres, sheaves of wheat, Roman Xs or coats of arms.

There was a curious, very high-legged stool with something like a saddle on top; this was so you could watch card games from behind the players. New, very large, comfortable upholstered sofas also made their appearance, along with glassed-in bookcases that could also serve as display cases. And beds, magnificent as ever, now showed more carving and less upholstery—the columns were always sculptured wood—while being covered with new feathered comforters.

Finally, another newcomer made its entrance: the dining-room table. Until then, people had eaten on small round tables or simply on big planks resting on wooden horses and hidden under floor-length tablecloths. Now proper dining tables, often of mahogany, were made so that leaves could be inserted or removed.

No less important than the table was its décor. Aside from the plates, silverware and crystal glasses, it bore rows of silver, silver-gilt or gold candlesticks and at least one great centerpiece, a vast silver or gold basket piled high with fruit and flowers. The remaining space might be covered with a profusion of cut flowers or, possibly, two layers of different-colored sand. Decorative motifs would be drawn in the upper layer, thus making the bottom layer visible. Or, more spectacular still, a whole landscape would spread across the board. The diners, as they walked in, could see whole valleys and hills, trees and flowers, even a river, all covered with frost and snow. Then, as warmth reached the table top from the lighted candles, the "snow," which was actually made of starch, would begin to melt. The trees would become verdant, the flowers bright, and the river would fill with water. It must have been an enchanting spectacle.

Along with the fashion for flowers everywhere went a preference for cheerful upholstery material. Armchairs were covered with light-colored silk or velvet, often with stripes: blue and yellow together were favorites, while flower patterns were more often seen on chairs. They might also be covered with *toile de Jouy*. And some of those armchairs were actually recliners—you pushed a lever and the back came down to whatever level you wished.

These rooms, which eschewed the splendor of Louis XIV and the complications of Louis XV, were small paradises of simple yet luxurious boiseries, hanging silks and original, striking furniture. Of course, not all rooms were new; many people kept some or all of the furniture made thirty years earlier and left to them, along with the house, by their parents; but they managed to integrate it into a new whole. It may now be revealing to take a look at the bedroom of the widowed marquise de Rochechouart, who lived in comfort, but on a dowager's pension. It is a mixture of the decorative fashions of her youth, when crimson was the favorite color, and the newer trends. As it was, it must have had a great deal of charm.

On the walls was a gray boiserie framed in gold with a painting in the middle. The bed was covered in crimson taffeta, but it also had a blue taffeta eiderdown. Some armchairs were upholstered in cut velvet, others were gilded and had tapestried backs and seats, still others bore the fashionable stripes, but in white and crimson. In a corner stood a crimson taffeta screen, with close to it a little painted tin table (the marquise undoubtedly washed in it), and a walnut dressing table with a mirror. Toward the middle of the room there were two writing tables, one in inlaid wood with a marble top, the other, smaller one, with a copper-gilt openwork gallery.

Back near the walls stood two chests of drawers, one in inlaid wood, the other covered in Chinese lacquer with a marble top, and a bookcase with doors hung in crimson and white taffeta. On the chests stood a copper-gilt clock, two white marble candleholders and two little porcelain figures.

This was obviously a large, well-appointed room, pleasant, not very luxurious and with enough writing tables to please a bored widow. Behind this room were two smaller dressing rooms and, farther on, a dining room, drawing room, etc. If we move now to the abode of another widow, things will get very much simpler.

Madame Kerber was the relict of a master clockmaker, and she lived in just one room—but a very large one. No boiseries here, but an Indian cloth printed with stripes and bouquets of flowers. She had two curtained windows, and another pair of curtains to close off an alcove with a low bed—no columns, no eiderdown. And right near the bed was a *chaise percée* with its chamber pot. She didn't own much furniture, only a gaming table, a round dining table, an inlaid console with two drawers, a writing table and a chest of drawers. It was all valued at a mere four hundred livres and, presumably, poor Madame Kerber had all her meals sent in from outside.

Of course, one single armchair could cost as much as Madame Kerber's entire furnishings. Marie Antoinette, who knew the work of a great cabinetmaker when she saw it, kept Weisweiler, Roentgen, Leleu, Riesener and Jacob busy designing and carving furniture for Versailles, Fontainebleau, Compiègne and Saint-Cloud. A carved, gilded wooden armchair by Georges Jacob is a good example of this.

The feet are decorated with vertical acanthus leaves curving out at the top from which the fluted legs, each fluting bearing a bronze rod, rise to Ionic capitals. The wood all around the seat is adorned with an ivy garland which continues along the arm's vertical support and ends in a caryatid with the head of a woman topped by a basket. The horizontal part of the arm, which is upholstered in the middle, is linked with this basket by a sinuous ivy stem. Carved ribbons frame the central upholstery, and the arm is linked to the back by a large acanthus leaf. The upright members of the back emerge from a vase and each is then decorated with an acanthus leaf and fluted, finally ending in a Doric capital which supports a little vase. Across the top we see a motif of oval forms surmounted in the middle by a shield bearing the letters MA and framed, as well as linked to the back, by a garland of flowers. The seat, back and arms are upholstered in white silk with a motif of small draperies and leafy branches.

This description seems impossibly complicated, but in fact the armchair, sumptuous as it is, exemplifies the simple lines of the Louis XVI style. The ornamentation is, of course, abundant—hardly a surprise since this was a chair literally fit for a queen, but it is never heavy. And, as always, the quality of the details is remarkable. There is never an awkward or unfinished passage; no matter how closely we look at the folds of an acanthus leaf, the lines of a Doric capital, or the petals of the flowers, they remain perfection itself, proof of that inspiring alliance of true dedication and great talent.

Of course these splendid rooms had to be kept clean, and their owners expected a response when they pulled one of the numerous bells. Everybody who wasn't altogether destitute had servants; a prosperous shopkeeper usually had a maid of all work who lived in his house and was helped in the kitchen by her employer's wife. A duke or a *fermier général* might have forty or fifty servants.

Some of these you never saw. There were the chefs, their helpers and scullery maids in the kitchen, some ten to twelve people altogether. Then, in the stables, with their twenty to thirty horses, a complement of five or six stableboys made sure the animals looked their best, and two or three coachmen, in resplendent livery, ruled the roost.

In the house itself there were cleaning women. Then, going up the ladder, we come to the liveried servants. Every great house, every employer of more than two or three servants had a special livery worn by all visible male servants—the King's was blue and gold, the Queen's red and silver. There were footmen, who waited at the doors of the main rooms, announced visitors, fetched and carried, ran errands and stood, in pairs, behind the carriage. They also served at table and might, in a great house, number anywhere from ten to twenty-five. Closer to the top came a maître d'hôtel, the French version of the all-powerful English butler. Finally the master had a valet or two who curled and powdered his hair, dressed him, took care of his clothes and often turned into a confidant, even a purveyor of easy women. As for the mistress, she had from two to six maids to take care of her hair, clothes and jewelry, much of which might be sewn on a dress. These maids also had to dress her, no mean task at a time when clothes were laced or, more often, pinned together—a very convenient arrangement if your weight kept changing, but one that implied the presence of several maids, a long time spent in getting dressed and a stately way of moving. It was no surprise that when Madame de Staël, coming to be presented at court, jumped out of her carriage with her usual impetuousness her train stayed behind and had to be hastily pinned back on—but it was considered amusing.

Obviously it was all too splendid to last, those harmonious rooms, full of masterpieces, inhabited by a society whose clothes were as elegant as their surroundings, whose lives were so easy, so pleasant. The world that made all this possible was based on hard, unchanging privilege, the right of a very few to rule and pay no taxes. While houses, inside and out, set a new standard of beauty, gilded carriages were running over the poor; while silken ladies chattered or played their harps, the people of France were working. No, it could not last; all too soon the Revolution came and swept it all away. Of course, people went on being rich and living in grand houses—but they were just that: rich. Wealth replaced perfection; pomp, amiability. Empire furniture took the place of Louis XVI masterpieces, but those last twenty years before the great change remained a golden, shimmering dream in men's memories.

Chapter Four

THE ESTABLISHMENT: ARISTOCRACY, PARLEMENT AND CHURCH

Nothing could have been more fashionable, in the 1770s and 1780s, than to show one's interest in the welfare of the people and nation; nothing could have been more false. France was firmly divided between a small establishment of perhaps forty to fifty thousand people, and a vast, still inchoate lower class whose primary purpose was, apparently, to support the aristocracy, the Church and those peculiar institutions, the parlements.

It was easy to tell just which of the two categories you belonged to: establishmentarians paid virtually no taxes; the rest of the nation did. It was a system which didn't do much for public finance since the poor, and only the poor, supported all public expenditure; it didn't do much for the poor either, since their already small incomes were reduced, sometimes by more than half, in order to pay the government taxes on land, income and roads, and the tithe, the Church's claim to ten per cent of all they made. A political cartoon, published in 1789, shows a peasant bearing a nobleman and a priest on his back, with the caption, "This has to stop." That it did was the most incontrovertible achievement of the Revolution.

The nobility, as such, was a curious body, composed of discordant, sometimes warring parts, and united only in its claims: freedom from taxation, immutability of feudal dues. Originally, all nobles had been warriors, and their privileges had been fair compensation for a life in which they might find themselves smiting the infidel or merely the lord next door. By the eighteenth century all this had receded to a very distant past, and even Saint-Simon, that upholder of aristocratic privilege, bemoaned the uselessness of his class.

There was a *noblesse d'épée* (nobility of the sword) and a *noblesse de robe* (nobility of the—judicial—gown), a country nobility, a Paris nobility and a court nobility. A rich and fashionable duke who was also a First Gentleman of the Bedchamber had very little in common with an impoverished baron who starved on a few ancestral acres, which he might even be seen plowing, sword at his side, or with a judge whose patent of nobility went back a mere fifty years.

There lay the paradox and the flaw: a courtier had nothing but contempt for a man recently ennobled, and showed it on every occasion. You could not be presented at court unless you could prove four hundred years of nobility: what could be more wounding for a man of great wealth, who, further, was legally noble, than to be told he was not good enough to attend his sovereign? And how could he help resenting the arrogant scion of an old family whose only achievement was that he had deigned to be born? He was bound to hope, even work, for a change that would give him his fair share of social status and political power. Yet he was legally a noble, with all the exemptions and privileges of that state, and therefore quite unwilling to contemplate any change which might set back his class as a whole. The net result was a frozen society in which the enormous mass of the underprivileged could look for no change, but in which the nobility was constantly at war with itself, and thus inviting disestablishment since it was providing its enemies with their best arguments. The only wonder is that the Revolution did not come sooner.

There were several ways of becoming noble if, alas, you were born a commoner. You could render the King some signal service, or just please him, and be ennobled as a reward; you could be appointed to an office so powerful that the King would ennoble you; or, easiest of all, you could buy a function which carried nobility. If, for instance, you purchased the unsalaried and purely theoretical position of Secretary to the King, you automatically received a patent of nobility (as Beaumarchais was to do), and it would only cost you about twenty thousand livres. Finally, you could buy a piece of land to which a title was attached; with luck, and good planning, you could go in one day from humble commoner to noble count.

Voltaire is a good if somewhat surprising illustration of the process. He was born a commoner, the son of a notary. It was all very well to be considered the greatest writer alive, but it didn't do much for him in the way of privilege or precedence; so, by dint of steady intrigue, and after much lavish flattery of Louis XV's mistress, the marquise de Pompadour, he bagged an appointment as Gentleman of the Bedchamber in Ordinary. This was a menial court post, but Voltaire was now allowed to attend the King in his bedroom and, more important, he became, ipso facto, noble. Then came a hitch: Voltaire had an unfortunate way of noticing injustice and writing about it. In short order he became persona non grata and, since courts never change, he was told to resign or be fired, so he resigned—only, by resigning, he automatically lost his nobility.

After a pause—Voltaire found it safer to leave France for a while—he returned and purchased the estates of Ferney and Tournay which, besides being conveniently near the Swiss border, carried with them the title of baron; while discreetly forbearing to use his new title (he had a keen sense of the ridiculous), the new owner proceeded to exercise all his rights and never again paid a cent in taxes.

-—≼ ⊱—-

The *noblesse d'épée* was composed of the families whose forebears had formed a medieval fighting caste—and they were proud of it. Its members always wore swords as a reminder of their origins and still under Louis XVI were prepared to lead the French armies in time of war. It was assumed that the young men of the nobility would, by definition, make competent officers. Most of them entered the army at sixteen or seventeen—not, of course, as enlisted men, only commoners did that, but, if worse came to worst, as ensigns. They were not expected to spend much time with their regiments in time of peace and they counted on court favor for promotion. Thus a really influential family, like the Noailles or the Rohans, usually managed to have their offspring made colonels of their regiments at the age of six or seven.

This worked splendidly except in case of actual war, when sheer incompetence tended to have unpleasant results; so Louis XV founded the École Militaire where selected young men received a thorough grounding in all the arts of war. Of course the quality of military leadership improved as a result until an ugly fact came to light: some of these brilliant new officers were commoners. Clearly, there was only one solution. In 1781 the War Minister decreed that henceforth noble birth would be required for any army rank above that of sergeant. Many promising careers were ended—or so it seemed until the Revolution; and a young Corsican destined for the École Militaire, one Napoleone Buonaparte, was forced to scramble very hard to produce his proof of nobility.

Here again we see the stultification of the system: in the seventeenth century it was still possible for a talented commoner to make good in the army, rise to a high rank and found a noble family; by the end of the eighteenth, the *noblesse d'épée* had become a closed caste which carefully shut out any new recruit. In 1789, not surprisingly, most of the army joined the revolutionaries and the officers emigrated.

Only the lesser members of the *noblesse d'épée* depended on the army for an income. Most had hereditary estates, and almost all counted on the King's favor for a pension. In any event, the nobility had no choice: the only career it could embrace without losing caste was the military. While, in England, great nobles settled on their estates to improve them, governed the country through their control of Parliament and speculated in trade, their French counterparts forgot that they had estates and lived at court, attending on the King and looking to him only for political and financial plums.

There, indeed, ran the great cleavage within the *noblesse d'épée*. On the one hand, courtiers who could boast either high rank or a substantial income considered it beneath them to show concern about estates which they never visited, so they relied on a major-domo to take care of their affairs and spent all their time in display and intrigues. On the other, small noblemen, living in the country, did their best to wring an inadequate income from far too few acres and therefore put almost unbearable pressure on their tenants. They had no hope of ever being given a remunerative office or pension; and, while they were often quite as unpopular as the courtiers, they hated the court and all it stood for just as much as the peasants among whom they lived. Nor could they, like younger sons in England, become lawyers, politicians or even clergymen: noblemen didn't work, and preference in the Church came from Versailles.

Only the middle class thought about money: aristocrats simply spent it and, when it ran out, went into debt. Paying tradesmen, always an unpleasant obligation, could be put off, for years at a time if need be. Leading a sumptuous life was the main thing. When the duc de Choiseul fell from office in 1770 and was exiled, he retired to his castle of Chanteloup, which he promptly enlarged. Aside from the huge reception salons, there were libraries and game rooms, and rooms for a collection of coins said to rival the King's. A minimum of twenty people always showed up for dinner; forty came closer to the norm, and the cost of all this ran to over a million livres a year. Choiseul was rich, but not that rich. By 1780 he had to sell off his paintings.[1]

Few other great nobles were reduced to that painful necessity: there were endless plums in the King's gift. Pluralism of office was a way of life. You could be at the same time a Marshal of France (5,000 livres p.a.), a governor of a province (around 35,000 livres p.a.) which you were expected to visit for a week or so every other year, the holder of a Household post and the recipient, besides, of a yearly pension. Then, if your six-year-old child was made a colonel, or given an abbey, you could add that to your income. With luck and enterprise, you could be made a Knight of the Order of the Holy Ghost: this highest of the King's honors which carried a stipend as well, was all the more sought after since it had only one hundred members besides the members of the royal family. Finally, if you were really short of money and you caught the King in a good mood, he might give you an *acquis du comptant* (or cash voucher) which you would then present to the Treasurer; he could even undertake to pay your daughter's dowry. In fact, to the plebeian eye, it looked strangely as if the State existed for the single purpose of supporting the aristocracy.

When all else failed, or proved insufficient, there was always one last resource. As the duchesse de Chaulnes remarked to her son, "To marry advantageously beneath oneself is merely taking dung to manure one's acres." The

[1] The whole collection was bought by Catherine the Great and hangs in the Hermitage today.

dowry, in such cases, was apt to be really impressive; the young bride, a duchess now, usually spent the rest of her life ignored by her new family, though there were exceptions. The duc de Choiseul, for instance, married Mademoiselle Crozat, the orphaned daughter of a rich financier with a dowry of over four million livres; but, in spite of his wife's middle-class origins, he was always kind and attentive to her.

Of course, people sometimes vanished to their estates while their income went to pay their debts; still everyone was shocked when, in 1783, the prince de Guéménée, a member of the powerful Rohan family, whose wife was Governess of the King's Children, went bankrupt: he owed thirty million livres. Translated into a dollar equivalent of ninety million, it is a huge sum; but, put in perspective, it becomes more immense still: it was over one eighth of the national budget—which, today, would come to some ninety billion dollars. The prince begged the King to save him; the King declined: he didn't much like him, and it really was too much money. The Guéménées left Versailles and vanished into the provinces; their relatives got together and paid up; but, for the first time, people began to wonder why they had assumed it was all right for noblemen to have debts.

The prince de Guéménée, in fact, wasn't alone in going bankrupt: he took his whole order with him. Increasingly, as the century passed, people wondered just why the *noblesse d'épée* should consider itself so superior to everyone else. It now began to dawn on them that, as a class, it had lost its purpose. It seemed to exist only in order to spend money it often didn't have. Why should the prince, people asked, have been able to accumulate such a mountain of debt? And why should the King either rescue or pension his peers when the State no longer needed them? By the eighties, and not counting the distant American war, France had been at peace for more than twenty years, and it seemed as if all the *noblesse d'épée* ever did was intrigue at court. Six years after the prince vanished, the whole *noblesse d'épée* followed him—not to an obscure retreat but to exile or the guillotine.

—◄[ ]►—

The officeholding monopoly of the *noblesse d'épée* did not stop with the State and court: it extended to the Church as well. The eldest son would go to court, the youngest be made a bishop—it was all settled at birth, and easily achieved. By the concordat of 1516, the King named the bishops, who were then confirmed by the Pope, whether they were worthy or not. He also, once a month, worked on the list of benefices, distributing abbeys and other income-bearing ecclesiastical positions just as he pleased. Knowledge of theology or a saintly life was hardly relevant: here, as always, birth was everything.

There was scarcely a bishop who did not belong to an aristocratic family— a recent development. There would have been no chance of the great Bossuet becoming a bishop, if he had lived under Louis XVI because of his modest origins. The Rohans (who practically owned the bishopric of Strasbourg), the Montmorencys, the La Rochefoucaulds, the Talleyrands and the La Roche-Aymons came first and foremost.

Some of the bishoprics also carried actual titles: the Bishops of Cambrai, Laon, Reims and Mende were ex officio dukes and peers of the realm. The Bishop of Strasbourg was a prince of the Holy Roman Empire, and treated as such. Then there were "noble" chapters whose canons had to prove at least four generations of nobility and received an income to which no duty whatever was attached.

Aside from the bishoprics, the King also made abbés, whose income was derived from that of an abbey. In the Middle Ages the abbot had lived and ruled over his monks; now it was possible—indeed frequent—for an abbey to be given en commende: a set portion of its income, varying from a third to nine tenths, went to a person named by the King and quite free from any obligation of residence. The monks, left abbotless, would make do with whatever remained. It was not necessary for an abbé to have received holy orders: Princes of the Blood, for instance, were often given some of the richest abbeys to boost their income. By 1770, four fifths of all abbeys in France were en commende, with disastrous results. Between 1770 and 1790 the number of monks living in French abbeys fell exactly by half and since, further, they were left unsupervised, their standards of observance quickly declined. Some abbeys, indeed whole orders of monks, became bywords for various vices, the Carmes and Cordeliers foremost among these, who were known for their proverbial sexual ardor.

Women's convents were a little better, although some eighteenth-century nuns became famous for their sexual peccadilloes. The atmosphere of religious fervor was, in any case, hardly improved by the custom of making nuns out of girls with no vocation but even less dowry.

The Church of France was the first of the three orders of the realm; it was also the richest. Its income came from two sources: it collected a ten per cent tax on all non-noble income and it owned a great deal of land. The exact amount of that income is almost impossible to ascertain, since all Church possessions were tax exempt, and beneficiaries were often anxious to conceal the extent of their wealth. Still, we do know that the bishopric of Strasbourg brought in eight hundred thousand livres a year and that its holder, the Cardinal de Rohan, had a total Church income of over three million livres. We owe another way of estimating Church income to the Revolution. When, in 1789–1790, the National Assembly prepared to nationalize the estates of the Church, Talleyrand, then Bishop of Autun and the man in France who best understood the clergy's finances, suggested that the State provide a yearly subsidy of a hundred million livres. Since this figure was supposed to be substantially lower than that of the income derived from the abolished *dime* (tithe) and confiscated lands, we can surmise that the Church's real revenues were in the range of two to three hundred million livres. By comparison, the French national budget for 1781 ran to two hundred and fifty million.

As for the Church's cash reserves, they must have been huge: during this same crisis one of the bishops, Monsieur de Boisgelin, offered to give the State a onetime contribution of four hundred million livres, an almost unthinkable sum.

Most bishops and abbés had very little to do with religious activities. The Abbé de Chaulieu was famous for his obscene verse; the Abbé de Boufflers was an atheist, the Abbé Galiani a deist; the Abbé, later Cardinal, de Bernis obtained preferment by writing pretty verse for Madame de Pompadour and was generally nicknamed *Babet la Bouquetière* (Chatty the Flower Girl). The Cardinal de Rohan, of whom we shall hear more, shocked the Empress Maria Theresa, when he was ambassador to Vienna, by the extreme luxury he displayed; she also objected to his public wenching and to his hunting, in civilian clothing, on Sundays when he was supposed to be saying mass. The Abbé de Périgord, who became Bishop of Autun in 1788, was known for his wit, his success with fashionable women and his gambling. None of this was out of the ordinary: the Church was divided between *grands seigneurs*, who took the money and spent it as they pleased, and a proletariat of country priests who did the actual work. Most bishops had nothing but scorn for the lowborn priests, the priests nothing but hatred for their bishops.

There were, in fact, two kinds of priests: *curés décimataires* (ten per cent tax-collecting priests), who were appointed to the living by its patron, usually the local lord, seldom the bishop (Voltaire, at Ferney, could appoint two priests), and *curés congruistes*. These were appointed by the *curés décimataires*, who had better things to do than serve mass and attend to the needs of the poor. The *curés congruistes* received at most two hundred and fifty livres a year, not nearly enough to live on. As a result, village churches were ruinous and village priests more likely to look after their fields than the faithful.

By 1789 the French Church was split right in two: there was no longer anything in common between its aristocracy and its proletariat, except for being objects of scorn to anyone with any pretension to intelligence or fashion. "We felt a secret pleasure in watching the attacks on that old assemblage [the Church], which we considered gothic and ridiculous; we enjoyed at the same time the advantages of a patrician life and a plebeian philosophy," wrote the vicomte de Ségur, son of the War Minister brought to office by Besenval. Depending on your point of view, the Church could stand for fiscal greed (it made a "voluntary gift" of only fifteen million livres a year to the government), debauchery in high places or grotesque old-fashioned intolerance. And yet it went on performing, perhaps through force of habit, a number of useful functions: it educated, it took care of the sick, it helped the poor.

Education was virtually a Church monopoly. There was a primary school in every parish, usually run by a priest. The Jesuits and later the Oratorians ran six hundred secondary colleges in which grammar, history, geography, mathematics, Latin, theology and the classics were taught by highly competent masters. There were, it is true, a few secular universities; but even there some of the professors were ecclesiastics.

Land improvement, curiously, was also largely due to the Church; some resident bishops had the interest and the capital which lay landlords so often lacked.

All the hospitals were religious. They were, on the whole, places to die in. There were very few cures, not surprisingly, since four patients were put into every bed and hygiene was non-existent. Still, toward the end of the century there was a slight improvement; and, if it came to that, it was better to die indoors and in a bed than to be left to expire on the street.

Finally, the Church clung, albeit not very passionately, to its tradition of relieving poverty. There was a state tax to help the poor, but it usually produced no more than four or five hundred thousand livres a year. How far the ecclesiastical authorities would go in assisting the poor varied widely from diocese to diocese; still, it was a last resort for the truly desperate.

Even the doctrine taught and accepted by the Gallican Church was rather peculiar. The Pope's bulls and encyclicals could be published only after they had been approved by King and the Parlement de Paris; over the centuries a number of these had been withheld or even burned at the stake by the public executioner. A whole separate Church had thus come into being. It acknowledged the Pope's authority in theory but within well-defined limits; it held that the Sorbonne knew more about true doctrine than the College of Cardinals; in fact there were many resemblances between the Gallican Church and the Church of England and, as such, it was a constant source of annoyance to Rome.

Like the *noblesse d'épée*, the Church managed to put itself in the most dangerous position possible: it was split down the middle, its leadership weak and corrupt, its numbers poor and angry. It had lost the support of the ruling classes and the respect of the people. Unable to count on either Rome or itself, it stood exposed to attack from every corner, a tempting prey which provided both a convenient political target and a source of seemingly endless money. It is no wonder that the confiscation of Church property and the establishment of a Gallican episcopal Church wholly independent of the Pope were among the first reforms of the Revolution.

—⁂ ⁂—

The last element of the establishment trinity was also the oddest. The *noblesse d'épée* and the Church, in one form or another, existed all over Europe; but the parlements were a peculiarly French institution whose absurdity had long been understood and denounced—uselessly, since they seemed able to survive just about anything.

Each of the thirteen parlements had its own jurisdiction, corresponding to the ancient limits of a province. The Parlement de Paris, however, played a dominant role: it was the ultimate court of appeal from the provincial parlements; it had far and away the widest jurisdiction, its circuit stretching in a large circle around Paris. It was the only parlement joined by the peers of France on certain great occasions and thus the only one able to judge a peer. Finally, by virtue of its location in the capital, it frequently tried to usurp a political role.

Unlike their English namesake, the parlements were neither elected nor in any way representative of the people. The members were not even appointed by the King; they simply bought their offices. Money was the only standard. Neither competence nor even moderate intelligence was required; as for honesty and incorruptibility, they would have been positive hindrances.

Nor did the parlements, even that of Paris, exist as one body. The Parlement de Paris, alone, was the reunion of nine judicial chambers composed of two hundred and forty members of differing status. Its most important section, the *Grande Chambre,* was led by a *Premier Président* (First President) who was named by the King but had to buy his office; then came nine *Présidents à mortier,*[2] twenty lay counselors (*conseillers*) and twelve clerical counselors who sat only on cases concerning the Church and its doctrine.

The main function of the Parlement de Paris was judicial: it was the principal court of the realm. Its all-embracing jurisdiction covered criminal as well as civil suits; it was also competent to determine religious dogma; it could suppress any published material, and frequently did; it was the court of record: no new law or edict, no creation of a duke and peer, no new tax could be valid until it had been registered by the Parlement. Finally, as an outcome of this last function, it was entitled to present remonstrances to the King if it disapproved of the text it was asked to register.

From this right came the Parlement's political pretensions until, at the end of the Ancien Régime, its members tried to prove it was entitled to the same powers as its English counterpart.

The counselors and presidents of the Parlement de Paris, like their provincial colleagues, came from the top crust of the bourgeoisie. Their offices, after all, were expensive: in 1789, in Paris, the *Premier Président's* place was worth 150,000 livres, and a *conseiller's* seat 50,000 livres. As it was, this represented a sharp decline: just as the King grew increasingly stricter about the genealogies of his courtiers, so the Parlement de Paris, seized with the same madness, decreed that no one could join its ranks unless he could produce four noble grandparents. Of course, the office of president or counselor, in itself, conferred nobility upon its holder; and so a few great parliamentary

[2] The *mortiers* were fur-lined hats which they wore when they walked into the court.

families, the Ormessons, Aguesseaus, Aligres, inter alia, passed their seats on from father to son.

By 1770, in fact, the Parlement de Paris had come to include the elite of the middle class—the *ennobled* middle class. Président d'Aligre, for instance, had a capital sum of 5,000,000 livres invested in the Bank of England, and an income of 700,000 livres. Président Lepelletier de Saint-Fargeau's income was well over 500,000 livres, and, rich as they were, those two were by no means alone. A new, intermediary class had come into being: it was ex-tremely wealthy—but not prestigious; it was legally noble, and thus privi-leged—but it claimed to speak for the bourgeoisie and the people; it often married into the *real* nobility (those huge dowries)—but it could never be received at court; it had enormous financial power—but had nowhere to go politically.

This uneasy situation maddened the parlements; in an effort to assert their supposed powers, they spent most of the eighteenth century in systematic op-position to the King, first on religious, then on financial questions. Time after time they refused to register the tax edicts sent to them by Louis XV.

A King faced with this kind of obstruction had a traditional solution: he could hold a *lit de justice* in which, face to face with the assembled parlement, he gave it the order to register the edict. In French constitutional practice the King's will must, in the last resort, be obeyed.[3] When Louis XVI, that mild monarch, was accused by the duc d'Orléans of resorting to il-legality, he answered: "It's legal because it's my will," and he was right. But by the 1760s the parlements, in defiance of this principle, started meeting again after a *lit de justice* to reject the very edict they had been forced to register in the King's presence. By 1771 the confrontation had reached such a pitch that Louis XV was driven to take a radical step: he abolished the parlements.

Of course there was an uproar—but no lower-class uprising. All the rich families whose power was suddenly gone shrieked in frenzied protest, to no avail. New courts were created, and within a year justice was being rendered better and faster than it had in centuries. A grateful public began to see the parlements for what they had really been, corrupt and greedy bodies, unin-terested in justice or anything else outside their own interests.

Justice may always be costly; within the jurisdiction of the parlements, it was ruinous. Although the King did pay the members a small salary, most of their large income came directly from the people involved in civil suits. First there were the *épices*, official preliminary bribes; they could bring in as much as fifty thousand livres a year per judge. Then there were the *vacations* and *offices*, additional, recurring, multiplying charges, all of which had to be paid in full before the case actually came to trial. All this took time; innu-merable documents had to be composed, copied, stamped and filed with the clerk of the court. And then the judges had other things to do: after all,

---

[3] "*Si veut le roi, veut la loi* [The law wants what the king wants]," ran the maxim.

great properties take some looking after. In consequence the progress of justice was, at best, extremely slow. Suits were expected to last for years; and even then fair and impartial judges were rare exceptions.

One of the worst characteristics of the thirteen parlements was their blind solidarity. If you were on bad terms with any member of any one of them, or if you belonged to a group they didn't approve of, such as the intellectuals, and you had to go to law, you could expect to lose regardless of the merits of your case. And if you were arrested for any reason the chances of your being ever found not guilty were horrendously slim: despite all attempt to shame them, the parlements insisted on the use of the two dreaded "questions," the *question préalable* and the *question préliminaire*, i.e., torture by water, the rack, thumbscrews and *brodequins,* which slowly crushed the leg bones from the top of the thigh to the ankles. It was by no means unusual for a man to be carried in to his trial: you can't walk very well with crushed, broken, bleeding legs. Then, if the accused was found guilty, he could be condemned without a public statement of cause; as the penalty was carried out the same day it was imposed, there was no way mistakes could be rectified.

The new court, on the other hand, the Grand Conseil, was composed of magistrates appointed for life by the King and paid by him; offices could neither be bought nor inherited. The magistrates, who did not have to be noble, received their patent of nobility at the same time as their office.

At first the public was indifferent. Voltaire and the philosophers, though, who were acutely aware of the old parlements' frequent denials of justice, immediately backed the reform. Soon people realized that here they could find relatively efficient and fair trials. The old problem had finally been solved, and justice stopped being the property of a small, prejudiced and selfish class.

Unfortunately the man responsible for these reforms, the Lord Chancellor de Maupeou, had come to power as part of a ministry firmly backed by Madame du Barry. The Dauphin, who was both very Catholic and very prudish, loathed his grandfather's mistress and all her works. When the old King died in May 1774, and the Dauphin succeeded him as Louis XVI, his first act was to dismiss the hated ministry, and with the ministry went the Grand Conseil.

Louis XV had been hated; Louis XVI seemed the answer to every hope. His accession was greeted with almost delirious joy by everyone except Madame du Barry's party—who promptly started to slander him. And in the first flush of his popularity the King proceeded to cancel his grandfather's reforms —besides, he couldn't stand Maupeou. On October 27, 1774, he recalled the parlements. This liberal move was widely applauded: any institution capable of resisting new taxes must be on the side of liberty and the people. In fact, no assumption could have been further off the mark. What Louis XVI had done was to recall a selfish oligarchy whose opposition to change was carefully hidden by hypocritical phraseology.

The Parlement de Paris promptly showed its mettle. The edicts recalling it had specified that, henceforth, remonstrances could be made only *after* the registration of an edict: it was the only way to prevent the kind of sterile and systematic opposition the Parlement had so often displayed earlier. On December 2 the reborn court assembled and refused to register the very edicts which had brought it back into being, on the grounds that it had no need to be re-created since it existed as of right. The edict prescribing registration before remonstrance was therefore equally invalid, and on the same grounds. With that flourish, having set history firmly back, the Parlement returned delightedly to the collection of bribes and the breaking of limbs.

For the rest of the reign the Parlement's position was simple: it claimed that it was a legislature and tried to stop every reform as it came along. On March 12, 1776, the King had to hold a *lit de justice* to register an edict abolishing the provincial customs which made trade almost impossible (see Chapter Ten), and another abolishing the *corvée*: the two weeks a year peasants were forced to spend making and repairing roads was to be replaced by a universal land tax. Of course, all the judges were men of property; they could only oppose a new law which shifted, even slightly, any burden from the overtaxed, overworked peasantry onto their own shoulders. The *noblesse de robe* enjoyed the same privileges as the *noblesse d'épée*, after all. "Feudal rights," said Président Séguier, that great defender of the people, "are an integral part of an owner's property."

The Parlement then proceeded to oppose, in quick succession, an edict abolishing the old, restrictive medieval guilds and another establishing the free circulation of grains throughout the kingdom; and all these reactionary stands were cloaked under claims that it was defending the subjects' freedom (in this case, clearly, the right to starve).

In 1777 the King appointed a liberal ministry under Necker; of course, the Parlement was against it. In 1780 Louis XVI abolished the use of pretrial torture; the Parlement was shocked and scandalized, though it was soothing to remember that it retained the use of torture during or after the trial. In 1781 Necker tried to create a network of provincial assemblies to advise the King. Without wasting a second, the Parlement ended this attempt at forming the roots of a true parliamentary system. All through these and other similar conflicts, it persisted in its old claim that it was speaking for France itself, when it was, at best, a small, non-representative oligarchy whose jurisdiction was limited to the provinces surrounding Paris.

All through the eighties the Parlement's opposition to the King's policies persisted; it could, therefore, hardly believe its luck when that foolish, bumbling monarch thrust the Necklace affair into its lap.

The events themselves were relatively simple. In the early seventies the court jewelers, Boehmer & Bassange, had assembled a diamond necklace of a size and quality never seen before. They had to borrow heavily, at a high interest, in order to buy the stones, so they were naturally anxious to sell it as fast as possible. Given the cost and splendor of the piece, the Queen was the obvious client—but she wouldn't buy it. Since she was well known to love diamonds and had gone into debt in order to purchase ever more, Boehmer & Bassange couldn't believe their ears.

The next step was for them to see the King and talk him into buying the necklace as a present for his wife. That worked, briefly; but Marie Antoinette refused the necklace on the legitimate grounds that 1,600,000 livres could be better spent elsewhere. The desperate jewelers then offered it all over Europe, but still to no avail. At that point Boehmer asked Marie Antoinette for an audience and, falling to his knees, told her he would kill himself if she didn't buy the necklace. Justifiably angry, the Queen had him thrown out.

Then, in 1784, things changed. Cardinal de Rohan, whom we have already met as Bishop of Strasbourg, came to Boehmer and explained that the Queen, after all, had decided she wanted the necklace but the transaction had to remain a secret (one wonders whether she was also supposed to wear all those diamonds only when she was quite alone), and that she had chosen him, the cardinal, as the intermediary. The jeweler, with a great sigh of relief, handed him the necklace, nodded happily when he was told payment would be made in several installments, the first to come soon, and settled down to wait.

The first question is, of course, whyever should Marie Antoinette have chosen the cardinal to represent her? The answer is very simple: she didn't. In fact she disliked Rohan so much that, although he was Grand Almoner of France, and thus in charge of all religious ceremonies at court, she always refused to speak to him. It wasn't just that she found his manner odious; her mother, the Empress, had been shocked by the cardinal's behavior in Vienna and, even worse, a letter he wrote home from Vienna after the first partition of Poland had been shown, by helpful friends, to the then Dauphine. "I have actually seen Maria Theresa weep over the sufferings of the downtrodden Poles," Rohan had written, "but that princess . . . seems to cry on command: in one hand, she holds a handkerchief to wipe away her tears while, with the other, she seizes a sword so as to be a co-sharer." It was funny, it was also true, but the words rankled and Marie Antoinette never forgave.

The cardinal found this situation awkward and unpleasant. No courtier ever liked to be out of favor; besides, he considered himself a cardinal in the line of Richelieu, Mazarin and Fleury: he, too, ought to be Prime Minister. And there was no chance of that without the Queen's favor. Early in 1783, through Joseph Balsamo, a charlatan whose hold on the cardinal was a claim that he could transmute lead into gold, he met an adventuress, Madame de la Motte-Valois, who mendaciously represented herself as belonging to the Queen's intimate circle. Like everyone else in Paris, she knew about the necklace. Little by little she led the cardinal to believe not just that the

Queen was ready to forgive him but even that she felt strongly attracted to him. The necklace was to be the occasion of his return to favor. As the go-between, he would pick up the necklace and take it to the Queen, who would pay for it over a period of time.

Just in case the cardinal had any doubts, Madame de la Motte now produced several highly amiable letters signed "Marie Antoinette de France." The cardinal, because of his position at court, should have known that Queens never signed themselves "de France," and merely used their first name, but he fell into the trap. Soon after, a meeting (on August 11, 1784) was arranged, for midnight, in the park of Versailles (which was open to the public). At the appointed hour a young woman who looked strikingly like Marie Antoinette but was in fact a prostitute found by Madame de la Motte and called Mademoiselle Oliva appeared, muttered a few words and quickly ran away when Madame de la Motte rushed forth, frantically whispering, "Quick, quick, here comes the comtesse d'Artois."

The cardinal was now completely dazzled. He fetched the necklace from the jewelers and gave it to Madame de la Motte, who would, in her turn, give it to the Queen—or so she said. That Sunday Rohan went to Versailles, expecting the Queen to shine forth with diamonds and friendliness. Instead, both were conspicuously absent, and she ignored the cardinal just as usual. Undaunted, the cardinal, to whom Madame de la Motte explained that these things take time, waited and waited and waited. In the meantime Madame de la Motte, who had suddenly gone from poverty to extreme affluence, bought herself some carriages and prudently moved out of Paris.

Nothing further happened until the beginning of 1786 when Boehmer & Bassange, who were about to go bankrupt and to whom the scheduled payments were long overdue, went straight to the Queen and complained. She sent them to the King and the cat was out of the bag.

At first there was immense confusion; but as the cardinal's role began to emerge Louis XVI made his first mistake by having him arrested, on a Sunday afternoon, after mass, wearing full canonicals and in the middle of the Hall of Mirrors. The scandal was immense. Then, as the story unfolded, people found it hard to believe the cardinal could have been quite that foolish. Still, one by one, all the little group was arrested and the sequence of events became clear enough.

Of course, many people who hated the Queen could hardly contain their joy: it was very easy to make her look bad. Now Madame de la Motte (minus the diamonds; she had sent them to London) was in jail, along with Mademoiselle Oliva; as for the cardinal, he had offered to pay for the necklace out of his own pocket and was in the Bastille as befitted his rank.[4] From there, he wrote the King, asking to be declared an innocent dupe. "If," he asked, "I could hope that the inquiries which may have been made, but which I know nothing about, had led Your Majesty to decide that I am

[4] It was the traditional prison for misbehaving nobles.

guilty only of having been fooled, I would then make bold to beg you, Sir, to pronounce on my case with both justice and kindness." A *lettre de cachet*, exiling the cardinal, could have ended it all; another could have kept Madame de la Motte in jail, where she certainly deserved to be; and the affair would have been over. Instead, a stupid King and a Queen both blind and intent on public vengeance decided to refer the whole mess to the Parlement.

Instantly the scandal rebounded. The Parlement, at first unable to believe its luck, gloated. "What a great and happy business! A crook of a cardinal, the Queen implicated in forgeries! What slime on the crozier and the scepter! What a triumph for the ideals of liberty! What importance given to the Parlement!" wrote the *conseiller* Préteau de Saint-Just, one of the future judges. As for the Princes of the Blood and the peers, who sat in the Parlement, they simply excused themselves.

The trial was short, the result predictable. On May 31, 1786, Rohan was declared innocent (and the Queen guilty by implication); only Madame de la Motte, who, after all, had the diamonds, was condemned as a thief; as such, she was to be branded with a V-shaped red-hot iron on both shoulders; and, shortly after, despite her shrieks and contortions, she had to endure both pain and infamy.

It was immediately obvious that the Parlement had capped its many years of opposition. "That trial created a shock which rent the foundations of the State," Goethe wrote. "It destroyed all the respect the people felt for the Queen and, generally, for the upper classes. For, alas, each of the actors only made plainer the corruption in which the court and people of the highest rank were mired. . . . The Affair of the Necklace is the preface of the Revolution."

The Parlement had never felt more powerful. It went on to oppose every one of the measures taken by the Finance Minister to remedy the desperate state of the Treasury, to such an extent that its systematic denials led directly to the calling of the Estates-General; and then, aghast, it realized what it had done: a genuinely representative assembly would gather, for the first time since 1614, and take unto itself all claims to speak for the people's rights and wishes.

In one last desperate attempt to regain the lost ground, the Parlement then launched iself into the current controversy: were the Estates-General to gather as they had in 1614? If so, while voting would take place inside each of the three orders,[5] each order would have one vote in the final decision so that, once again, the clergy and nobility could combine to keep down the Third Estate. Further, members of one order had been permitted, in 1614, if elected, to sit with another: i.e., members of the *noblesse de robe*, although they were noble, could be, and often were, elected for the Third Estate,

[5] Clergy, nobility, Third Estate.

whose interests they did not share. It was immediately obvious to everyone that this solution would ensure the impotence of the Estates-General.

The other possibility, hotly backed by liberal nobles like La Fayette, gave each deputy one vote; and since the Third Estate had twice as many deputies as each of the other orders; since, further, most priests from the clergy could be counted on to support the Third Estate instead of the hated bishops, it was equally clear that something like a real Parliament would quickly appear.

Without a moment's hesitation—privileges were privileges—the Parlement backed the first solution, thus at last showing its true colors. Within a week it had lost all the popularity so carefully gathered during the entire century. It was prorogued in October 1789 and dissolved on March 24, 1790. Many of its members ended on the scaffold; almost all were ruined as their cherished institution collapsed under the ruins of the monarchy it had helped to destroy.

—◦❈ ❈◦—

The establishment, in those last twenty years of the Ancien Régime, had become an elite left behind by changing times because it was incapable of reform; worse, it undermined the very pillars which had so long supported it. The Parlement, that gathering of spoiled and selfish plutocrats, could not exist outside the system; yet it did its best to ruin that system. The Church, as it became more worldly, more corrupt, was clearly seen as failing in its every duty; yet its prelates led ever more splendid and dissolute lives. The nobility, now functionless, demanded ever greater rewards while performing ever smaller services; yet it joined, with glee, the ranks of those who were slandering the monarchy.

There are many examples in modern history of ossified structures, of reactionary elites swept away by the winds of change; but the French upper classes were almost unique in banding together to destroy their own privileges. The two nobilities fought each other; the clergy refused to help the State in its hour of need; the liberal noblemen attacked the King, Queen and court; the Parlement cooperated in the attack: they seemed not to realize they were bringing about their own downfall along with that of their enemies. The establishment, having carefully engineered its destruction, sat back in dumb amazement, apparently paralyzed, as it watched its own success. The crisis it had labored so hard and so unconsciously to bring about came with startling suddenness. The Estates-General met at Versailles in May 1789; and, having endured almost a thousand years, the nobility, Church and Parlement were all swept away in the few months from May to November.

4. *Galerie des Modes: Lady wearing a pouf adorned with oak leaves and feathers, and a court dress. The complex array of gauze, lace, flowers, ribbons and tassels decorating the huge skirt demonstrates the skills which brought fame to Mademoiselle Bertin.*

Chapter Five

THE RULE OF FASHION

Fashion was all-encompassing, and it changed from one day to the next. "You look very dowdy today," one smartly dressed nobleman was heard telling another as they walked in the Tuileries gardens.

"Dowdy!" the other man exclaimed. "Dowdy! My tailor brought me this suit no later than last night!"

"No wonder, then!" the first nobleman rejoined disdainfully. "Didn't you know the fashion had changed this morning?"

"You want to know what the fashion is today? Oh, little dogs and physics lessons, riding at noon in the Bois de Boulogne and, of course, Beaumarchais's new play!" a young woman about town might have answered when asked about the latest mode; and, if pressed, she might have gone on to talk about the American War of Independence, a new way of balancing the budget, snuffboxes, hats, essence of beef and the new color for dresses. We tend to think of fashion only in terms of clothes, but in France, between 1770 and 1790, fashion ruled every aspect of life, every amusement, every interest, even the very hour at which you woke or went to sleep. Soon after her accession to the throne in 1774, Marie Antoinette admitted her ambition was not to be a great Queen: she merely wanted to be the most fashionable lady in the kingdom.

The fashions in politics, economics, physics and literature varied almost as quickly as did those in clothes, carriages and even manners. Keeping up with the new mode became a full-time occupation for people in Paris and at court. It might be upsetting to lose a husband or a child, but it was tragic to be out of fashion: after all, you could always marry again; you might have another child; but there was no recovery from being once thought old-fashioned.

Paris counted several leaders of fashion, but for dresses and hats one designer reigned supreme: the great Rose Bertin. She was a small, plump woman with a turned-up nose and a fitting appreciation of the greatness of her calling. When a husband once complained that her bill was too high, she stared. "Is a great painter only paid the cost of his canvas and paints?" she asked.

The Queen's Minister of Fashion, as she called herself, was a decorator, not a dressmaker. The sumptuous dresses, with their stiff, pointed bodices, tiny waists and huge hoop skirts (they sometimes reached eighteen feet in circumference) came to her plain (if you can call silk, velvet or brocade plain). She then ornamented them with gold and silver embroidery, flounces, lace, sometimes gathered and drawn across the skirt in great loops and bouquets or garlands of silk flowers so that the vast skirt almost vanished under its colorful, rich and often asymmetrical décor. A dress worn at court by the duchesse de Choiseul gives a rather simple example of this style: it was made of blue satin, garnished with marten fur, embroidered with gold, adorned with diamonds, each diamond shining in the center of a silver star underlined by gold spangles, and with this dress, further enriched by lace sleeves, the duchesse wore her hair curled and powdered in a coiffure over three feet high which displayed a whole garden with a brook (made of mirror), a little jeweled clockwork windmill spinning away, flowers and grass.

Of course, that was a court coiffure. Mademoiselle Bertin also provided *poufs,* huge, mushroom-shaped hats of silk or velvet adorned with jewels, lace, ribbons and feathers, usually in fairly large numbers. A *pouf* usually cost about 60 livres (about $180), and a really elegant woman owed it to herself to order them by the dozen. A plain hat—straw, with just a bouquet of flowers or a few feathers—came cheap: 20 to 40 livres ($60 to $120), but then you could only wear it in the morning or the early afternoon. As for a proper court dress, even if you supplied your own diamonds it might cost as little as 1,900 livres ($5,700) or as much as 2,800 ($8,400). As a consequence, Mademoiselle Bertin's bills ran up rather quickly. In 1784, a year in which Marie Antoinette announced she was no longer interested in clothes, she spent 87,597 livres ($262,701) just on Mademoiselle Bertin's creations. Her total dress bill for the year (including everything—cloaks, shoes, gloves, underwear, etc.) was 285,000 livres ($855,000), exactly double her official allowance.

Mademoiselle Bertin's shop on the Rue Saint-Honoré was one of the curiosities of the capital. Its façade was painted to look like yellow marble and sported purple fanlights and green medallions. Once inside, amid the bustle of buyers and pretty shopgirls, the visitor found himself faced with the portraits of the designer's royal clients: the Queens of France, Spain, Portugal and Naples, the hereditary Grand Duchess of Russia and several archduchesses, and with a constantly changing display of the great modiste's latest creations. Thus, in 1781, you might have seen an exhibition of two hundred and eighty court dresses ordered by the Queens of Spain and Portugal for which Their Majesties were being charged 500,000 livres ($1,500,000). Twice a month dolls dressed in the current fashion were sent all over Europe so that lesser mortals might keep up with the latest from Paris.

Visiting the shop was easy; it was much harder to see Mademoiselle Bertin. Twice a week she would vanish to Versailles. "I'm going to work with Her Majesty," she would say, to the horror of the titled ladies who overheard her; and in fact her conferences with Marie Antoinette were so lengthy that she was forced to rent an apartment at Versailles. This aroused immense resentment at court, where etiquette reigned supreme and four hundred years of nobility were required before anyone could be officially presented. The Queen's attendants were ladies of the highest ranks, and they treasured those rights which had been established, once and for all, by Louis XIV. It hardly seemed fair that when you had finally been appointed a lady in waiting, after years of intrigues, and received the right to attend the Queen in her bedchamber, Her Majesty should suddenly turn around, nod, and vanish for the rest of the day into the privacy of her study, there to discuss with that little shopkeeper just what the fashion would be next week.

Keeping up with the changes in style was not enough: colors changed just as quickly, and a lady with any pretension to elegance would not be caught dead in a dress of last year's color. The subtleties were so great that fashion developed a new vocabulary: the chic color, in the fall of 1779, was puce, a grayish brown. When the King first saw a dress in this new shade he grimaced and remarked: "Why, that is the color of a flea!" The word caught on. Soon there was not only flea color, but back of a flea, belly of a flea, thigh of a flea and blushing flea—a pinkish gray-brown—as well as angry flea. Every new color must have its name: when Marie Antoinette came to the throne a nuance called "hair of the Queen" (ash blond) was developed; when her first son, the Dauphin, was born, so was *caca-dauphin,* a brownish shade inspired by the diapers of a baby who is not yet toilet-trained, a little lighter in color than *boue de Paris* (Paris mud); and shy salmon had a moment of great popularity.

The passion for names extended throughout fashion's domain. A reporter attending the opera in 1788 noticed the toilette worn by Mademoiselle Duthé, a famous actress. He described her as wearing a dress of withheld sighs (split with an underskirt), adorned with superfluous regrets (a gathered, looped band of material), with, in the middle, some perfect naïveté (knots of lace); it was garnished with indiscreet complaints (appliqué silk flowers) and ribbons of marked attention (wide bows); her shoes were hair-of-the-Queen color, embroidered with diamonds in perfidious attack (a raylike design) with the come-hithers (embroidery on the back of the heels)

Nouvelle Coëffure dite
la Frégate la Junon

5. *Galerie des Modes: A new (1779) coiffure entitled "The frigate La Junon." The recent participation of the French navy in the American war inspired another fashion in which a ship, anchored down with pearls, sails on a sea of curls.*

in emeralds. And, most amazing, this seemingly incomprehensible jargon was spoken as currently as if the French had suddenly developed a second language.

Of course Mademoiselle Bertin had competition: Madame Augier also counted the Queen among her clients, as did Madame Lompey, but neither ever equaled her in international fame. And there was a fashionable shoemaker, a neighbor of Mademoiselle Bertin on the Rue Saint-Honoré, Charpentier, who fancied himself quite a great man, invited dukes for dinner (they didn't come) and held private theatricals, a pastime until then reserved for the higher classes.

There was a right shop (and a thousand wrong ones) for everything: for instance the only possible jeweler, a sort of super-Cartier of the seventies and eighties, was Le Petit Dunkerque. Only there could you find enameled gold watches, chains, seals, fobs and rings you could wear without blushing; but here too you must keep a sharp lookout: one year's watch was next year's shame. In 1780 an elegant young man had to wear two watches. In 1781 only servants did, and last year's double watches were put away for good. At Le Petit Dunkerque you could also find gold snuffboxes, candy boxes, fans and, in general, the costly trinkets without which no campaign of seduction could succeed.

Still, dresses and jewelery were no more important than a successful coiffure; and here again there was one fashionable master, the great Léonard. Until Léonard, the Queen's hairdresser had not been permitted to attend other ladies; but Marie Antoinette, who paid him a mere 1,574 livres ($4,722) in 1784, was so frightened he might lose his flair that she broke this rule, much to everyone's shock. No lady of fashion would attend any of the great court functions unless Léonard had done her hair; so many a duchesse, whose coiffure was built, curled and powdered as early as twenty-four hours in advance, had to sleep sitting up, her head held high by a special cushion so as not to upset Léonard's masterpiece.

Hair powder (a mixture of starch and perfumed powders) had been in use throughout the century; but now you could not be in fashion unless you wore towers of hair piled up nearly three feet high and generously supplemented with cushions and hair pieces. This edifice was adorned with curls, a hat, ostrich feathers and jewels, but to be really modish you had to wear a headdress *de circonstance*. Thus, when Admiral d'Estaing won his battle over the English fleet, ladies wore an entire ship, almost a foot high and dangling a jeweled anchor in the back (see illustration ✂5); they adorned themselves with flowers which drew water from flat bottles concealed deep within the structure, or with a mechanical jeweled bird which suddenly started to trill; there was even a hair-do called *à la grandmère* which could be lowered a full foot by concealed springs so as not to shock elderly ladies (the grandmothers in question).

These coiffures naturally took hours to build, so there was no question of taking your hair down every night, and many ladies, rather than disturb the edifices on their heads, would postpone washing their hair until the cushion used to give it body was quite eaten away with dirt.

The Queen herself had a passion for ostrich feathers, so they figured prominently, usually in bunches of two or three, in these majestic creations, along with whole strings of pearls and diamonds. While they provided a startling, often beautiful spectacle, the inconvenience of these architectural masterpieces was great: ladies often had to kneel in their carriages and bend through doorways so as not to disturb their coiffures.

The preoccupation with these coiffures was constant, and, even when Léonard was not called upon, fashionable ladies were constantly pondering improvements—and treating them as great matters indeed. John Moore, an English traveler, tells this story: "I found," he writes, "Madame de M. at her toilette in consultation with a general officer and two abbés concerning a new headdress which she had just invented. It was smart and fanciful and, after a few corrections, received the sanction of all these critics. They declared it to be a valuable discovery and foretold that it would immediately become the general mode of Paris and do immortal honor to the genius of Madame de M."

Men's coiffures never reached quite such extravagant heights; still, everyone in Paris wore his hair curled and powdered. Fashions varied somewhat—now you had to wear four tight horizontal curls on the side of your head, now only two; toupees sometimes rose quite high, and then they collapsed again—but the general look remained constant: a pigtail in back, tied with a ribbon, and side curls. A man could no more dress his hair himself than could a woman: in 1780, in Paris alone, there were twelve hundred men's hairdressers who employed six thousand assistants, not counting the many valets who attended to their masters' hair.

It would take a good hour to have your hair done: it must be curled, covered with pomade, then powdered. While you were being powdered, you hid inside a great wrapper, which covered you from neck to foot, and shielded your face with a paper cone. Prince Kaunitz, who was particular, would station twenty valets, ten on each side, down a gallery, and then run the gantlet in the midst of a cloud of perfumed powder. Such evenness, indeed such perfection, was finally reached that soon the fashion changed again. Around 1785 elegant young men would put their hats on as soon as their hair had been powdered, thus slightly disarranging their coiffures: it was smarter to hint that you really didn't care about such frivolities as dress and coiffure—when, in fact, they were the main topic of your thoughts.

Life was impossible without two hats made by Poupart: one classic three-cornered hat to be carried with court or evening dress, and one of the new tall round hats in the English fashion. These top hats, which came in grays,

6.   Lavréince, What Does the Abbé Think? *A fashionable lady at her toilette is consulting an abbé on the merits of a new fabric, a scene just like the one described in this chapter. The décor of the room, with its pilasters, antique motifs, draped curtains and straight-lined furniture, is a perfect example of the Louis XVI style.*

pale browns, even soft mauves, were actually worn: three-cornered ones never were. Soon after arriving in Paris, Benjamin Franklin wrote: "The French dress their heads so that a hat cannot be put on them, and then wear their hats under their arms."

Even if her hair had just been dressed by Léonard, even if one of Mademoiselle Bertin's newest creations was awaiting her, a lady could not rest unless she wore the right make-up—which consisted chiefly of rouge applied in a patch around the cheekbones. The precise shade was all-important: at court, only a very dark red would do; a lady of the nobility in Paris needed a lighter shade of red, while actresses wore an almost purple rouge and women of the middle class were content with a modest rose. A woman wearing pink rouge at Versailles must be very ignorant or very courageous: in short order, she would find herself laughed out of the palace.

Fashion did not stop with clothes or make-up: it ruled the very way in which you spent your day. No woman of fashion ever woke before eleven, some not until afternoon; as they never saw the light of day, they were called "lamps."

Breakfast consisted of a cup of chocolate in bed; then came the first, secret toilette, when corset and petticoats went on, as well as those powders, creams and scents which can transform a hag into a pretty woman; then came the second, public toilette. It was a real levée, and any acquaintance might visit. It was now just a matter of patting a curl into place or adjusting the rouge. This always took place in a room with a northern exposure, so the light would not deceive. The dressing table was covered with lace, every toilet article was gold or ivory; and before the personal maid brought in the dress, leg and bosom were generously exposed to the visitor's gaze.

Fashion then ordered a ride in the Bois de Boulogne, and, for that, a Parisian lady dressed in men's clothes. She wore her hair in a pigtail, put on a man's riding habit with a triple collar, a waistcoat and a shirt, and topped it all with a huge hat richly covered in feathers. This masculine look soon reached the court, and one day Marie Antoinette appeared dressed for her ride in this latest manner. Louis XVI watched her and said nothing; but the next day he came to see her off, wearing a lady's full coiffure. The Queen was not amused, but she learned her lesson and went back to a more feminine style.

After her ride, in the company of several fashionable young men, our elegant lady returned home and changed into an afternoon dress, then went out again, to look at the week's novelties or to spend an hour or two in quick visits: she would walk into a friend's sitting room, sit down, say three words and go out again; then, perhaps, she would attend a lecture or go back home and change into an evening gown of embroidered silk worn over a huge hoop; then out again, to dinner, the theater, the opera, and a late supper.

Through most of that day our fashionable lady was surrounded by a cloud of friends and admirers, a few young men, a poet or a philosopher, an abbé[1] or two, and, most important, a little dog: she could not survive without that faithful companion, that focus of all her feelings—provided he was the right kind of dog. He must not be too large or too lively; he must be white, or partly white; he really should have slightly curly hair—and then he would sleep on his own gilt and velvet bed[2] at his mistress' side, accompany her everywhere, sit next to her in her carriage, be carried under her arm to her friends' houses and bark, to the audience's great annoyance, from her box at the theater or the opera. Of course it sometimes happened that our lady, weighed down as she was by her many occupations, forgot to take her little dog with her. What a catastrophe that would be! One of the attending young men must be dispatched home instantly, and her heart's favorite promptly brought to her.

Second in importance to the dog was a "tender friend." Until 1775 our lady's closest friend was usually young, male and handsome. Now suddenly it was the fashion to have a woman friend with whom to share the secrets of one's heart. No one could be dearer to our lady than her friend. Her least illness would cause tears and vapors, her recovery, ecstasy. Here is one proof of the sincerity of these ardent feelings: the princesse d'Hénin, who professed the tenderest love for the princesse de Poix, was obliged to go to Versailles one evening to attend to her duty as a lady in waiting while her young friend was ill. The next morning Madame de Poix received a letter from her friend: "She writes after having been awake the entire night; she counted each hour and, when the time came for the fever to break, she herself felt a kind of shiver. She is in such a fright! Can it have been a premonition? She can hardly bear the anguish and is sending a servant right over; she won't live until his return and begs for reassurance."

Madame de Poix, much moved by this, quickly wrote that she had spent a rather good night and had the servant called in to give him the letter: "Quick, take this to Madame d'Hénin. . . . She must have spent a terrible night."

"I don't know, Princess."

"Was she very unwell this morning?"

"Her door was not yet open when I left."

"But didn't she give you this letter herself?"

"Yes, Princess, she did, she gave it to me last night."

Madame de Poix was somewhat amused by her friend's anguish; but they remained as fast friends as ever.

---

[1] An abbé, originally the head of an abbey, had come to be merely a man of good family, usually a younger son who, needing an income, had gone into the Church and received the revenue of one or more abbeys. These young men were more interested in women and the good life than in their spiritual duties.

[2] We can still see a carved, gilt wood and blue velvet doghouse made for Marie Antoinette at The Metropolitan Museum of Art in New York.

Along with this tender love for their friends, our ladies constantly displayed the most outré kind of sentimentality. Tears, whether real or contrived, poured out all day and night; you cried your way through the latest novel, you cried at the sunset, you cried at the opera. In fact, when one day Marie Antoinette and the Princesse de Lamballe sat down together to eat strawberries and cream on a bench in the Tuileries gardens, immediately all the ladies present burst into tears, moved as they were by the Queen's simplicity. All through the late seventies and the eighties, Paris and Versailles were awash with the tears of these very ladies who, a very few years later, would walk up the steps of the guillotine, dry-eyed, straight-backed and impassive.

There was also a fashion for chemistry and physics. All the smart young women attended lectures given by scientists and talked about them constantly; the new topics were Lavoisier's discoveries on the composition of air, Franklin's work on electricity and Mesmer's use of "magnetic fluid"—a mysterious kind of electricity which was gathered by him into a large vat from which metal rods emerged; to the naked eye, of course, the vat looked empty. All you had to do, Mesmer would explain, was to grasp one of these rods and let the magnetic fluid course through your body: not only would it cure various ailments, it would also strengthen you and make you live longer. For several years Mesmer was all the rage, and his consulting room was filled with the cream of society, all come for their dose of magnetic fluid. While a very few said they felt nothing, most swooned, cried, trembled, blushed or even fell into convulsions.

Conversations were not confined to the nature of hydrogen or the existence of phlogiston; current events were often the topic of the day, and first among these were the American war and Dr. Franklin, who soon after his arrival found himself the idol of Paris. One of the Queen's ladies wrote: "Franklin had appeared at court wearing the costume of an American farmer. His straight, unpowdered hair, his round hat, his brown cloth coat were in sharp contrast with the embroidered, glittering clothes, the powdered and scented coiffures of the Versailles courtiers. This novelty charmed the lively heads of the French ladies. Many elegant parties were soon given for Dr. Franklin." And so Franklin became all the rage, along with his new country. There were hairdos à la Liberté in which pearls and feathers were replaced by stalks of wheat and oak leaves; everywhere people wanted to meet Franklin; all were charmed by his simple—artfully simple—manners and pithy conversation. Naturally, he thought that it was all more than a mere fashion. "All Europe is on our side of the question . . . ," he wrote. "Those who live under arbitrary power do nevertheless approve of liberty and wish for it. . . . Hence it is a common observation here that our cause is the cause of all mankind and that we are fighting for the liberty in defending our own." (May 1, 1777.) A little later he added: "The Ameri-

7. Fragonard, Design for the Franklin Medal. *The medal itself became highly desirable and was given, in a somewhat unusual setting, by Louis XVI to Madame de Polignac.*

cans are received and treated here in France with a cordiality, respect and affection which they never experienced in England." (February 12, 1778.)

This was all very well for some forward-looking people. Louis XVI supported American independence because he thought it would weaken England, but he found all this talk of liberty a little grating, especially when he noticed that members of his court were wearing medals stamped on one side with Franklin's portrait and on the other with a motto reading: *"Eripuit caelo fulmen sceptrumque tyrannis* [He has vanquished the lightning from heaven and the tyrant's scepter]." The comtesse Diane de Polignac, sister-in-law of Marie Antoinette's great favorite, the duchesse de Polignac, shared the general rage in her capacity as a woman of fashion; and, for the New Year, she received from the King a Sèvres porcelain chamber pot in the bottom of which the famous medal had been inserted.

World events were all very well, but you could hardly hold up your head if you had not been vaccinated against smallpox. The reason was simple and had relatively little to do with the fear of that prevalent, disfiguring and often deadly disease. Louis XV died of smallpox in 1774 and the new Queen, who had been vaccinated in Vienna, convinced her husband and brothers-in-law to be among the first Frenchmen to follow suit. After a few days of anguished suspense (would the twenty-year-old King follow his grandfather to the grave?), the obligatory pustule came and went, and the royal family was seen to be in splendid health. Within a week a coiffure *à l'inoculation* had been invented, and there was scarcely a pretty woman in Paris who could resist a passionate desire for the new vaccine.

Just as it prescribed vaccination, fashion determined where and when its devotees might go for a walk, so that the crowds were always dense: thus you might go to the Tuileries gardens only around five in the afternoon; you might stroll on the boulevards in the early evening, ride in the Bois de Boulogne between twelve and three or drive out to Longchamps just one special Sunday in April; and always the rest of the world (the other fashionables, that is) were there with you. As a result, these promenades were perfect occasions for displaying the latest fashions. You dared not appear wearing last week's dress or hat, for fear of deadly ridicule; and reporters would describe each week exactly what they had seen. Thus, in 1780, foreign and provincial readers were stunned to discover that, while ornate silk and velvet dresses were still worn at court and in the evening, simplicity ruled the day.

Suddenly everything was white. Dresses were made of gauze, muslin, linen, and their deep décolletés were veiled with transparent kerchiefs. Skirts were split in front and ballooned out in back over a bustle called a *cul de Paris*: it was, everyone said, a revolution. It was also too simple to last. Soon the simple materials were embroidered; then lace was used, then silk came back. Stripes, new shapes, contrasts between over- and underskirt, sleeves, no sleeves, colored or striped stockings, all had their moment: there was no end to change. Never had there been such a contrast between day and evening clothes: simplicity of line and materials before sunset, huge, hooped, embroidered skirts and stiff bodices after dark—but always tall hairdos and always powder.

For men, too, clothes changed around 1780. The new fashions came from England: tall, round hats, coats cut much closer to the body, on much simpler lines, and made of plain materials; wool and cloth replaced the embroidered silk and velvet coats, which were only worn at night; but embroidered waistcoats endured, indeed grew more richly decorated, as their length receded. Knee breeches were still worn, but white stockings gave way to stripes. Hair was still powdered but arranged more simply, with just one curl on each side of the head and a short pigtail.

Along with the new clothes, new amusements were discovered. Horse racing was imported from England and in 1777, for the first time on French soil, a race was held. Only three horses ran on a makeshift track in the Longchamps plain, one belonging to the comte d'Artois, the King's youngest brother, one to the duc d'Orléans, his cousin, and the third to the duc de Lauzun, the model of all fashionable young men. The Queen attended the race, watching from a platform especially built for her. It is hard to say which caused the greatest scandal: the behavior of His Royal Highness, jumping up and down and cursing horribly all through the race, or the spectacle of Her Majesty, skirts blown about in the breeze, applauding the winner and allowing herself to be surrounded by a melee of young men in boots (as opposed to court dress) who treated her more like a kept woman than like a Queen. There was such a tremendous fuss, in fact, that Marie Antoinette promised never to go back to the races; but even without her royal patronage racing continued, prospered and became the most fashionable pastime for smart (and rich) young men. As for the jockeys, mostly imported from England, they were soon to be seen in the most fashionable company, where they were treated rather like pets and gave great offense to other social climbers.

Another major innovation, and one which, like racing, was to endure, was the café. Coffee, tea and chocolate had reached France in the 1660s and were used at first sparsely—they were very expensive—and medicinally. Like hot baths, they were thought a dangerous though sometimes necessary remedy. Soon, however, their cost went down, their use became frequent and the first coffeehouses opened. At first a convenience—you didn't have to invest in a whole pound of coffee at once—they soon turned into pleasant meeting places where you gathered with your friends, read the newspaper and talked interminably. Certain cafés, like the Procope on the Left Bank, or the Régence on the Right, were the salons of the philosophers. There you might see Diderot holding forth on religion or mechanics, Grimm storing up anecdotes for his letters to Frederick II and Catherine the Great, and Helvétius discussing the economy.

At the Café Mécanique in the Palais-Royal the ubiquitous waiter was gone: you sat down at your table and found a piece of slate on it. You wrote down your order and the whole table vanished into the basement, soon to reappear with a bill. You paid your money, the table vanished once more and came up again, bearing your order. Other cafés were peopled by the solid Parisian middle class, others still by pretty girls in whose bedrooms, close by, you might finish the conversation started by the flash of a shapely leg.

Of course the writers who came to the cafés were not all great men; many were pamphleteers, needy, vicious, ill-paid men who fawned on their patrons but filled a real need. In a time when the monarch ruled absolutely and was almost the sole dispenser of offices, pensions, bishoprics and other assorted favors, and when books, like newspapers, were strictly censored and often banned, pamphlets were the only way the dissatisfied could publish their views and take their revenge. These *libelles*, generally printed abroad, usually in Holland, were short productions, sometimes just a sheet of paper with a few lines of verse; but they were legion and they were vitriolic. They were read feverishly and openly in Paris, just as avidly in Versailles, where they were dropped in the royal apartments and even, on several occasions, placed under Marie Antoinette's pillow. They attacked the powerful—ministers, cardinals, the royal family—and especially the Queen. They were violently defamatory and accused her of every turpitude: she was a nymphomaniac, insatiably calling guards and footmen to her bed; she was a lesbian and her friendship with Madame de Polignac concealed the most perverted practices; she stole money and jewels from the King to give to her baseborn lovers; she was forming her own party and planning to take over the government; she passed on all the State secrets to Austria (this came closer to the truth); her children were bastards; they were not her children at all; and so on ad infinitum. Today they read just like the wild accusations made a few years later by the revolutionaries who, after killing the princesse de Lamballe, would parade her private parts, stuck on a pike, before Marie Antoinette's window. Yet these pamphlets were inspired and financed by the King's brothers: the comte de Provence, who wanted to replace his elder brother; the comte d'Artois, who wanted his children to inherit the throne; and the duc d'Orléans, the King's cousin, who thought of himself as the French William III;[3] as well as by the great families—the Rohans, the Noailles—who chafed at the favor shown by the Queen to the Polignacs and their coterie. Nothing could have been more fashionable than these pamphlets: they were read everywhere and passed from hand to hand, their contents were recited again and

[3] William III, the Stadholder of the Netherlands, replaced his father-in-law, James II, on the English throne as the result of the Revolution of 1688.

again by both court and town. Slowly, they made their way down to the people, who came to believe—it must be true if it's printed—that the royal family and court were corrupt, debauched and incapable. The lesson was well learned, and often recited when the Revolution turned against the very people who, having undermined their own regime, now had to choose between impoverished exile or death on the guillotine.

In the meantime, though, there were many new amusements. Society had always attended the opera or the theater, sitting in the great boxes on the first and second tiers, proudly displaying its sumptuous clothes and glittering jewels. Now this display became a great bore. It was much more fun, much more comfortable, to sit in a small box, shut in front by a grille so that people could not look in. You could take your little dog with you, even go wearing a *déshabillé* dress under a great cloak. And when that palled, you could always go to the Tuileries gardens or the Jardin du Roi and watch the launching of that mad new invention, a balloon.

On December 1, 1783, with the Queen watching, the brothers Charles and Robert de Montgolfier made their first ascension in a hot-air balloon kept aloft by an iron basketful of burning straw. The marvel was made of cloth, all in one piece, with a gallery at the bottom where the two men stood, and was painted blue and gold with great interlaced *L*s (for Louis XVI) and swathes of draped material. Mercier, who witnessed the event, wrote that "two hundred thousand men raised their arms to the skies in an attitude of surprise, admiration, joy and amazement; some wept with fright; others, choked with surprise, terror and emotion, fell to their knees; the weather was superb." Immediately, balloons appeared everywhere, on commemorative medals and Sèvres porcelain, on printed cloth and jeweled pins. A coiffure à la Montgolfier was created—you carried a small balloon in your hair—and everyone rushed to see the next take-offs of the real thing. Finally, if all other amusements palled, you could always rent a nightingale and shed fashionable tears as you listened to its melancholy song.

It is a common mistake—corrected, notably, by Marcel Proust—to think that attending elegant events and doing elegant things will confer elegance. In fact, only elegant people decide who will belong among the elect. Who, then, was in fashion, in Paris, after 1774? Marie Antoinette, for one, not because she was Queen but because she cared so much about fashion, and her friend, the silly but shrewd duchesse Jules de Polignac, who cried at least three times a day and was a little richer after every tear; and the duchesse's set at court: her sister-in-law (to whom the King sent that chamber pot), her lover, the comte de Vaudreuil, and her other friends: the smart, young and pretty women of the court and the handsome young men headed by the duc de Lauzun, a man so fashionable that the Queen could not spend a moment without him until, mistaking love of chic for love itself, he tried to seduce her. The comte d'Artois, nicknamed Galaor the Fair, whose 355 pairs of shoes and shoe buckles were probably fewer than the number of his mistresses. The duc d'Orléans, much pressed to find time for a wife whom he seldom visited, an official mistress, Madame de Genlis, whom he saw a little oftener, and wild orgies attended by pretty girls, some of whom came directly from their beat on the neighboring streets.

On the other hand, Franklin, that amiable American, was also in fashion, as were some writers. "Men of letters," wrote a surprised English traveler, "are received at the houses of the first nobility on the most liberal footing. You can scarcely believe the influence which this body of men has. . . . They have considerable weight on the manners and sentiments of people of rank, of the public in general and, consequently, are not without effect on the measures of government."

The people who did and said fashionable things were in fashion, even if they belonged to the upper bourgeoisie; but the comte de Provence, King's brother though he was, was not in fashion. He was very fat; but then so was the duc de Guines, whose every suit had two pairs of breeches, one for standing up, the other, a little less tight, for occasions where he might have to sit down—and he was in fashion. What actually told against Provence were his pedantry and lack of agreeable wit.

Foreigners were in fashion: "Next to a lady, the most respected character in Paris is that of a stranger," our English traveler wrote, adding: "I went to a revue; these two gentlemen are foreigners, the people around us said, and we were allowed in front." However, old people were beyond the pale. The young Queen (she was eighteen at her accession, her husband twenty) called the older ladies "packages"—they were bundled up like packages—or "centuries"; youth was the only right age. Anyone who worked for a living could never be in fashion, but a superlatively rich, preferably retired, financier could be. Foremost among these was Monsieur Necker, the Swiss banker, whom Louis XVI made his Minister of Finance and who helped bring about the Revolution; his daughter, Madame de Staël, used her talents to stay in fashion until her death in 1816.

Mesmer, with his magnetism, and the comte de Saint-Germain, who claimed to be two thousand years old and recounted his chats with Caesar, Charlemagne and Michelangelo, were in fashion, along with Lavoisier, a great scientist in his own right, and Buffon, who first described fauna and flora scientifically; but so were witty young abbés, and the eighty-six-year-old Maréchal de Richelieu, whose conquests far outnumbered Don Juan's and who had only just remarried.

Actresses could be in fashion, as could singers and dancers (but they were not received in the great houses). There was, however, one category of people who never, never could be in fashion: the provincials. They knew nothing, understood nothing, felt nothing. They wore clothes that looked like last year's, discussed six-month-old books, had no idea of the latest gossip. Even their manners were grotesque. One day a lady of fashion came across a cousin, a provincial countess, in some old relation's salon. With polite insincerity, she invited the package to dinner, only to find with horror that she had been taken at her word: the provincial lady came to dinner that very night, not having realized that "You must come to dinner" meant "I hope I never see you again."

But then, of course, the poor countess did not speak the fashionable language. In Paris you "died" if you had to leave your little dog behind for the evening; you "loved outrageously," "praised miraculously," were "prodigiously obsessed" when, in fact, you were mildly interested; if you actually liked something, you were "so mad about it as to lose all appetite." Only exaggeration would do. The French language had exhausted, it seemed, its ability to convey the simplest feeling; yet the very ladies who spoke this jargon would write, speak and behave with the noblest simplicity when, a few years later, they found themselves in jail or mounting the steps of the guillotine.

All this was only a veneer; there is general agreement among foreigners who came to France, as well as among French diarists and memoirists, that the French, always famed for their manners, had at this time brought them to a rare degree of perfection. "Politeness and good manners," wrote John Moore, "may be traced through every rank, from the greatest of the nobility to the lowest mechanic. . . . [They] pervade every situation and profession. A stranger is never laughed at, even when he utters the oddest solecism or equivocal expression. 'I am afraid,' said I yesterday to a French gentleman, 'the phrase I used just now is not French.'

" 'Monsieur,' he replied, 'this sentence indeed is not French, but it deserves to be.' "

The comtesse de Boigne, who as a young woman met the survivors of pre-Revolutionary society, wrote that the elegant simplicity of their manners and the grace of their conversation was unequaled.

It would have been considered bad manners for anyone, no matter how brilliant, to hold forth in a salon. The conversation was general, passing easily from light to weighty matters; wit was openly appreciated, young people encouraged. L'usage du monde was everything, though: a man of genius who lacked it would go unrecognized, a superficial but polished talker might be praised to excess. Exaggerated politeness was considered bad form, but then, "The language of society is that of compliments," a contemporary wrote.

With all this went certain conventions. In great houses you were expected, when you left after dinner, to forgo all the many and complex farewells ordinary politeness called for: you just walked out of the room. The mistress of the house would shout a vague word which you would just answer with a mumble. But when you came in at the beginning of the evening, in full dress, your sword at your side, you were expected to go through the usual formalities.

The food you ate, at that dinner, could also be fashionable: rather like today, a *nouvelle cuisine* had just been developed. It was subtle, alchemical almost, and created curious, exotic dishes. For the first time the French ate turtle steaks and turtle soup. The great trick was to produce dishes having neither the name nor the appearance of what they actually were. Thus, when confronted with roast hare, chances were that you would find yourself eating fish, and that a dish of cauliflower would turn out to be chicken. It was dull, ordinary, common, even, if a dish was what it seemed: the palate must be surprised, each course a novelty.

The eighteenth century knew nothing of artificial flavors and colors: how then was it all done? Simply, but very expensively, by the reduction of almost every ingredient into a very small amount of mush or bouillon in which the taste was highly concentrated. These essences formed the base of the *nouvelle cuisine,* and the greatest chefs were the ones whose essences were the strongest and most varied, and who were the cleverest at imitating, with combinations of puréed foods and essences, the appearance of altogether different ingredients. Naturally, there was tremendous waste: you needed over ten pounds of beef to make a bare cup of concentrate.

Fashionable women in the late seventies merely nibbled; soon they refused to eat at all, at least in public. They would merely drink a little of the new essences, claiming that they were so concentrated as to be nourishment enough. Only low, common people actually ate food you had to chew, they said; just the thought of sinking your teeth into something solid was enough to make you quite faint. Although it was also the fashion for women to be thin—in the rest of Europe, plumpness was popular—one wonders whether they really survived on a few sips of essences; but no chronicler has been so ungallant as to record secret banquets or hidden feasts.

In one respect, at least, fashionable women were not quite the ethereal creatures they liked to seem: the flesh was not just weak, it was enthusiastically abandoned. Infidelity was nothing new. Chamfort, in his *Maximes et Anecdotes,* recounts this conversation between a man and a woman, both in their sixties: "If you only knew," the duc d'Antin said to the Maréchale de Mirepoix, "how much I desired you when you were young!"

"Heavens," the Maréchale answered naïvely, "why didn't you tell me? You could have had me just like all the others."

Another observer wrote that "women come out shy and reserved from the convents where they have been educated; within six months, they become fashionable, take a lover and no longer see their husbands."

All marriages were arranged; the groom and bride often met for the first time at the altar. When, in spite of this, a few couples fell in love and actually remained faithful to each other, it was considered to be in thoroughly bad taste. Every fashionable woman had an official lover (often supplemented by quick flings), every man an official mistress; and only a provincial would invite husband and wife to the same dinner. Since fashionable couples lived in large houses, they had completely separate apartments. One day a husband decided to visit his wife. Much to his surprise, he found room after room with the doors unlocked and with nary a footman. Finally, opening one last door, he understood why: there was the footman, caught in the act with his wife. The lady, looking a little embarrassed, flung her skirts down. The husband bowed to her and merely remarked: "Think, madame, how embarrassing this would have been if someone else had come in!"

Many couples were scarcely on speaking terms. "I am writing you because I have nothing else to do and ending because I have nothing to say to you," ran a letter from one aristocratic wife to her husband, while another, asked by her husband of a few days to use the intimate *tu* form, answered: "*Eh bien, va t'en* [Well, go thou away]!"

Discretion was not considered the better part of valor; young men were expected to brag of their conquests, young women to make their affections plain; when, now and again, a child was the outcome of these excursions, the name of the real father was quickly established. There was so little attempt at hiding anything that, when the comtesse de Flahaut who, as everyone knew, had been having an affair with Talleyrand, then Bishop of Autun, produced a son, not even her husband was annoyed that she named the baby Charles, Talleyrand's first names being Charles-Maurice. And not only were those affairs topics for casual gossip, but so were the gentlemen's performances. The same Madame de Flahaut remarked to her friend Gouverneur Morris that Talleyrand was not quite enough for her: he was, she said, *suaviter in modo* but lacked *fortiter in re*.

In most cases like married like—the daughter of a great nobleman married another, an attorney's son wed a judge's daughter. Sometimes a noble but impoverished house took into its ranks the daughter of a financier and then, all too often, treated her with scorn. Moore tells a typical story of the standard marriage. The marquis de F.'s mother had arranged with another noble family that her son should marry their daughter; she so informed the marquis, who acquiesced with the greatest of ease and professed himself already in love with his affianced bride although he had never met her. After a few weeks he was actually introduced to her and owned himself conquered by her charms. A few weeks later still the young woman's father came to visit the marquis' mother and told her, with all the politeness imaginable, that he had received new information which prevented him from giving his consent to the marriage. Moore saw the marquis just then and, finding him perfectly cheerful, asked him if he were not sad to lose the woman he loved. Monsieur de F. answered that he cared not in the least and had loved her only because he must; adding that, in any event, he would not have ended the liaison which then occupied his heart.

Not all unmarried girls, convent education notwithstanding, were quite as virginal as their future husbands supposed: an apothecary had just invented an astringent vinegar which, applied to the right place, caused a tightening such as to fool even an experienced bridegroom.

Women had their lovers, men had their mistresses; but, beyond that, a whole new, fashionable social category came into being: the kept woman—of whom there were some ten thousand. Kept women were not exactly prostitutes: they lived in prosperous, elegant style and sometimes set fashions; they were often kept by one man only (though sometimes by two or three), and often had a profession besides: they were actresses or dancers or opera singers. They had to be pretty, of course, and accommodating; but they were also expected to be bright, witty, well dressed and well mannered. A kept woman, if she watched her step, might rise to almost any heights: Madame du Barry, Louis XV's last mistress, showed her colleagues the way to fame and fortune. The comte d'Artois kept Mademoiselle Duthé, of the Opéra, and was reliably rumored to be giving her over 100,000 livres ($300,000) a year. Many of these ladies lived in great, though never gross, luxury. They had sumptuous private houses, bought their dresses from Mademoiselle Bertin, had their hair done by Léonard and drove out in luxurious, often trend-setting carriages, as did the lady who one day appeared in a town coach completely covered with Sèvres porcelain tiles.

Kept women gave suppers which were famous for their refinement but sometimes ended in orgies. They invited the greatest nobles, who came and were delighted—the men only, of course. By 1780 almost no man of fashion failed to keep one of these women, besides having a mistress in society. It was new, it was fashionable, it was also enduring: the custom lasted until World War I.

Well below these courtesans were some thirty thousand prostitutes, plain and simple. Theirs may have been the oldest profession, but certainly they had never flourished before as they did now. You saw them everywhere, in all the fashionable promenades, in the cafés, hitching their skirts up to their waists to attract a client, and baring décolletés that reached to the navel. It was the done thing to gather a dozen or so of these girls from the streets now and again, get drunk, and all have an orgy together—five or six men, twelve or so women. After that you were often faced with unpleasant consequences: syphilis was even more prevalent than it is now. The prince de Lamballe, a great-grandson of Louis XIV from the wrong side of the blanket, died of it at the age of thirty-four after having infected his wife—and he was by no means alone. In 1781 it seemed as if there was hope: a "doctor" claimed he had produced an unguent which, if applied before intercourse, prevented one from catching any venereal disease. There was immediate and general interest in his product and, as proof, he offered to give a show. His offer was taken up and soon he was demonstrating the efficacy of the unguent by performing on the most notoriously diseased whore in Paris in front of His

Royal Highness the duc d'Orléans and assorted gentlemen of the highest nobility. There followed a short period of feverish suspense, at the end of
which it became clear the unguent was a sad failure.

The fashion for prostitution reached unexpected quarters. Once a year a
great public ball was given at the Opéra to which all women came cloaked
and masked, so you could not tell if you were propositioning a duchess, a
proper bourgeoise or a kept woman. One year, in great secrecy, Marie Antoinette attended the ball. She was quite thrilled when she was offered two
hundred livres for the night—though she did turn the offer down.

On a very different level, perhaps, but in much the same way, fashion
ruled politics, that universal topic of conversation between 1780 and 1790.
Much of the early Revolution resulted from these fashionable chats. This
will be discussed at greater length a little later, but a fact remains: in
France, between 1774 and 1790, there was not a single area of society, government, the arts, not a single aspect of life itself which was not subjected to
the passing fashion.

For those few thousand people who made the visible part of the nation,
fashion was everything, everywhere. You might be ruined, you might be ill,
you might die, even, of an excess of fashion, as did Voltaire in 1778:[4] still, it
was as nothing as long as you did not become unfashionable. In a society
where the *douceur de vivre* had been brought to a perfection unrivaled before or since, only capricious fashion could still provide the excitement
needed to enliven a surfeit of pleasures; and, surprisingly, the power of fashion outlived the society it had thrived on: in the midst of the Reign of Terror, when all those noble heads were falling under the guillotine, fashion
continued to rule and Robespierre himself, the Incorruptible, bowed his
curled and powdered head to its sway.

[4] The old man, who had been living at Ferney for over twenty years, returned to Paris
and was so mobbed by his admirers' frenzy that he died of a kidney infection brought
on by exhaustion.

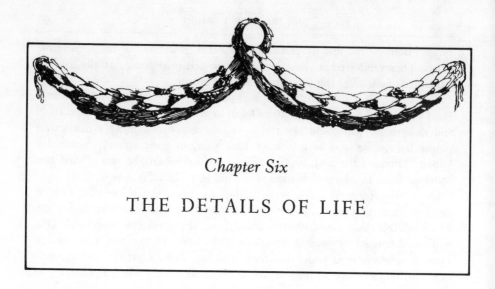

Chapter Six

THE DETAILS OF LIFE

Even when fashion rules supreme, everyday life must go on: we eat, we spend money, we become ill. Elegant ladies might sup on a cup of essence, but the rest of humanity was being served substantial meals made from widely available, but new, recipes. There were rules to be respected, lingering customs, bold new departures.

Then it must all be paid for. What were people's incomes and what were their investments? How did they keep their money and pay their bills? Could they save? All these questions must be answered if we are to understand the very mechanics of a society.

And finally we must all, one day, feel unwell, whether it be a bad cold, a dangerous contagious disease or the ravages of age. While there has never been a time in which medicine was unimportant, our period was one in which the prestige and incomes of doctors rose rapidly. Could they cure their patients, now, when their forebears had failed? The answer was of burning importance to all, both in their personal lives and in the wider political sphere: it made a world of difference whether kings lived or died.

Taken together, these three topics—food, money, medicine—make up a good deal of life, absorb people's thoughts and occupy much of their conversations. They also define the texture of ordinary days: we never stop eating and spending, we often worry about our health. But though fashion is always with us, we in the 1980s live in an age of instant, frozen food, omnipresent banks offering easy loans, and do-it-yourself medicine—pills to sleep and to wake, pills for colds and constipation and pain and just about every conceivable ill. Life in 1770 was a good deal less convenient and very much slower.

⸺⧱ ⧽⸺

"The old cuisine was very complicated and infinitely detailed. Modern cuisine is a sort of chemistry. The cook's science consists in knowing how to decompose, help the digestion and extract the quintessence of meats, in obtaining nourishing, yet light, juices, in mixing them and commingling them in such a way that nothing will dominate while everything can be tasted," wrote Marin in *The Gifts of Comus, or the Delights of the Table*. That was the ideal. In practice, essences proved an irresistible temptation. They were so mixed that strange new flavors emerged; it became impossible to know just what you were eating.

There were two kinds of essences: the *fonds clairs*, which were made from veal and poultry, and the *fonds bruns*, extracted from beef. These were so strong that they were undrinkable as such, but they could be used as bases for sauces. It thus became possible to serve a roast with a sauce, a great step forward since a first-rate cut of meat was combined with the tasty sauces which, until then, had come only from long-simmered stews. Soon new essences were made, such as mushroom and ham, and wine was added to the cooking process so as to provide a wide range of different *fonds*.

The very word "restaurant" comes from these *fonds*. It was the custom to give invalids a very concentrated bouillon—a *fond*, really—to restore their strength. The very first restaurants served nothing but these "restoring" liquids, though they soon added a variety of foods to their menus.

A number of other innovations graced the new cuisine. Mayonnaise was most probably invented by the Maréchal de Richelieu's cook during the siege of Port Mahon on the island of Minorca (hence *sauce Mahonnaise*), as an answer to the lack of supplies: what could a harried chef make with only olive oil, mustard, vinegar and eggs, that unlikely combination? The result was brought back to France and quickly became popular; by 1770 it was entering the standard repertory of French chefs.

Truffled foie gras, that expensive but blissful marriage of specially fattened goose liver with fresh truffles, also came into being; the demand for this unctuous, velvety masterpiece has never slackened since.

Less luxurious but delicious too, meringues made their appearance at every elegant dinner, though they did not become universally popular—perhaps because wood-burning ovens were unreliable. All this food was washed down with a fizzy wine invented by Dom Perignon in 1714: champagne may have already been fifty-six years old in 1770, but it was only just reaching a peak of popularity. For the first time, people agreed you could drink champagne with every course, even oysters.

Shellfish, of course, was nothing new; it had been eaten right through the Middle Ages: but an elegant new meal now became popular: the *souper d'huîtres* (oyster supper) during which nothing but oysters, buttered bread and white wine were consumed. It was understood that several hundreds of the plump, fresh *belons* or *marennes* would be eaten, but at fifteen livres per hundred only the rich could afford to indulge.

With the exception of mayonnaise, all these innovations were reserved for the well to do; ordinary kitchens might have one *fond* or two, but only grand establishments could afford the rich repertory needed for the *nouvelle cuisine*. There, dishes became increasingly complex; chefs displayed virtuosity so great that, leaving truly modern trends aside, it returned straight to those medieval rules by which disguise was all. Contrary to the style that had developed in the sixteenth and seventeenth centuries, the new cuisine would produce meals consisting exclusively of one sort of meat, cooked in twenty different ways, or dishes in which so many potent essences were mingled that, just as colors indiscriminately mixed finally produce a muddy brown, they achieved curious, unrecognizable and not altogether pleasant tastes. It is perhaps no wonder that, by 1780, chefs were complaining that people ate much too fast to appreciate what was being served them: a meal composed of one mystifying, strange-tasting dish after another does not seem very inviting.

Luckily, French cuisine continued to progress in less exalted circles. The first modern cookbook was published in 1779. Entitled *La Cuisinière bourgeoise*, it achieved instant and lasting popularity—it continued selling well into the nineteenth century, and it is easy to see why. It starts out by defining a long list of utensils and culinary terms: a *contractier* is an open oven, a *cannelon* is a mold, a *chevrette* is a trivet. It then goes on to give typical menus for each of the seasons. Before we look at one of these, it is important to remember that different foods were available in different seasons; we are accustomed to eating strawberries, peas and lettuce all the year round. In 1779 strawberries came in late June and were finished by late July; lettuce was a summer produce, peas an expensive rarity in late spring and easily available in July and August. Some fruit ripened in early summer, some, like grapes, in the fall. Almost nothing, except spices, came from the tropics —the trip took too long. Even oranges and lemons were rare and costly. Fish came in winter, because it traveled better in the cold weather, and so did shellfish, which you ate only during the months with an *r* in their names.

Ice was relatively abundant in winter, scarce in summer, though it was preserved in large underground icehouses. While ice cream and sherbets were popular (and not cheap), iced drinks appeared only in very grand houses. Naturally, food didn't keep very well. The cook went to the market every morning and bought just enough for the day. Even so, she often had trouble finding what she wanted: royal and aristocratic households sent their butlers to the markets at dawn to buy the best of everything.

If you were reasonably prosperous and wanted to give a dinner for fifteen in the summer, *La Cuisinière bourgeoise* advised the following menu:

One large roast beef
to be placed in the center of the table

FIRST SERVICE

Two soups:
Cucumber soup
Green pea soup with croutons

Four appetizers:
Fried mutton feet
Veal roast in pastry
Small pâtés
Melons

SECOND SERVICE

Boiled leg of mutton
Roast veal marinated in cream
Duckling with peas
Squab with herbs
Two chickens with little white onions
Rabbit steaks with cucumbers

THIRD SERVICE

Replace the roast beef in the center
by a large brioche.

Four roasts:
One small turkey
One capon
Four partridges
Six squabs roasted like quails

Two green salads

FOURTH SERVICE

Apricot tartlets
Scrambled eggs
Vine-leaf fritters
Cookies
Small white beans in cream
Artichokes with butter sauce

FIFTH SERVICE: DESSERT

A large bowl of fresh fruit
to be placed in the center of the table

Four compotes:
Peaches
Prunes
Pears
Green grapes

Four plates of ice cream

One plate of cream cheese

One plate of pastries

Of course, not everybody ate every dish. Most people would choose one, or at most two, offerings from any given service, and the quantities eaten of anything were very small. Even so, our fifteen middle-class people, who probably spent some three or four hours over their meal, could hardly have left the table hungry. This dinner was the only large meal of the day; it was eaten any time between 2 and 4 P.M. and was preceded only by a very light morning breakfast, most often bread and coffee. The other meal, supper, was taken at nine or ten, later in more elegant circles, and usually consisted of cold meat and perhaps a vegetable, though when it became a *souper fin* in the smart set it could turn into quite a meal.

No wines are mentioned in our menu because a variety of open bottles were set up on the sideboard. You would turn to one of the servants and ask for whatever you wanted to drink, white, red or rosé, as often as your glass was empty. In great houses it was the custom for each guest to bring his own servant, who stood behind him throughout the meal and attended to his wants. *La Cuisinière bourgeoise* aimed at a more modest milieu: it recommended having seven servants to pass the food and wine, six of whom were probably hired for the day.

An interesting aspect of our menu, besides its abundance, is its simplicity. No expensive, rare foods are served; no essences are used. The meats are plainly boiled, stewed or roasted. There is clearly no attempt at imitating the complex, costly fare served in more fashionable houses. And in all probability everything was cooked just right: for the first time since Apicius, *La Cuisinière bourgeoise* gave precise recipes with the ingredients in order and in stated amounts. Here is the recipe for the roast veal marinated in cream listed in the second service:

Put in a pan just the size of the filet of veal a pint of milk with a good piece of butter worked with flour (*beurre manié*), 2 cloves of garlic, 4 shallots, parsley, a whole spring onion with the green part, a bay leaf, thyme and basil to taste, 4 cloves, 2 sliced onions, salt and pepper. Warm the marinade, stirring constantly, until the butter melts. Take it off the fire, put in the veal filet and marinate for twelve hours.

Then take the veal out, dry it thoroughly and cover it with buttered paper. Roast it on a spit. Serve it with a *sauce piquante* made thus: Sauté 2 onions in butter; when the butter has browned, add a pinch of flour, then add bouillon, 2 tablespoons of vinegar, a glass of meat juice mixed with finely ground meat, salt and pepper. Boil for 15 minutes, skim off the fat and put through a sieve. Pour into the serving dish and add the veal on top.

We may not all have spits, but roasting the veal in a slow oven would do just as well; the buttered paper will stop it from drying out. Instead of the meat juice plus ground meat, use Bovril, and the recipe can easily be made today.

Since this was a summer menu, it did not include fish; still, on Friday no one was supposed to eat meat. Herring, the most popular seafood, was also quite cheap; all other fish tended to be expensive because the numerous convents kept the demand high. There might, too, be some disagreement about just what constituted meat. Some game birds, for instance, were exempt, thanks to Madame Sophie, one of Louis XV's daughters, who had a passion for plover. Loath to give it up, even during Lent, she explained to a bishop that game birds were not really meat; after much thought, the bishop ruled that if, when the bird was put down on a cold dish, the juices did not coagulate, the bird was indeed not meat. History does not tell us whether frantic skimming went on in the kitchens to get all fat out of the juices before the plover was set down on the crucial platter; but, after a minute of suspense, the juices stayed liquid and the princess rejoiced: for Friday and Lenten purposes, the bird was a fish.

This passion for food was characteristic of the royal family. Louis XV, alone, preferred quality over quantity; its other members took after Louis XIV, a notoriously voracious eater. Louis XVI, in turn, was famous for the amount he consumed; he was indeed extremely fat, which is no wonder when we look at one of his dinner menus, always keeping in mind that he ate in public and alone, and often sampled every dish.

He started with two *grandes entrées,* beef with cabbage and roast veal, went on to sixteen *petites entrées:* pâtés, chops, veal head, chickens, roast suckling pig, fowl, fowl legs, crown roast of lamb, turkey, sweetbreads, duckling, capon, veal marinated in cream;[1] then came four appetizers: filet of rab-

---

[1] Yes, the one from *La Cuisinière bourgeoise.*

bit, spit-roasted veal, consommé of veal, cold turkey; two side dishes: Westphalian ham and brioches arranged to look like a bush; sixteen small side dishes: vegetables, eggs, custards, poached eggs in meat broth, pastries, jams. All this was accompanied by Burgundy and Tokay wines, of which the King drank sparingly, and followed by liqueurs and cordials.

It is interesting to note that a serious eater like Louis XVI would have none of the *nouvelle cuisine;* any one of those dishes could have been served on a middle-class table. A number of items were quite expensive—suckling pig, hare, partridge, Westphalian ham—but all would have been immediately rejected by anyone with a sense of fashion.

There is, in fact, a curious correspondence between the *nouvelle cuisine*— which really was a revival of the *ancienne cuisine*—and the trend in chic young circles for a return to the past. The comte de Ségur, in his memoirs, tells us that along with other leaders of taste like Messieurs de Noailles, d'Havré, de Guéménée, de Dillon, de Durfort, de Coigny and de La Fayette, he spent a whole winter plotting to bring back sixteenth-century fashions, just as, today, dress designers revive the fashions of the 1940s. They almost succeeded; a costume ball turned out to be a great success; but the King, firmly, for once, forbade any change in court dress, and the whole movement petered out. It was as if a doomed society, unconsciously aware of its approaching end, were trying to reassure itself by a flight back to a safer time. Still, while the *nouvelle cuisine* died with the Revolution, the new *cuisine bourgeoise* went on to lasting fame and glory.

—◦◦{　}◦◦—

We are so thoroughly accustomed to paper money in its various forms— bank notes, checks, bonds, credit card charge slips, stock certificates—that it may be hard to visualize a way of life based almost entirely on the use of metal coins. There were no bank notes in France in 1770, no checks, no charge cards and almost no stock certificates; there wasn't even a stock market. Bonds existed, in a form very different from what we know, and so did promissory notes; but life was conducted in terms of gold, silver and copper which you carried with you, all representing non-existent units of currency.

Officially, and in all reckonings, the livre was the only unit of currency. It was divided into twenty sous, and that was that. But there was no such thing as a one-livre coin. The copper coinage was in multiples of a sou; the silver coinage was in écus, each of which was worth three livres; and the only circulating gold coin, the louis, was worth twenty-four livres. Since, after all, it was easier to speak in terms of existing coinage, we find people constantly referring to five hundred louis or a thousand écus—not twelve thousand or three thousand livres, even though all public and private accounts, firmly ignoring the actual currency, were drawn up in livres.

People who worked for a day's pay received it in coin, generally copper, since a worker would receive something between thirty and sixty sous a day. You shopped with coins; you paid your servants in coins; when you saved money it was in coins. Since households were larger, and almost everyone had servants, people were seldom robbed, a good thing, since they often kept a significant part of their fortune in coins in a metal box on the premises.

Of course there were banks; but they did not compete for small accounts by offering free saucepans or blankets. They were essentially speculative enterprises. The banker invested his own money along with that of a few rich clients: only the very rich had bank accounts, and they used them simply as investments. You did not draw on your banker to pay your bills, or your rent, or your creditors: that was all done in coins. Rather, your money stayed at the bank and, you hoped, multiplied. You might withdraw part of it to buy an estate or a town house, but nothing much smaller.

There were no lines of credit, no overdrafts; banks didn't make personal, house or car loans. We are used to living on credit; but in 1770 credit meant you took time paying your bills. Where, then, did people invest their funds? Sometimes in ships and their cargoes, whatever they might be: spices, brocades, Chinese lacquers or porcelain, or, most profitable of all, slaves. Sometimes in grains: the price of wheat fluctuated widely from month to month, as it still does today. It could be highly profitable to buy grains in July and hold them until the following April or May, those nasty months before the new crop came in. But the one great investment was land. If you had money, you bought an estate. Land was visible, relatively stable in price and always there: ships went down, grain rotted, but once you had land you were firmly established. It could, as we have seen, make you noble; it could give you a good deal of influence; it showed you were a man who mattered.

Most often, however, banks traded in state paper: it made no sense for a bank—as opposed to a person—to own land. Governments, then as now, borrowed money at varying rates of interest, and they were more or less likely to pay what they owed in time, although in France alone the State went through two partial bankruptcies, one in 1715–1718, the other in 1788–1789. In France the King was theoretically responsible for all borrowed money and undertook to pay its interest four times a year; but payments were sometimes late; in crises, they might not come for years. Then, even metallic currency can be tampered with. Legally, a coin was worth whatever it said on its face; thus it was possible to call in all louis and reissue them at a lighter weight. This had a double result: the first was to give relief to the Royal Treasury, since it now had gold left over with which to mint new coins; the other was to create just the kind of inflation we have been experiencing lately. Since the twenty-four-livre coin was suddenly only worth, say, seventeen, in *real* value (i.e., its weight in gold), the new twenty-four-livre lighter coin would pretty quickly lose purchasing power and prices would go up accordingly.

The value of your bond, which was a face value, would remain the same, however; so you would have suddenly lost seven livres out of every twenty-four.

All this influenced the value of bonds and kept them fluctuating. If it seemed that things were about to take a turn for the worse, you anticipated at least lateness in interest payments; and your hundred-livre bond might fluctuate all the way down to fifty livres or less. Bankers, who tried to keep themselves well informed, speculated on the market's fluctuations. Finally, they loaned the State money directly, sometimes as an advance on future taxes, and always at a very high rate of interest.

For most people, however, banks didn't exist. When they needed to borrow money, or to invest it, or just to put it somewhere safe, they went to their family *notaire*. A *notaire* was a powerful figure. He owned his office and employed a number of clerks—sometimes as many as twenty or thirty. All private transactions went through him. He wrote them up and made them legal. *Notaires* set up and sealed marriage contracts and mortgages; houses and land were bought and sold through them; they wrote wills and administered estates. So when you had too much money to keep in your safe at home, you took it, in coins, to your *notaire* and asked him to invest it for you; he would then find you a borrower who could offer good security, usually a hard-up landlord who could give a mortgage, and bring the two of you together in his office. Just as now, the maximum rate of interest was regulated by law, so you knew what to expect. You also knew how long it would be before you saw your capital again: if you gave a ten-year mortgage, then your money was invested for no less than that period of time and there was no way you could get it back earlier. If the mortgagee defaulted, you could, of course, after some legal maneuvers, seize the property. If necessity struck, your *notaire* could sometimes resell your mortgage for you, but you must expect to take a loss. Finally, if you were broke but stood to inherit money, you could always go to a moneylender and borrow against your future inheritance at a rate of interest which would make today's loan sharks envious.

Where did the money come from in the first place? For most of the well to do, it came from the land. France, in 1770, was still overwhelmingly an agrarian nation. And since most of the rest of the population worked the fields, their income, such as it was, came from the same source.

While commerce played a role and made some men rich, industry had not yet been born, and all people of means had estates. As a result, incomes fluctuated widely, depending on the crops, the weather and the honesty of one's peasants and bailiff. It was therefore quite normal for even very rich people to be in debt if it had been a bad year: they never thought of spending less, so they owed money to their tradesmen, who, knowing they would have to wait, padded their bills accordingly. This was true even of the King: Marie Antoinette's dress bills for 1784, for instance, were still being paid off in 1793 after Louis XVI had lost his head.

Money also came from the exercise of a profession. There were notaries, lawyers and doctors whose fees were quite as exaggerated as they often are today. It might also come from a trade—printer, carpenter, painter, etc.—or from a shop. Servants, who were legion, were hardly paid at all, sometimes a bare hundred livres a year, but they had food, shelter, clothing, laundry, sometimes their employers' castoff suits and dresses, and, of course, they helped tradesmen inflate the bills so as to share the difference with them.

Writers usually depended on a patron or a royal pension: it was almost impossible to make a living from your books. Restif de la Bretonne, a prolific and popular author, calculated he had made a mere 1,500 livres a year. Painters often worked on commission; they were seldom rich, though, if talented, never poor. A fashionable portrait painter, on the other hand, someone like Madame Vigée-Lebrun, could ask as much as 3,500 livres per picture and make over 75,000 livres a year.

And, of course, incomes varied hugely: the King's brothers, between them, spent 8,000,000 a year; of course, each had a Household numbering over four hundred persons. The duc d'Orléans had an income of over 2,000,000 a year. A wealthy nobleman might have anything from 100,000 to more than 1,000,000 livres. We have seen a cardinal with an income of 3,000,000 (but he was exceptional) and a président of the Parlement de Paris with over 500,000 livres. On the other hand, most of the population of Paris lived on 1,000 livres or so. Apprentices were often not paid at all, just given food and shelter. Successful lawyers and doctors might make as much as 50,000 to 60,000 livres while a clerk had to make do on 1,500 livres.

Where did the money go? Mostly where it does today, except that people didn't travel or buy appliances. You could rent a very nice apartment for 300 livres a quarter or a garret for 10. You could have a perfectly decent meal at an inn for 30 sous or 2 livres. A court gown cost at least 1,500 livres, but a very nice town dress could be had for 100 (no embroidery), and a working outfit for 10 or 15 livres. Cabs cost 30 sous an hour, a rented valet 2 livres a day. You could have a whore for anything from 2 to 40 livres, depending on her appearance, or keep an opera singer and, like the comte d'Artois, spend 100,000 livres a year. A small rented carriage set you back 10 livres a day plus fodder for the horse; you could buy a light two-wheeled gig for 500 livres or a magnificent carriage for 10,000. You could live very carefully on 5,000 livres a year, quite well on 10,000. If your income ranged from 20,000 to 50,000, you were very prosperous. Over that, you were rich. And if you kept your income, but moved out of Paris, your money would go two to three times as far.

Just as now, life was easier if you had some easily available capital, but very few people did. Since most people's wealth was invested in land, the capital was frozen; it could be a great inconvenience, especially since it rarely returned more than five per cent, and often as little as two or three per cent of the invested capital. Money did not circulate much since credit was almost unknown. The only major redistribution of income came in the form of feudal dues and taxes on the peasants; that money, or a large part of it, went toward supporting the court and the nobility.

In most respects people's ways of handling money had changed very little since 1670. And when change finally came, in 1788–90, it came brutally. In less than three years France passed from the Middle Ages to the modern era, to the accompaniment of endless theories, explanations and pamphlets. By 1800 France had experienced all the dubious blessings of fiat paper money, the use of credit and the growth of banks; but it took a political revolution to bring about financial progress.

—◄[ ]►—

Life, in 1770, was still short, dangerous and frequently painful. The great medieval epidemics of plague and cholera had somehow passed away, but they had been replaced by smallpox and, to a lesser degree, tuberculosis. Over sixty million people died of smallpox between 1700 and 1800. Almost everyone had smallpox at some time in his or her life; some survived intact; many sufferers were left pitted and scarred. Children who caught the disease seldom survived, but it killed impartially. In 1774 Louis XV was its most illustrious victim. His face horribly swollen and discolored, he was a week dying and suffered horribly. The eruption had come out, always a good sign, but then a sort of general infection set in so that, at the time of his death, the King had become completely unrecognizable, his head three times its normal size and black, his body rotting while he was still alive. The stench was such that the normal post-mortem had to be abandoned and the corpse hurriedly buried.

The young Queen Marie Antoinette had heard about vaccination in Vienna: her mother's doctor, van Swieten, one of the very best in Europe, knew that the Turks made a vaccine with pus taken from a sufferer, and that it was usually effective; at the same time Jenner, in England, was experimenting with cow vaccine and getting dazzling results: the entire English royal family thought it safe enough to ask for vaccination.

Smallpox was supposed to be its own cure: if you had it once and survived, you were immune; but Louis XV had suffered from a disease generally thought to be smallpox in 1737 and then had caught it again in 1774; besides, you might very well not survive your first bout. So the Queen insisted, and on June 8, 1774, Louis XVI, his brothers and sisters-in-law were vaccinated. The suspense was tremendous. A number of influential people predicted the demise of the entire royal family and blamed the Queen for this holocaust; but within two days the telltale pustule appeared: the vaccination had been successful. Of course, fashion promptly made vaccination a must, and a small group of smart young courtiers rushed to imitate the King. Still, the majority of the population remained untouched, and smallpox went on killing almost as many people as ever.

As for tuberculosis, or consumption as it was called, there was neither cure nor vaccine. If you caught it you were just out of luck. It killed Madame de Pompadour, and the Dauphin, son of Louis XV, and his two wives, and the first Dauphin, son of Louis XVI. Nobody understood the disease, or indeed any other: nothing had changed in medicine since the Middle Ages.

There were no real remedies for anything, no painkillers except opium pills, which were freely available but tended to become less and less effective the longer you used them. If you received an arm or a leg wound, the limb was generally amputated there and then to prevent gangrene, and even then it often set in. The state of surgery may be sufficiently described by pointing out that in most cases barbers were also surgeons. Simple, supposedly safe diseases like chicken pox could quickly become fatal if a doctor attended you: on the whole, it was safer to be left untreated.

Of course, then as now, doctors prescribed a variety of pills; the difference was that, in 1770, the pills were supposed to re-establish a theoretical equilibrium between four "humors" which existed only in the doctor's mind, so, at best, the pills did nothing; at worst, they killed you. Still, anything you swallowed was secondary. Medicine had three universal, constantly applied remedies: bleeding, purging and enemas.

It was thought advisable to be bled regularly. Very rarely, it actually helped: after giving birth to her first child in the midst of a mob of courtiers, Marie Antoinette fainted, overcome by heat and closeness more than by the pain of delivery. She revived when bled by her attendant physician. Further, in an age of appalling personal hygiene, when people tended to eat huge meals and, after a certain age, move very little, bleeding may have helped to relieve hypertension. On the other hand, there is almost no illness that cannot be made worse by frequent and repeated bleeding and purging; a TB sufferer went to his grave much faster if attended by a reputable physician. There was actually an etiquette of bleeding. Being bled once was thought sufficient, if accompanied by purges and enemas, for slight illnesses, sore throats, a broken leg, indigestion or just fatigue. Two bleedings would indicate a more serious illness; three bleedings and you were advised to send for a priest. After that it was a tossup as to whether you died of disease or just plain exhaustion.

Purging was simple enough, and frequent: you took a violent laxative (if it produced blood, then you could tell it was really doing its job). It was so much a part of everyday life that it became a standard excuse—you got out of seeing a bore by saying you were being purged.

As for enemas, they had developed into an almost separate branch of medicine. There were emollient enemas, blood-thinning or -thickening enemas, enemas to combat the excess of wet or dry humors, enemas to be taken in conjunction with bleeding, summer enemas and winter enemas. Like bleeding, of course, repeated enemas would make just about any sickness worse.

Today we find pain unacceptable. In 1770 it was a normal part of life. There were no antibiotics to cure infections so they had a tendency to fester;

sometimes, if you had a dangerous infection, an abscess would be helped along so as to allow it a way out; and it would last, and last, and last. If you broke a leg you were simply held down while it was set. If rheumatism then set in, that was too bad. And there were always your teeth.

Dentists, as we think of them, did not exist. If you had a terrible toothache, well, you could have your tooth pulled. The upper classes tried to keep their teeth relatively clean, usually by rubbing them with a piece of coarse cloth; toothpaste and toothbrush had yet to be invented. And if, at the age of forty, you found yourself left with only two or three teeth, you could try wearing ivory dentures which you had to take out before eating.

Still, doctors never worried about their total lack of effectiveness. They had been graduated from the Paris Medical School, after several years of purely theoretical study, without ever actually seeing a sick person, and granted the title of "very illustrious physician doctor of the Paris School of Orthodox Medicine, keeper of the Hippocratic oath." They were conversant with Aristotle and Thomas Aquinas; they wrote Latin; they understood all about the humors and the volatile fluids, and the use of bleeding, purging and enemas. If, after all that, their patients dropped like flies, it was simply too bad. Besides, they were an impressive-looking lot, clad in long black gowns and huge wigs: one look, and you could see they meant business.

In medicine, however, new fashions now appeared. The treatments remained unchanged, but elegant young doctors began to doff their gowns and wigs to appear in civilian clothes. Soon they charged far more money than their predecessors had ever dared to contemplate, up to forty livres a visit, and were seen rushing about Paris in their own carriages. By the eighties, no self-respecting doctor went anywhere on foot, and the smarter members of the profession were invited to dinner, a great step up, socially.

Still, fashion aside, a new breed of doctors appeared, men like the Swiss Théodore Tronchin, who was a firm believer in preventive medicine and proper hygiene based on sufficient physical exercise and relative sobriety. He was a strong exponent of the smallpox vaccine, which he used as early as 1756 to immunize the duc d'Orléans's children. He is also justly credited with keeping the frail, often ailing Voltaire alive well into his eighties, an age then reached by very few people indeed.

Another doctor, a Frenchman, Anne-Charles Lorry, began the study of skin diseases. His *Tractatus de morbis cutaneis,* published in 1777, while elementary by today's standards, is a serious and worth-while study. At the same time two other doctors, Lassone and Vicq d'Azyr, founded the Société Royale de Médecine with Turgot's backing, while new periodicals—journals of medicine, surgery, pharmacy—began publication. The stage was being set for the rapid development of medical science in the nineteenth century.

Along with this real progress, a new sort of doctor also appeared: the fashionable charlatan. Of course there had always been phony physicians who, frequenting fairs and markets, sold miraculous elixirs. Now, however, several of these self-taught prophets became famous, Mesmer first and foremost.

Mesmer first came to Paris in 1778 from Austria and claimed he could cure any disease or disorder by the use of magnetism. At the Queen's request —she was always partial to things Austrian—Mesmer was actually given money by Louis XVI; in short order he opened a magnetism clinic on the Place Vendôme. There a huge vat filled with water, pieces of metal and bottles sat in the middle of a room, with metal rods protruding from it. In a carefully calculated environment, with dramatic lighting, soft music and perfumed vapors, Mesmer seems to have achieved some results by the use of hypnotism and collective suggestion. In no time at all he had become all the rage. Paris came to swoon and be cured, La Fayette first and foremost. It was not until 1784 that Mesmer was proved a fake by two of the new breed of doctors: Bailly, who was to be mayor of Paris in 1789 and end up on the machine perfected by the colleague who was assisting him, Dr. Guillotin.

Magnetism was soon replaced as a miracle cure by electricity. Volta had just discovered that, if you put copper and zinc in acid and water, you can generate an electrical current. Galvani studied its effect on the body and a young physician named Jean-Paul Marat published a *Study on Medical Electricity* in 1783. Like Dr. Guillotin, he was promised to later and greater fame.

There was another new development in 1778: the founding of the Hôpital Necker. Entirely financed by Monsieur and Madame Necker, it was the first attempt at creating a place where people might actually be cured, and thus very different from the dreadful Hôtel-Dieu where the sick came only to die. It was also the first non-religious hospital. Today, over two hundred years later, the modernized Hôpital Necker, now financed by the State, but still using, among others, its original buildings, is one of the best in Paris.

—◁{ }▷—

Politically, architecturally, artistically, France was rushing into the modern age; even its cuisine was setting the stage for later triumphs; but in those most sensitive areas, money and health, nothing much had changed since the Middle Ages. It is easy for us, as we look with hindsight, to see that great transformations were on the way; but people still felt rather uncomfortable in a money economy and didn't really quite know how to deal with it. They dreaded illness fully as much as their ancestors half a millennium earlier. Life was still very uncertain, infant mortality high, survival unpredictable.

Every historical period has its discrepancies, its contrasts between innovations and permanence, but those of the seventies and eighties created a very particular sort of tension: it can be very upsetting to believe that intelligence is able to understand and reorganize the world when every day is full of uncertainty and even dread.

Chapter Seven

THE ARTS:
PAINTING, SCULPTURE,
ARCHITECTURE

One fact, throughout our period, seemed indisputable to the French: France held the first place in the arts. In fact, the world of painting and sculpture, in the seventies and eighties, is more striking for its poverty than for its accomplishments. It was as if so much creative energy, care and money went into the decorative arts—and architecture—that there was almost nothing left over for the arts proper. In a country which, at other times, has produced a plethora of great artists, we find only one painter of the very first rank, David, and one great sculptor, Houdon. True, there were a number of highly competent secondary creators whose work, while not bearing the mark of genius, is nonetheless extremely pleasing.

The problem was that the visual arts, like the society, had become frozen. Of course, style had changed; here, too, the rococo was unfashionable and the great Fragonard, though he was doing work of extraordinary beauty, was finding it difficult to make a living; but most of the popular painters—Vernet, Vien, even the young David—simply went back to an earlier, well-established classical style. Part of the problem was the conservative influence of the Académie des Beaux-Arts to which every artist worthy of the name belonged: like almost every institution of the time, it looked firmly to the past; academicians liked what they knew; if Boucher was out of favor, then a reheated, second-rate imitation of Poussin would do nicely.

Compounding this, painters became literary and expressed, in paint, the intellectual fashions of the period. This can be a dangerous habit and result in lifeless, conventional work: the artist no longer speaks for himself, but simply repeats other people's ideas. The worst of it is that it looks good at the moment. Five or ten years later the lineaments of fashion have become visible; as the times change, the work is left behind and looks as awkward as yesterday's hat. Still, there is one thing to be said for the artists who appear in this chapter: they all had a superb technique. As a result, even when their main work appears stilted or dull, their portraits often still vibrate with life.

Ever since the mid-seventeenth century painting had been split into two categories: so-called history paintings, with grand religious, historical or mythological subjects, and genre painting, derived from the Dutch little masters and devoting itself to the humble incidents of everyday life. Poussin, Le Brun, Boucher and Fragonard had represented the first category, the brothers Le Nain and Chardin the second. Now genre painting coincided with the current fashion for sentimentality (see Chapter Five). The result was Greuze.

No one was more popular, more successful, for the thirty years between 1755 and 1785, than Greuze (born 1725). He did everything to please: his colors were fresh, light and attractive, his flesh tones Rubensian in their richness, his subjects always popular; but, more than that, his were paintings with a message. The rococo painters had thought it enough to express their own sensuality, thus awakening that of the viewer. Now, Greuze said that painting must have a moral content (and Diderot heartily agreed); each work would preach its own homily; each subject would be full of ready emotion; and, always, touching events would be enacted by those simple but clean peasants the age was so fond of.

Of course, it helped that Greuze's figures were all so pretty to look at; and, in fact, while his cheap sentimentalism may put us off today, his work is still pleasing: we may find the content mawkish, but the form is colorful, fresh, even enticing. There is more to be said for Greuze than most modern critics would allow.

By 1777 his work had become costly. His *Little Girl Holding a Dog* sold at auction for 7,200 livres, a high price for a living artist. Of course, the subject helped: the dog was dead. Then, with *La Cruche cassée* (the broken jug) he achieved temporary immortality. This painterly allegory of lost innocence—the symbolism is obvious: the girl has just ceased being a virgin—is full of pleasing details. The young girl, whose face is attractive yet sad (i.e., doubly attractive), stands by the well holding the broken jug; her dress is rather stiffly painted, with a dry brush and quick touches, as a contrast to the fleshy voluptuousness of the face; she is obviously a villager, yet the painting is full of those charming little notes—flowers, ribbons—the eighteenth century was so fond of. All in all, the work was a compendium of everything people liked: the return to nature à la Rousseau, the love of virtue allied with a touch of salaciousness, and a thoroughly sensual technique. No wonder the critics and the public were so thrilled.

From this, Greuze went on to still greater triumphs; his next two contributions to the Salons—where all the year's paintings judged worthy by an

Academic jury were hung for the public's enjoyment—just about brought
the house down. They were *A Father's Curse* (1777) and *The Punished
Son* (1778), and represented the essence of verbose, sentimental painting—
or so, at least, his contemporaries thought. In fact, while this is certainly true
of the subject matter, Greuze's technique was changing.

A Father's Curse is, of course, full of drama, or perhaps more accurately
melodrama. The participants, here again, are clearly villagers and dressed as
such. On the left the aged parent, both arms raised before him the better to
curse, is held back by a weeping daughter while, on the right, the wicked
son, one arm flung up in self-affirmation, prepares to depart through a doorway where a rascally-looking character is waiting for him. His mother and
sister are still clinging to him, and everyone looks thoroughly distraught.
Here are feeling, a theme, a lesson to be learned, all of which may tend to
make our more cynical age giggle. But on the other hand, the figures are
beautifully painted and full of movement; the composition, while remaining
purely frontal, is complex and successful; the two pyramidal groups of the father and the son balance each other and create great pictorial tension. In
fact, if it weren't for the subject matter, and the still rather Rubensian treatment of flesh, we might almost be looking at an early David. The lack of
decorative background is also typical of this new direction: a genre painter
was becoming classical. The work, as a whole, is too bombastic to be really
successful, yet it is good enough to deserve more than the traditional smirk.

In the other, succeeding, canvas, Greuze continues to be moral and didactic while denying himself any other easy success; again the figures move
against a dark, empty ground (the back wall of the room); the artist has
resisted the temptation of a fashionably attractive rural setting; the figures
are set in classical attitudes while the composition remains firmly planimetric.
The phony, exaggerated feeling is still there, however: after (one supposes)
several years, the son has returned. Alas, he is too late! On the left, his dead
father lies stiff on a bed, surrounded by his lamenting family. In the center,
the erring son's wife dramatically points to the corpse while her husband,
half collapsed on the right, is, as the title indicates, punished by the father's
death. Again, it's a little hard not to laugh.

It would not be fair to leave Greuze without mentioning his admirable,
and unjustly forgotten, portraits. They are true and vivid, and present the
sitter to us in a sympathetic, intelligent way: we feel we know how and
what he thinks; but also they are exquisitely painted in a style which is more
austere, less pretty and really much more effective than that of the history
paintings. There is no cuteness; a cool light bathes the subject and the often
plain gray background: this is sensitive, restrained, competent portraiture at
its very best. It seems probable that an exhibition composed solely of
Greuze's portraits would cause his reputation to rise considerably.

Curiously, the two most famous professional portraitists of the period are far less effective than either Greuze or David, both of whom seem to have given portraiture little thought. They are also women.

Adélaide Labille-Guiard and Marie-Anne-Élisabeth Vigée-Lebrun were highly successful rivals. Between them, they painted everybody who was anybody, thus leaving us a precious record, but one was far more ambitious than the other.

Madame Labille-Guiard was perfectly content to be a portrait painter, pure and simple. Her clientele, largely royal and aristocratic, was composed mostly of women whose slightly flattered charms she rendered with a competent brush; highly adept at depicting dresses and embroidery, jewelry, lace and feathers, she always did full justice to the sitter's costume. Indeed, we can see why these slightly too pretty portraits were so popular: they look so rich. That, unfortunately, was just the problem. In her acclaimed portrait of Madame Adélaide,[1] for instance, what we see first of all is a magnificently embroidered red velvet overdress, opening to reveal an enchanting *broché* silk skirt; our eye next travels to some very fine lace and the ladder of ribbons decorating the sitter's bodice; then to a trompe-l'oeil relief showing the medal-like profiles of the late King, his son and daughter-in-law. It is almost as an afterthought that we finally look at the princess' face—handsome, majestic and really rather young. It is, in fact, far and away the least interesting part of the painting and is highly flattered, besides. It is true that Madame Adélaide could look majestic, but she was also incredibly nasty, a prototype of the sour old maid who likes nothing better than punishing the world around her. She was also wrinkled and faded. None of this is apparent in what is, actually, a splendid still life. The same is true of the portrait of Madame Sophie, Madame Adélaide's sister: we would never guess that this plump, amiable woman was practically retarded.

Far preferable to this official work is Madame Labille-Guiard's self-portrait with students. She is seen dressed to kill, with her white embroidered satin shoe peeking from the edge of her skirt. Brushes in one hand, palette in the other, she is hard at work while two young women students behind her look on. It is possible she may have improved her own looks a little, but there is a freshness, a sense of reality, about this composition which, along with the light, attractive color, help to give it great charm. Quite obviously the artist was at her best when she was also at her most truthful.

Madame Vigée-Lebrun, her great rival, was far more ambitious; but it is an open question as to whether she was the better artist. Unlike Madame Labille-Guiard, she thought of herself as a history painter and espoused rather simplistic, neo-classical theories; born in 1755, she was the same age as that movement. This is all too apparent in one of her main attempts, a work characteristically entitled *Peace Bringing Back Abundance* (1780) in which two simpering, overweight ladies in Roman clothes are seen leaning toward

[1] One of Louis XVI's maiden aunts. She died in exile in 1799.

each other; Abundance is identifiable by its horn, far and away the best part of the painting because of its charming still life. As for the work itself, aside from its grotesque appearance, it is simply an uninspired imitation of the French seventeenth-century painter Laurent de La Hyre.

Still Madame Vigée-Lebrun was known for her portraits, not her allegories. In her lively, informative memoirs she tells us about her career, how she was taken up by the aristocracy, then by the Queen herself; in fact she became Marie Antoinette's painter, producing portrait after portrait: we see her in court dress, with the royal cloak, with a rose, with her children, indoors, outdoors, in summer, in winter, in velvet, in linen (this was the picture which caused such excitement—see Chapter Three). Her face also varies; sometimes it is quite realistic and sometimes altogether idealized. One would think that, amid this abundance, Madame Vigée-Lebrun would have come up with a speaking image of her sitter; yet the most alive, most vivid portrait of the Queen is an unfinished work by Kucharsky, a very minor artist.

Perhaps the painter felt too much admiration for her model; as we have seen (Chapter Two), she was devoted to the Queen; but that seems to have been a constant problem. The duchesse de Polignac may have been as enchanting as Madame Vigée-Lebrun depicts her, and so may Madame du Barry; but what about all the other ladies? And it was part of the artist's principles to paint only women who looked natural—so she asked all her sitters to forgo powder, rouge and their usual dress. What we see is a procession of pretty women in straw hats and linen scarves, and this considerably reduces the works' historical value. As a result, Madame Vigée-Lebrun's appeal is quite different from Madame Labille-Guiard's. Though she was capable of painting velvet and lace, she seldom did so, and the charm of her work, such as it is, comes from an appealing mock candor very much in the spirit of the times. It is no wonder her models were pleased: they all seemed to come out of the pages of Jean-Jacques Rousseau's stories. We can, at any rate, leave her that merit, along with that of having given us a thorough record of Marie Antoinette and some of the most elegant women in Paris. But if Madame Vigée-Lebrun's portraits can look very dull today, her memoirs[2] make up for her deficiency as an artist: they are lively and very informative. As we read them, we are given a clear, amusing and altogether valuable picture of life in Paris at the end of the Ancien Régime.

The classical trend which surfaces in the works of Madame Vigée-Lebrun and those of a number of other mediocre painters at the end of the century had never really died. All through the rococo, there had been a line of artists who looked back to Poussin and Raphael. Joseph Vernet (born 1714) fitted right into it and was immensely successful.

Like all other promising painters, Vernet was sent off to the French

[2] They were actually set down by her nephew.

Academy in Rome; he came back from Italy as a painter of the sea, and a very competent one at that. In a sense he can be described as a follower of Claude Lorrain: we see the same coasts, the same seaports, the same wide seas and spectacular sunsets, the same tiny figures in picturesque costumes. While he wasn't as great a painter as Claude—he lacked Lorrain's sense of mystery—he was nonetheless effective. His subject, always the same, always new, is the sea: in a port, by a wild rocky coast, on a sunny day, in a storm, at night, at dawn, at dusk. This allowed for very realistic renderings of the Italian coast, along with some wonderful light effects. Vernet had worked out a clever way of registering his impressions (shades of Monet!) before the light could change by assigning a letter to each nuance: it was thus enough to sketch the form roughly, adding whichever letters corresponded to the color as it then was. As a result, his work has a richness of hue and an immediacy which made it appealing to even so stern a critic as David.

Marie-Joseph Vien (born 1716) was also part of the classical tradition, but he infused it with his own realistic outlook. During and after the usual stay in Italy, he combined the study of antiquity with that of nature; in many ways his style announces that of David, whose master he was. It is typical of Vien that, in his school, he provided live models for his students to draw while discussing the art of the Greeks and Romans.

By the seventies Vien was famous; he received a pension from the King, was made rector of the Academy and instantly sold every canvas he could paint. While it is, perhaps, unfair to judge him after seeing David's work— after all, it hadn't yet been painted—he lacks real originality. His compositions all too often look like prettied-up Poussin or Bourdon; it is classicism with a desire to please, and as such it doesn't quite work. Still, Vien knew how to look: his portrait of an old man, now in Narbonne, is wonderfully real. Against a plain background (no distractions), we see a wrinkled, tired, still intelligent face and the hands, though in no way distorted, are posed so as to remind us of the stiffness of old age. All in all, it is a successful and moving work.

The same cannot be said, unfortunately, of his history painting. In *Lot and His Daughters* (Le Havre) we have a typical Italian landscape in which Poussinesque figures have been rather awkwardly placed—and they are much too charming: you would never guess that Mrs. Lot had just turned into a pillar of salt. However, the painting, like many other Viens, is partly redeemed by the ravishing still life placed next to Lot. On a stone base a large cloth has been draped: bread, a knife, an urn, a basket have been set down with a sure sense of reality; they are almost Caravaggio-like in their intensity.

The very worst aspect of Vien appears in his *Susanna and the Elders*: we see a sort of Boucher nude ogled by two Poussinesque figures, and the two styles clash irreconcilably; but in a later painting, *The Love Merchant*, the

artist finally reaches a synthesis. In a large room furnished in Louis XVI antique style we see a seated woman, her maid standing behind her. Another
woman, the merchant, kneels before her and holds up a little Cupid by the
wings. On a table there is, again, an enchanting still life, this time of a bou-
quet of flowers in a crystal vase, a rose and a necklace of gold beads lying on
the tablecloth, a smoking incense burner and a gold box with carved side
panels. Not a great work, perhaps, but this adaptation of an antique Roman
decorative painting cannot be ignored.

Vien's passion for the antique, along with his regard for reality, was absorbed by his star pupil, Jacques-Louis David, whose respect and admiration
for his master never faltered. However, with David, we enter a completely
different category, that of the artist of genius.

David (born 1748), after studying with Vien, went on to Rome where he
was able to see for himself the style he had already begun to practice. He
was still in Italy when he painted what is unquestionably his first masterpiece: the stunning equestrian portrait of Count Potocki. Curiously, David,
who ranks with the greatest of portrait painters, never took that genre very
seriously because, he felt, it suffered from a terrible defect: lack of moral
content. And here the artist shows himself a true man of his time: without
ever sinking into the mawkishness and sentimentality of Greuze, he, too,
wanted to paint didactic, moralizing paintings—only David's morality was
half political.

Still, Count Potocki is a very remarkable picture, an image of youth, elegance and energy painted in a highly restrained palette. Against the background of an old Roman wall supporting several large columns, cut off by
the frame right near their bases, we see this charming, athletic young man,
doffed hat waving in one hand, coatless, and dressed only in a shirt, waistcoat and skin-tight pants, his feet encased in ankle-high laced boots, riding
his prancing steed whose mane and tail billow like foam. The horse is in
profile and fills the whole width of the picture space, a powerful horizontal
form reacting against the vertical of the count, also in profile, except for his
three-quarter head, whose muscular leg, in those butter-colored tights, is ad-
mirably modeled.

While David has given us a stunning image—the old wall, the strong,
graceful young man, that fiery horse—he has also managed to produce a
composition based, essentially, on the intersection of the horizontal and vertical which, like a cross in the middle of a blank page, cannot help but fix
our attention, while it conveys to us the careless pride, the refinement, the
mastery of a young aristocrat. Content and form are perfectly blended—and,
besides, the painting is very beautiful.

A survey of David's portraits would take us well beyond 1790, but it was
in those pre-Revolutionary years that his style was formed. Just because he
painted Marat's death and Napoleon's coronation, he is often thought to be-

long to the new era; in fact, he only continued to apply principles that form an integral part of the Louis XVI style. His portrait of Lavoisier and his wife, which he painted in 1788,[3] now in The Metropolitan Museum of Art, New York, is certainly in the very top rank of his oeuvre (see the dust-jacket).

Art historians often oppose masters of color like Titian to masters of design like Michelangelo; and David is always placed in the second category. It is quite true, when we look at the Lavoisier portrait, that there is very little color: the background is dark, Lavoisier himself wears gray, his wife white. The red velvet tablecloth is the only splash of color. Yet this very restraint should give us a hint: all those gray and white tones, so full of light, so clear, so transparent, are in themselves quite as rich as the most dazzling hues; what we see is a symphony in nuances, a sure feeling for the infinite variety of what we might call black and white color. The art of using grays is carried quite as far here as it ever was by Van Eyck and Hugo van der Goes.

Of course, the Lavoisier portrait is no grisaille: there is that red tablecloth. What we see, in fact, is the great physicist bending over the table full of various instruments, pen in hand, with his wife standing behind him and bending over as well. He sits at the edge of the table so that we see his left leg. Here again, the composition is based on the coming together of several dynamics—the vertical of Madame de Lavoisier, the semi-vertical of Lavoisier himself, the horizontal of the red table with its instruments. Our eye moves back and forth, as it goes from the sensitively but realistically rendered couple to the instruments symbolizing Lavoisier's key role in late eighteenth-century science (see Chapter Eleven). It is all there, really, inside and outside, feeling and accomplishment. David managed to paint the several aspects of reality while producing a singularly beautiful image.

It was David's history paintings, however, that he cared about. From the very first he found his topics in the world of Greece and Rome; aesthetically, he really belonged to his time. Since the exhumation of Pompeii and Herculaneum the antique style was all the rage, and David shared the general passion. More important, the ancient world provided the artist with a rich hoard of political subject matter: Rome, after all, had once been a republic and its history gave the artist a chance to paint pictures with a high propaganda content.

David's first great success came in 1784 with his *Oath of the Horatii*. Against the background of an arcade held up by Doric columns, we see, on the left of the picture, a group of four men: the father holding out three swords, and the sons, their arms stretched out as they take their oath; they are dressed in absolutely authentic Roman costumes and vibrate with pur-

[3] He was paid seven thousand livres—double, it is nice to note, Madame Vigée-Lebrun's top fee.

8. *Martini, The Salon of* 1787. *In this depiction of the yearly painting exhibition, we can recognize David's* Death of Socrates (*bottom row, fourth to left of door*), *Madame Vigée-Lebrun's portrait of Marie Antoinette* (*second row, second to left of door*),

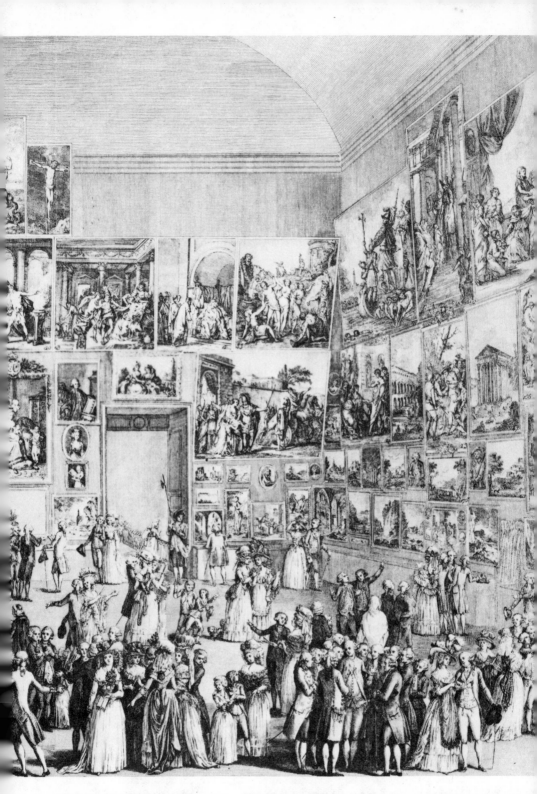

Madame Labille-Guiard's portrait of Madame Adélaide (second row, fourth to left of door) and several Hubert Robert landscapes (left wall) among the year's production. All of these are discussed in this chapter.

pose and energy. More, perhaps, than most artists, David makes us feel the body beneath the clothes: he always drew his figures in the nude before going on to dress them.[4] On the right, the women huddle in the corner and balance the first group, but they are much the weakest part of the composition, as contemporary critics were quick to notice. Still, it is a wonderfully simple, eloquent picture. The fact that David also returns to classical physical standards adds to the beauty of the painting: the figures look like animated Greek statuary; while his arrangement remains always purely frontal, the movement across the surface of the picture plane unites strength and simplicity. And, of course, archaeological authenticity is a key part of the image.

The moral content of the *Oath* is clear enough: honor before everything. That of the *Death of Socrates* (1785), at The Metropolitan Museum of Art, New York, is more pointed still. It was an unjust state which forced the great philosopher to die for teaching and speaking the truth. The application of this idea to a regime based on censorship and state prisons was obvious enough, and no one missed it. Although propaganda alone does not a good painting make, the *Death* manages to be both moving and beautiful.

David chose the moment when one of the disciples hands the philosopher a cup filled with poison. The two main figures in this intensely dramatic scene are Socrates himself, half reclining, but one arm raised high in exhortation, and a young man, his broad back turned toward us, covering his eyes with one hand and holding out the cup with the other. Socrates is surrounded by a group of his students. The scene takes place in a torchlit prison cell: we see its wall and grated openings. Yet this tragic scene is rendered with great restraint. Only the cupbearer shows vivid emotion—and we don't see his face. Socrates himself is perfectly calm as he teaches his last lesson. The painting is all the more effective for its lack of melodrama.

For the Salon of 1789, that key political year, David produced another masterpiece: *Brutus Receiving the Bodies of His Dead Sons*. The theme is, of course, the struggle against tyranny, and David substituted this painting for a projected *Belisarius* in order to make his point. The work represents a turning point in other ways as well. While the artist had always yearned for authenticity in his renderings of antique subjects, he now went so far as to order special furniture from Georges Jacob (whom we met in Chapter Three). It was made from sketches of the real thing represented in first-century frescoes which David had seen during his stay in Italy.

Brutus, an older man, sits almost crouched in the left foreground; he stares at us as the corpses of his sons are brought in behind him; on the right, his wife and daughter point, horrified, to the bodies being carried in. The composition is far more complex than that of the earlier paintings. The strict planimetry gives way to an interaction of foreground and background; and Brutus' emotion is most vividly evoked by his complete lack of drama; the

---

[4] Some of his sketches are not without their comic side. A nude coronation of Napoleon is a case in point. . . .

women supply the obvious emotion. Here, as in David's other paintings of this period, color is almost completely absent: we see a harmony of grays, rusts, browns and whites.

Everything works: the feeling, powerful yet controlled, the eloquent composition, the very simplicity of the strictly authentic setting; and the tragedy is made even more poignant by a beautiful still-life detail, a basket full of yarn and cloth on the table. The women were working at their domestic tasks when the dreadful news arrived. David richly deserved the praise showered on him by critics and public alike. And he was well fitted, by conviction as well as by talent, to become the official painter of the Revolution.

Another painter who was as fond of Rome as David, and a good deal more attracted by ruins, did not fare quite so well; of course, it didn't help that he was the Queen's favorite artist and Keeper of the King's Pictures. Hubert Robert (born 1733) went to Rome in 1754 at the height of the excavation fever. He caught it and never recovered, so he specialized in the representation of ruins and the Italian landscape, much the way Vernet specialized in seascapes.

His early work is an exuberant mixture of real and imagined ruins, often placed in fantasy landscapes. He was much given to the use of deep, careful perspectives angled so as to leave an impression of mystery. Colossal architecture is often cut off by the frame: we live in a world of imagination rather than strict reality. And while Robert was also fond of depicting real buildings and sites, his effects are never dry, precise or mechanical. The lines are softened, the play of light and shadow, carefully observed, is given great importance: it is a painter whom we see at work, not a technician.

Life itself always comes along to form a part of Hubert Robert's compositions; paintings are typically called *The Italian Cook* or *The Italian Weaver*. There is no moral here, nothing grand, except for the architecture: everyday occupations form the subject of the painter's art.

From this it was an easy step to realistic landscape depictions. We see the Villa Medici in one work, the bridge over the Gard in another. Soon Robert had become a painter of gardens as well as ruins, and of current events. We owe to him depictions of the gardens at Trianon, which he helped to design, and images of the park at Versailles in 1775, when Louis XVI ordered many trees taken down and replaced by new plantings—those trees whose fall the Abbé Delille was to sing (see Chapter Eight). In one of these paintings Marie Antoinette bends over two children and the King, in a pink suit, watches as the trunks come tumbling down. Leafing through Robert's work is not unlike looking at a beautifully made newsreel or travelogue: we see the Paris Opéra fire of 1781, the demolition of the medieval houses on the Pont Notre Dame, and the Bastille just as it began to come down, but also the Vigier public baths on a bank of the Seine, and the Grand Gallery of the Louvre.

Robert even helped to create the environments he painted. When the trees

9. *Rousseau, Hôtel de Salm, entrance from the street.* The arched central portal, with its reliefs of Fame blowing her trumpet, the colonnades and the pavilions, with their openings conforming to simple geometric forms and surmounted by rectangular reliefs, are typical of the new, classical style. Here, at its best, it blends sobriety and grace. For a description of the other façade, see page 127.

around the Bain d'Apollon, in the park of Versailles, came down, he was asked to design a new setting, and did, mixing rocks and water, vegetation and sculpture; it still looks wonderful.

However, if Hubert Robert had done no more than paint pretty landscapes, charming ruins and current events, he would be justly forgotten by all except eighteenth-century scholars. That such is not the case is due to his delicacy of palette, grace of manner and wonderful sense of light. We like Impressionist painting for its style, not its subject matter; a hundred years before the Impressionists, Robert had been fascinated by the color and look of the outdoors at different seasons and times of the day. There is a real magic in his work, compounded of a sense for the instant and a feeling for the passage of time: millenary ruins are represented as they were at that one, unrepeated moment.

Another artist chose, like Robert, to depict his times; but he showed men (or women), not events, and with such genius that he is very probably the greatest portrait sculptor who ever lived. His name was Houdon, and he was both famous and unrivaled.

Like all his colleagues, Houdon (born 1741) went to Rome and was influenced by antiquity; but more perhaps, by the Romans than by the Greeks, and by their realistic portrait sculpture. His first major work, an écorché, an anatomical study of a man, is remarkable for the knowledge it so openly displays. By 1771 Houdon had moved on to portrait busts and scored his first great triumphs.

The bust of Diderot "establishes at the very beginning of Houdon's career the qualities that made his portraits outstanding in his time and in many ways unique in the history of portrait sculpture. . . . [They have] a marvellous quality of alertness and immediacy," H. H. Arnason has written. Indeed, Diderot is in the middle of speaking; his mouth is open, his eyes, which look slightly to the side as if he were addressing someone in the next seat, are remarkably lifelike thanks to the deep incision of the pupil and the play of light and shadow it creates. The hair "is modelled lightly and freely to suggest the texture of actual hair. . . . The illusion is remarkable that the hair might yield to the touch."[5] It was Houdon's great gift that he was able to seize upon the sitter's main characteristics, psychological as well as physical, and embody them in his sculpture, which is, appropriately, almost always life size.

It was almost impossible to be famous, in the seventies and eighties, and not be sculpted by Houdon (yes, there is even a bust of Louis XVI); it was therefore obvious that when the aged Voltaire came to Paris in 1778 he would sit to the great sculptor. The resulting full-length statue of Voltaire would be enough, if all his other works were to vanish, to make Houdon famous.

We see the writer and philosopher, looking very frail (he died within the

[5] H. H. Arnason, *The Sculptures of Houdon* (New York, 1975).

next month), but intense, alert and intelligent, sitting in a Roman-inspired chair and clad in a toga-like dressing gown which suggests his importance and lasting fame. His sparse hair, held back by a band around the forehead, floats down around his head; but what is most remarkable is the way Houdon has captured Voltaire's look of thoughtful awareness, that irony, that vitality, still intense despite the writer's great age. There is nothing left, it seems, but skin and bones; and yet that half-smile of Voltaire's which so many contemporaries tried unsuccessfully to describe, we see it now on Houdon's statue: it is the true expression of the man who wrote *Candide*.

Popular though he was, Houdon did not limit himself to portraits. His *Diana*, graceful, slim, caught in mid-movement, with one foot off the ground and the other lifting up, reminds one of Mannerist art at its best; but this is more real and, curiously, more nude: an athlete on her way. Almost the opposite of the Diana, his *Winter (La Frileuse)* is a masterpiece of voluptuous grace. Here is another naked young woman, but this time soft, inviting, sexy. Her torso is wrapped in a shawl which forms a cowl around her head; she is bare from the waist down and has the look of a woman who has just come out of a warm bed into a very cold room: we want to cover her, we also want to caress her.

Houdon was far too much a man of his time to ignore the United States. He made a wonderfully eloquent bust of Franklin in 1778, went on to sculpt John Paul Jones in 1781 and Thomas Jefferson in 1789. While his is the standard depiction of Franklin, he is perhaps best known in this country for his full-size statue of George Washington in the Capitol at Richmond, Virginia. It was obvious to everyone, in America in 1785, that only one artist was great enough to provide a marble image of its first citizen; so correspondence went back and forth and, on October 2, 1785, Houdon arrived in Mount Vernon. Washington sat to him for a little over two weeks (October 2–19) and then, with a plaster model, Houdon went home. His fee for the completed statue was 25,000 livres, plus 12,500 livres for expenses.

The sculpture shows us the great man, tall and dignified, if slightly portly, looking almost severe. He is dressed in full regimentals, a reminder of his role as Commander-in-Chief, but, while his right hand rests on a cane, his left leans on a huge fasces from which his sword is hanging—the symbol of Cincinnatus who, having won the war, abandoned public office and returned to his plow. While this comes as close to official portraiture as Houdon ever did, it still conveys the essence of the man, his unemotional steadfastness, his majesty of demeanor, his extraordinary presence. The statue, when Houdon sent it to the United States, was well received: he had indeed become the most admired artist on both continents.

Painting and sculpture, in our period, always seem to fit their time; but architecture had its own revolution, some twenty years before the real event, and a number of visionary architects reached spectacularly new solutions

10. *Ledoux, Barrière du Trône. This is one of the entrances to Paris where the excise tax on all merchandise entering the city had to be paid. (See Chapter One.) The side pavilions are composed of simple volumes, as are the bases of the two columns. These, however, display Ledoux's visionary quality while remaining functional (notice the little rectangular windows).*

which have never looked more appropriate than they do today in this age of the postmodern style.

The two leaders of this movement produced plans so new, so different from the current fashion, that they ended up with very few actual buildings. Both Étienne-Louis Boullée and Claude-Nicolas Ledoux developed a new style in which buildings were composed of a combination of large geometric masses. From the outside, their titanic constructions, made more massive still because they are pierced with only a few small windows, look enormous and impressive. Inside, they are wonderfully gracious. While both preserved some traces of classicism—mostly some columns and an occasional Palladian motif—they are characterized by the boldness with which they handled traditional but enlarged forms, and the skill with which they brought old features, like the barrel vault, into new combinations; above all, their work reflects a sense of grandeur conceived in a wholly original way.

Among other unbuilt ideas is Boullée's design for a huge library. The inner space is topped by an enormous coffered barrel vault, opened up on both sides by parallel skylights. It rests on a row of rather short, stout columns which spring from the top of the bookcase wall. What we have, essentially, are two elementary geometric forms, a rectangle topped by half a cylinder. "The coffers, the books on the shelves and the columns bring some unrest into the hall. But the decisive compositional elements are the barrel vaulting, the colonnade and the bookstacks. From this arrangement, a tremendous tension becomes apparent between the disparate elements," writes Kaufmann[6] in his brilliant study, and the final result is an immensely lively interior space. It was Boullée who produced the plans for the rebuilding of Versailles; we can only dream of what the palace might have been if the King's intentions had been carried out.

Ledoux, like Boullée, was fascinated by simple geometric shapes, but his combinations are a good deal more complex. In one of a series of tax-collecting pavilions he designed—they were actually built—the one at the Barrière de la Santé we see a prismatic building rising from a prismatic, windowless base. Each of the four entrances is topped by a half cylinder; a cylindrical belvedere capped by a hemisphere springs up from the middle: it is both striking and startlingly modern. Another design, unfortunately never carried out, would have been more extraordinary still, though it does not, like the Barrière de la Santé, depend on the relationships of disparate geometrical masses. His Shelter for Rural Guards is simply a huge globe set in the middle of the country. On each side a bridgelike staircase gives access to an entrance composed of a large Palladian motif. The simplicity of the form, never seen before then, and its size seem to place this building squarely in the mid-twentieth century. And since town planning was coming into its own,

[6] Emil Kaufmann, *Architecture in the Age of Reason* (Harvard University Press, 1955).

Ledoux designed a whole city where the look of the buildings would reflect their function: the brothel, for instance, was shaped like a phallus.

There were more traditional architects who simply followed in Gabriel's footsteps. Grace, elegance, happiness of proportions—those are the characteristics of the Louis XVI style, along with a firm adherence to the classical vocabulary of columns, pilasters, pediments and framed windows. The major innovation is the frequent use of rounded forms projecting from the main mass of the building. The Hôtel de Salm, in Paris,[7] designed by Rousseau in 1782, is as beautiful as it is typical of the current style. The river façade is lightly rusticated and pierced by large rectangular windows with stone frames and triangular half pediments; above each window is a round niche in which an antique-looking bust has been placed. The center of the façade comes forward in a semicircular movement; it is adorned with columns between the slightly wider windows, which are topped by plaques sculpted in low relief. Above each plaque is one of the circular niches with its bust, and the whole building is surmounted by a wide cornice which supports statues continuing the line of the columns into the sky. It is worth noting that this charming, restrained façade, while far less revolutionary or stark than Ledoux's buildings, nonetheless consists of two simple geometric forms: a hemicycle protruding from a cube.

Of course there were also architects who, like David in painting, tried for a return to the antique. De Wailly, who designed the Théâtre de l'Odéon (1779), belongs to that school. His building is an elongated block with plain, undecorated walls and framed openings preceded by an austere, majestic colonnade. And there were builders who simply put up many of the plain houses we see today in Paris; but even they strove successfully for graceful proportions.

While the visual arts, in our period, may have produced few geniuses, they did maintain a generally very high level; when put together with the decorative arts, they form a truly impressive ensemble. And it may perhaps be said that, for the French of the seventies and eighties, words came first; no people ever talked so much or so well: the literature of the age turned out to be a worthy rival, in its domain, to Houdon and David in theirs.

[7] Now the Museum of the Legion of Honor.

Chapter Eight

THE ARTS:
LITERATURE
AND THE THEATER

All through the eighteenth century the primacy of French writers over their European colleagues remained unquestioned; here, too, all eyes turned toward Paris. Frederick the Great, who wrote only French and had difficulty expressing himself in German, spent years trying to lure Voltaire to Prussia; Catherine II of Russia directed the same wiles at Diderot. All over the Continent, people waited for the newest French books, novels, philosophy, plays, history.

They had good reason to do so: all the new ideas came from the French *philosophes*. Montesquieu, earlier in the century, had analyzed and refined the new concepts which, though they originated in part with Locke, he made uniquely his own; his precepts are embodied today in the Constitution of the United States. The *encyclopédistes*, Voltaire, Rousseau, took up where he left off. Bold new ideas, whether about the iniquities of religious bigotry, the excesses of monarchical power or the very nature of knowledge, all came from France.

And there was more. Marivaux, in mid-century, not content with creating his own kind of urbane comedy, brought the novel to a new state of perfection—though it must be said that the English novelists were greatly admired even in France. Voltaire's tragedies, cast in a Racinian mold, enthralled audiences and his short stories—*Candide* is, today, the most famous of them— were eagerly awaited. Only poetry was lacking, but somehow no one noticed.

More remarkably still, everyone in France seemed to write easily, elegantly, just by instinct: never, perhaps, has the literary level of an entire nation been so high. Scientists today seem to be engaged in a competition to see whose style will be the most obscure. Redundancies, vagueness, heaviness all come naturally to our contemporaries; but in the eighteenth century even quite undistinguished people wrote light, charming, informative letters. One expects that writers will know how to write, and today one is often disappointed. Then, even semi-illiterates, when they put pen to paper, could express themselves clearly and vividly. Courtiers whose educations had been sketchy, and who had never had to write a word in their lives, would sit down to produce volumes of lively, informative and highly amusing memoirs, all in a style which many twentieth-century professional authors might well envy.

No subject, it seemed, was too abstruse for comprehension: Voltaire felt perfectly able to explain Newton's theories to the non-English world. It is no accident that a naturalist like Buffon (see Chapter Eleven) is usually included in histories of French literature. He was a scientist, but he could still describe the lives of the birds or animals and the aging of the earth in such a way as to make it pleasant, easy reading. And if a work was obscure or heavy going, then it was clearly the author's fault.

Within this general framework, however, the extraordinary explosion of talent that had characterized the mid-century was beginning to die down. Voltaire, probably the most famous man in Europe, died in 1778 at the age of eighty-four. Diderot lived a little longer and was still publishing: the *Essay on the Reigns of Claudius and Nero* is dated 1778, as are his *Elements of Physiology*, but this was simply a continuation of his early thought. Most of the others were dead or dying and, though people somehow remained unaware of it, they were, for the most part, not replaced. It is almost as if exhaustion were setting in.

Jean-Jacques Rousseau was unquestionably the greatest literary figure of the seventies and eighties even though he died in 1778. While his first works were published in the fifties, two major books, the *Confessions* and the *Rêveries du promeneur solitaire* came out only after his death; and his novel, *La Nouvelle Héloïse* (1761), continued to be read and discussed until well after the Revolution.

Unlike most of his colleagues, who thought that their social lives were quite as important as their literary productions, Rousseau was a recluse, a misanthrope who constantly expected the worst of his fellow man and not infrequently provoked it. But this attitude was consistent with his views: civilization was just another word for corruption, he said. Still, his books were read feverishly, passionately, by those very denizens of a sophisticated world who should have been repulsed by his every thought. More than just a literary fashion, Jean-Jacques books helped to shape European culture for well on half a century, and his political theories provided the underpinning of the French Revolution.

Two main themes run through Rousseau's work: all truth comes from nature and we should stay close to it; inequality, far from being ordained by God, is wrong, artificial, and should be ended. The two ideas are complementary. In a state of nature, men are both virtuous and equal; they love, they live freely. Nothing could have been more startling to a culture founded on the rule of a monarch appointed by God, a hierarchical Church whose head was Christ's vicar, and the legally established inequality of men.

"Madmen who complain ceaselessly about nature, know that your ills come from yourselves," Rousseau wrote in the *Confessions*; and, indeed, to him, the only good life was rustic and patriarchal; society brought nothing but problems. And since all men are equal, it also follows that a street sweeper is as good as a duke—a notion which may have become familiar two centuries later but which struck the French government as wholly destructive. Rousseau was obviously a dangerous man.

His first major work, the *Discourse on the Origins of Inequality*, explains how a hierarchical society came into being. "The first man who, having enclosed a piece of land, thought of saying: this is mine, and who found people stupid enough to believe him, was the founder of civil law. How many crimes, how many wars, how many murders, how much misery and sorrow he would have spared humankind, the man who, uprooting the fence or filling up the moat, would have cried to his equals: '. . . You are lost if you forget that this fruit belongs to all and this land to no one.'" This was a truly revolutionary idea, and many readers were upset, among them Voltaire who, inaugurating an argument much used by conservatives ever since, wrote: "What, the man who has sowed on this enclosed ground would be deprived of the fruit of his labor! What, that unjust man, that thief, would be a benefactor to humankind! That is the philosophy of a ne'er-do-well who wants the rich to be robbed by the poor."

Voltaire, who was very rich indeed, belonged to the old order; and, while we live in a society as firmly based on property as ever, we can at least appreciate the boldness of Rousseau's thought—as have revolutionaries from that day to this.

From that first enclosure, Rousseau went on, came private property and the civil laws which regulate it. The next step came when magistrates were chosen to make sure the laws were obeyed: a social hierarchy came into being and men were no longer equal. After that it was a short easy step to modern times: the magistrates, after seizing powers greater than those originally entrusted to them, declared themselves to be hereditary instead of elective. Despotism was born; and, looking around him, remembering that Louis XV had come to the throne at the age of six, he added: "It is obviously against all natural law to have a child giving orders to an old man, an imbecile leading a wise man, and a handful of people keeping far more than they need while the starving multitude lacks for every necessity." The revolutionaries, who worshiped Rousseau, said nothing more and nothing less.

Not all Rousseau's works were political. His next major success, *La Nouvelle Héloïse* (*The New Heloise*), was the first romantic novel ever written (1761). As such, it influenced both people's lives and the other books they read. This passionate, sentimental love story has two main themes, directly linked to those of the *Discours sur l'inégalité*. Jean-Jacques has told us that civilization corrupts all native virtue and that only the passions are natural. Here the passions are given free play, but we are soon led to see that true virtue can be found only in the control of these same passions: nature is contained by morals.

Allied with this theme, the reader also finds lyrical descriptions of the country. Until Rousseau, nature had been used only for allegorical purposes: river nymphs would praise, in verse, the hero. Now, for the first time, the author sees and describes with real feeling the woods, the mountains and the fields; Rousseau even points out how the landscape can reflect our emotions. Of course this goes together with a panegyric for the healthy, useful lives that people can live only in the country.

With all this, the novel often depicts true feelings, and that was why it became such a huge best seller. Julie and Saint-Preux, the leading characters, are passionately in love, a love not crowned by success. Julie will marry an older man, Wolmar, who will take in Saint-Preux and seek to better the ex-lovers on his model estate at Clarens. Here were all the themes to charm Rousseau's readers: a burning love very different from the trifling intrigues depicted until then; a feeling for justice, always appealing in an unjust society; and, finally, an almost passionate love of nature.

La Nouvelle Héloïse is an epistolary novel. One of Saint-Preux's letters to Julie is a perfect example of this new understanding of nature. "The country in which I am may contribute to my melancholy: it is sad and horrible, but thus all the more fitting to the state of my soul; I should not like to live in a more pleasant region. A line of sterile rocks, bordering the sea, surrounds my dwelling, made uglier still by winter. Ah! how well I know, my Julie, that if I had to give you up, there would be no other season or sojourn for me.

"Moved by violent feelings, I cannot stay in place: I run, I climb with ardor, I leap onto the rocks, I pace through all the surroundings and find everywhere in the world the same horror that rules within me. There is no more greenery to be seen, the grass is sere and yellow, the trees bare and the cold winds accumulate snow and ice; all nature is as dead before my eyes as hope in my heart."

La Nouvelle Héloïse was not just a huge, prolonged success: it changed the way people lived their lives. Suddenly, nature existed again; the fashion for English gardens and village life derive from this book. Passions, as opposed to polite feelings, were allowed, even worshiped. The Romantic Age was born.

Rousseau's next book was very far from being a novel. *Émile* (1762) was a lengthy treatise on education; and again it caused a revolution (see Chapter Nine). In 1760 children were brought up just the way they had been in 1660; by 1770 parents and governesses had entered the modern age.

In that same year Jean-Jacques published another precedent-shattering work, *Du contrat social* (*The Social Contract*). It is divided into four parts: the first deals with the general principles governing the social contract, i.e., the basic agreement between ruler and ruled, and between the ruled together; the second analyzes the nature of the sovereign and its ways of functioning (the people is the sovereign); the third considers the various possible forms of government; the last, certain acts of that government.

In this book Rousseau, realizing that natural freedoms, once lost, cannot be recovered, tries to find a way of ensuring the new civil liberties. These are to be protected by a freely chosen sovereign, by frequent voting and by an evolution in which people will give up personal independence to join in the general will so that the good of the society will come before that of the individual. The two bases for this ideal society are liberty and equality: all men are free and equal before the law, an idea the French Revolution and the United States Constitution were to put into practice. Laws must answer only to the general good and have a universal (within the country) application: there can be no more privileged classes and all must bow to a desire for the common good.

So far, there has been nothing to surprise us; these are the very principles on which our government is founded, though, of course, in monarchical France, the book was promptly banned. But *Du contrat social* goes a good deal further: wealth and luxury must be controlled and restrained, Rousseau says, because there can be no political equality without its economic and social counterpart. This point is obviously a good one; recent federal legislation on political contributions is just one application of it.

As for the actual form of government, the laws are to be made, or unmade, directly by the sovereign people through the use of referendums. The executive's task is to make sure those laws are obeyed. In some respects, of course, Rousseau was naïve. When he writes, "Since the sovereign is made only of private people who come together, he neither has nor is capable of having a will contrary to theirs; and so the sovereign power needs no limits in respect to its subjects, since it is impossible for the body to wish harm to any of its parts," of course, he is quite wrong; our century has shown that abundantly. Still, *Du contrat social* is an immense innovation; and while it was little read in the sixties, the revolutionaries made it their bible in the nineties.

Rousseau published nothing more of importance before his death; but he went on writing and produced what may well be, to our modern eye, his best book. "I am starting on an enterprise," he writes on the first page of the *Confessions*, "which is unexampled. . . . I want to show my fellow men a man just as he really is; and I shall be that man. . . . I am not like anyone else I have known; I dare to believe that I am not like anybody else on earth. I may be no better, but I am, at least, different. . . . Let the last judgment's trumpet sound when it will, and I will come, holding this book in my hand, before my judge. I will say firmly: 'This is what I have done, what I have thought, what I have been. I have recounted good and evil with the same frankness. I have hidden nothing bad, added nothing good. . . .' I may have supposed to be true that which I knew might be so, never what I knew was not. I have shown myself such as I was: contemptible and vile when I was so, good, generous, sublime when that was the case."

He was right: no one had, ever before, so bared himself to the reader. With sensitivity and eloquence, Rousseau recounts his feelings, his intellect, even his sex life, and, while we have become accustomed to tell-it-all books, we should not forget that this was the first, and, probably still the best, example of a man candidly showing us what he is and trying to understand himself at the same time. Of course, the *Confessions* are not a great book just because they are so true and so revealing; they were, after all, written by a man of genius. But in their freshness and their immediacy, in the fascinating, sometimes horrifying portrait they give us of a man, his life and his soul, the *Confessions* read today just as they did in 1782; they have neither aged nor lost interest.

Rousseau was the only giant; his disciples were numerous, but none began to even approach his stature. Still, Bernardin de Saint-Pierre, though not considered the master's equal, achieved tremendous popularity with a romantic novel of young love, *Paul et Virginie*, which was first published in 1788. To Jean-Jacques's now well-known formula—passion, virtue, nature—Bernardin added the ever potent charms of exoticism. He had spent two years on the island of Martinique, and that was where he placed his novel, whose two main protagonists are young, innocent and in love. Society intervenes by forcing Virginie to leave the island and play her proper role in Old World society. Her ship founders in a storm and the lovers are separated by death, a highly affecting theme, which caused many tears to flow.

Unlike Julie and Saint-Preux, Paul and Virginie are just as nature fashioned them: their passions have not yet been corrupted, they are, in fact, virtuous and so, in the Rousseauan sense, legitimate; but of course civilization spoils everything. The new tradition was firmly established and was to be continued, twenty years later, by Chateaubriand in his *Atala*. In *Paul et Virginie*, as in *La Nouvelle Héloïse*, landscapes play a vital role, but melancholy and sadness dominate. The very weather now answers to the characters' feelings; it is frequently and poetically described. "It was one of those delicious nights, so frequent in the tropics, whose beauty the cleverest brush could never fully paint. The moon appeared in the middle of the skies and was surrounded by a veil of clouds which its rays pierced by degrees. Its light spread slowly over the island's mountains and its peaks which shone with a silvery green. The winds held their breath. One could hear in the

woods, deep in the valleys, at the end of the rocks, little cries, the sweet mur-
murs of birds caressing one another in their nests, gladdened as they were by
the clarity of the night and the quiet of the air. . . . The stars were dazzling
in the sky and were reflected in the sea where their shimmering images were
repeated."

Altogether, this is a charming, exotic depiction of pastoral life in the
tropics, of pure young souls, of awakening love, all told sweetly, poetically
and very sentimentally. Even today *Paul et Virginie* retains some of its
magic; but it is mostly read by young adolescents and lacks the power of the
two other great masters of the genre, Rousseau and Chateaubriand.

Bernardin represents one side of Rousseau's legacy. A provincial typogra-
pher who wanted to simplify spelling picked up the other. Restif de la Bretonne (born 1734), who soon moved from Auxerre to Paris, was so easy and
prolific an author that he never bothered to write his books: he just composed the printing plates directly. He was also tremendously successful, appealing both to the upper classes and to the bourgeoisie by his curious mixture of naïveté and sophistication, vividness and moralizing; today, very
unjustly, he is almost completely forgotten.

Restif's world was Paris, and a Paris described in that realistic technique
inaugurated by Rousseau; he also picked up one of Rousseau's main themes,
that of the virtuous man (in this case, from the country too) who is corrupted by city life. But he went a good deal further: he recounted all he
saw, and he was a sharp observer. No detail was beneath his interest, no un-
pleasantness glossed over: although his literary heirs, the Goncourts, Zola
and Maupassant, did not start writing until nearly a hundred years later,
Restif is unquestionably the originator of the realistic novel.

Never before Restif had the life of the poor been thought a fit subject for
a book; nor had the daily incidents of street life in Paris seemed of any interest to a society whose eyes were firmly fixed on the rich and titled. And since
literary profits were so small, Restif never had to resist the temptation to join
the more comfortable part of his beloved city.

This brilliant observer and gifted writer, always busy, always running,
managed to produce over two hundred volumes between 1767, when he published his first book, and his death in 1806. In order to do so, he spent almost
as much time roaming the streets of the city as he did actually writing. He
never married—he had a taste for prostitutes—never, apparently, bought
new clothes and, shabby as he was, managed to frequent a few salons where
the nobility mixed with the bourgeoisie; and through the eighties, he received the backing of another successful eccentric, Beaumarchais.

Of course, you can scarcely write two hundred volumes and be always at
your best: Restif's books, marked as they all are by a unique directness, can
be extremely uneven. Like many self-taught men, he couldn't tell the good
from the mediocre; apparently lacking judgment, he was also short on taste

and discernment. "Make more cuts, or the public will make them for you," Mercier wrote him. The verse captioning Restif's portrait in the *Journal de Genève* on October 9, 1785, sums up the way his contemporaries felt about him:

> *Son esprit libre et fier, sans guide et sans modèle,*
> *Même alors qu'il s'égare étonne ses rivaux,*
> *Amant de la nature, il lui dut ses pinceaux,*
> *Et fut simple, inégal et sublime comme elle.*

> [His proud and free mind, without guide or model,
> Even when it wanders amazes his rivals.
> This lover of nature owes his brushes to her,
> And, like her, is simple, unequal and sublime.]

This is particularly true of his endless but often fascinating *Nuits de Paris* (*Nights of Paris*), which is simply a collection of incidents noted by Restif as he walked about the city. Some of these can be wonderfully vivid. There is the story (is it strictly accurate? one wonders) of Restif noticing four strong men in a dark street, who were busy making a hole in the side of a house. Undaunted, Restif ran to the main door and knocked frantically until the doorman and servants, issuing forth, caused the robbers to flee hastily; and the story of the young washerwomen who, having noticed that the linen they got from their elegant clients was still quite clean, rented it or lent it to various people for a few days before washing it and returning it to the rightful owners; and the story of the lost dog, barking away at a whole terrified street until pacified by the providential Restif. Many of these anecdotes are just hackneyed tales of the "dog bites man" variety, but they are easy enough to skip, and even today the *Nuits de Paris* often make wonderful reading as they give us a fascinating picture of Paris in the eighties.

Restif was far too prolific to confine himself merely to these observations; he also wrote a number of semi-autobiographical novels in which Rousseau's themes echo from page to page, although never in such a way as to bore the reader. The very title of perhaps his most successful book, *Le Paysan perverti* (*The Perverted Peasant*), is in itself characteristic: the peasant has been perverted by remaining away from country simplicity and virtue. As for the lure of the city, Restif describes it eloquently: "No, my dear brother, I will no longer enjoy the happiness of life in the country; my fate is cast; I love the city and hate it all at once; but I realize I cannot leave it. . . . When I try to find out why I like the city, I see that it is because of its politeness, so much more pleasant than mere cordiality, its grace of manners; people who seem elegant in the country are just ridiculous here: the natural result of this is that one slowly grows accustomed to finding oneself their superior. . . . Life in the city is more cheerful, the environment more pleasant, the way of thinking cleverer and more developed. . . . You will say that people in the cities are wickeder: I cannot defend them. . . . Women here are beautiful flowers, enchanting sirens who give one pleasures of a thousand different kinds. . . . The frequentation of the fair sex here is charming, the conversations seductive; their manners have such ease, such graceful lightness that time spent with them is passed in a continual ecstasy. One would think they were created only to please; and they give it all their care." Our peasant has obviously been well and truly perverted.

Along with his attempted reform of spelling, Restif felt called upon to improve a very imperfect world. He was interested in politics, of course. "Property is the source of all vices, crimes and corruption," he wrote after Rousseau. He did go on, though, to a variety of other subjects. *Le Pornographe* offers model legislation to govern the practice of prostitution; *Le Mimographe* contains a plan for a reformed national theater; *Le Gynographe* is a "suggested project of regulations which will result in the happiness of both sexes"; *L'Andrographe* "will bring about a general reformation of customs and thus the happiness of mankind"; *Le Thesmographe* embodies a general reform of the legal system; and, finally, *Le Glossographe* was to establish a more rational way of spelling, but Restif never got around to preaching what he practiced. This explosion of improving works—none of which was taken seriously—is, in a way, characteristic of a self-taught man who was convinced that nothing was beyond him; but it also reflects the dissatisfaction, the yearning for change that were so generally felt at the end of the Ancien Régime.

Restif's friend, Sébastien Mercier, quite agreed with him: France desperately needed reforms and he made his opinion plain throughout the twelve volumes of his *Tableau de Paris* (written from 1778–86). Like Restif, he resented systematic inequality and the concentration of wealth in a few private hands; he deplored the absolutism which allowed, among other abuses, the King to imprison his subjects at will; and he fought censorship very effectively by publishing his books in Amsterdam, whence they returned, as contraband, to Paris.

Between them, Restif and Mercier are providential for the historian. Their works are rich with details of life in the Paris of the seventies and eighties; they were both keen observers and vivid writers; but where Restif's taste leans to anecdote and the sensational, Mercier was a true reporter. The *Tableau* is not just a description of Paris, though it is certainly that, but also an account of how people lived, what they did, where they went and when, what they said and ate and bought. It told you who the fashionable jeweler was and what to do if you had left your belongings in a cab, as well as how many servants people had, what plays were successful and how to behave in society. Under Mercier's pen, a whole civilization comes alive again, in its own décor, amid its own customs; and while the *Tableau* does paint a rather golden picture, that is only because it shows us the reality of Paris. The author never hesitates to criticize and does so often—the hospitals are filthy, you can see obscenities scrawled on every wall, there are no great public buildings to speak of, the rich squander their money in a profligate and useless way. Still, like so many other Parisians before or since, he was in love with his city, and that feeling registers clearly. The most remarkable thing of all, though, is that Mercier manages never to be dull; his book is divided into hundreds of short, unconnected descriptions, which keep the reader moving and interested. The *Tableau* is not just an unprecedented—and unequaled—enterprise; it is also a highly entertaining book.

Restif and Mercier have largely been forgotten; Rousseau remains justly famous; there is another, infamous, author whose books are seldom read but whose name has become a household word: the marquis de Sade. While it is true that his work often has a sexual content,[1] it is in no way erotic. The sex is there to prove something about the society. Of course, everyone knows that, in his books, he defends cruelty, that women are whipped, raped, mutilated, killed, that sadism was named after him; and he is then unfairly dismissed.

All that, of course, is true; it is also a very small part of the total work. Before anything else, it should be mentioned that Sade is a good writer, one with a polished, literate, readable style; all sex aside—and it is really allegorical, anyway—his books and his very remarkable letters make wonderful reading.

The scion of a noble Provençal family,[2] the marquis de Sade started life in a perfectly conventional way: he fought, as an officer, in the Seven Years' War, then married, somewhat beneath him, the daughter of a rich parlement man, the Président de Montreuil. After living with his wife for a few years, quite happily, it seems, he was imprisoned at his mother-in-law's request, in theory because he made too free with the servants, in fact because he was spending his wife's money too fast. He remained in and out of prison until, like other prisoners kept at the King's pleasure, the Revolution freed him in 1790 and, in 1801, was clapped right back into jail—actually an insane asylum—because he had published a *roman à clef* called *Zoë et ses deux acolytes* which discussed Josephine's many love affairs a little too candidly.

There would be much to be said for his books if they did no more than legitimize sexual fantasies. In his recognition of their existence, Sade can be considered the precursor of Krafft-Ebing and Freud. "You know I respect all tastes, all fantasies; however strange they may be, I find them respectable, both because one is not able to control having them and because the oddest, the most bizarre of them, if properly analyzed, always proceeds from an origin of wounded delicacy," he wrote his wife from the Bastille. It is a thoroughly modern attitude; but as we know, precursors tend to be unwelcome.

[1] But not more so than many recent best sellers.
[2] He was descended from Petrarch's Laura.

It shows no mean insight to trace the origin of sexual bizarreness to a long-ago wound, no mean courage to describe its manifestations, especially since it involved looking into himself. Nor is there any use looking scandalized and pretending that Sade invented it all: sadism predates him by many millennia. Why then shun him and his works, when, in the world of medicine, diseases are named after their discoverers as a signal honor?

His books, however, are about much more than sex. His main point is that we must always recognize reality. Things are what they are, he keeps saying; most men are not virtuous; cruelty is rife (and who in our century could deny that?) and the only way to survive is to be aware. The marquis makes it all very clear in *Juliette, ou les infortunes de la vertu*. The two sisters, Juliette and Justine, are exact opposites: Justine is highly virtuous; she is religious, pure and perfectly blind to reality. As a result, she is repeatedly raped, flogged, bled, hanged (but taken down at the last moment) and abused in every possible way; when she finally comes across a man who seems uninterested in her charms, it turns out he's a homosexual and, since she surprises him having sex with his valet, she's flogged yet again. Juliette, on the other hand, thinks religion a bad joke; she uses her beauty to get what she wants; she is aware of men's faults and takes advantage of them: she ends up rich, powerful and respected. "Justine is the woman as she was, enslaved, miserable and less than human; Juliette, on the other hand, represents the new woman [Sade] could begin to see, a being as yet unthought of . . . who will have wings and renew the universe," Guillaume Apollinaire wrote, and he was perfectly right: in many ways, Sade was the first feminist.

He was also very much a man of his time. Like so many others, from Voltaire to Babeuf, he fought for liberty, religious, political, intellectual liberty, by his constant rejection of all convention. In his most philosophical work, *La Philosophie au boudoir,* Sade explains at great length the shortcomings of organized religion and preaches atheism, at a time when even advanced thinkers were usually deists. He does so partly by pointing out the hypocrisy of most religious practice, the discrepancy between preaching and life as well as the way in which organized churches always try to monopolize money and power; but more than this, Sade exemplifies the metaphysical rejection of God, a God who limits man's freedom and his responsibilities.

Perhaps most astonishing, though, is the ground on which Sade feels free to disregard current customs and prejudices: cultural relativity. The first in modern times, he points out that creeds and laws differ widely from place to place; that what, in some faraway country, would be a crime is, in another, highly praiseworthy; that some Greek habits, even, would seem heinous to the eighteenth-century French. This perfectly valid, highly sophisticated argument bespeaks great intelligence and an amazingly wide culture. Instead of being, as usual, summarily dismissed, Sade deserves recognition as a precursor and libertarian.

Poetry, all through the century, was weakly represented: people seemed to like pretty occasional verse above everything; as a result, we cannot find a single great poet. In our period one man, the Abbé Delille (born 1738), was overwhelmingly famous; his fame endured until the 1830s, when Sainte-Beuve wrote a devastating, and wholly justified, review of his work; he then sank into complete oblivion where he has remained to this day.

It is a little difficult for the modern reader to see where Delille's merit lies. His automatic, pedestrian verse, full of the most stilted classical references (the wind is always a zephyr, for instance), trudges down the long dusty road of imitation. Not for nothing did the abbé translate Virgil's *Georgics* into French verse (1769); we keep coming across invocations like this:

> *O plaines de la Grèce! O champs de l'Ausonie,*
> *Lieux toujours inspirants, toujours chers au génie . . .*
> *Hélas, je n'ai point vu ce séjour enchanté,*
> *Ces beaux lieux où Virgile a tant de fois chanté.*

> [O plains of Greece! O fields of Ausonia,
> Ever inspiring places, ever dear to genius . . .
> Alas, I have not seen this enchanted sojourn,
> Those beautiful places where often Virgil sang.]

His contemporaries, who were still apt to know Latin and besides were in the throes of "antiquomania," loved this kind of appeal; it tends to leave us very cold.

Still, the Abbé Delille was not wholly without merit; he had a real feeling for nature and its beauties, though he tended to express it in stilted, mechanical language. In 1782 he published a long poem called *Les Jardins* (*The Gardens*) which, while it often reads like a rhymed nursery catalogue, now and again rings with convincing emotion, as does this passage mourning the replanting of the park of Versailles:

> *O Versailles! O regrets! O bosquets ravissants,*
> *Chef d'oeuvre d'un grand roi, de Lenôtre et des ans,*
> *La hache est à vos pieds et votre heure est venue.*
> *Ces arbres dont l'orgueil s'élancant dans la nue*
> *Frappés dans leur racine et balancant dans l'air*
> *Leurs superbes sommets ébranlés par le fer*
> *Tombent. . . .*

> [O Versailles! O regrets! O ravishing woods,
> The masterpiece of a great king, of Lenôtre, of the years,
> The ax is at your feet and your hour is come.
> Those trees whose pride rose up to the clouds
> Struck now at the root, and swinging through the air,
> Their superb summits shaken by cold steel,
> Fall. . . .]

That description of the falling trees is at least pre-Romantic and can be considered a faint beginning of the great landscape verse written, some fifty years later, by Lamartine.

The fame of *Les Jardins* was such that when Madame Élisabeth, the King's sister, heard the book would soon be published, she deferred the changes she had planned to make in her own gardens so as to conform with Delille's prescriptions. What she and everyone else failed to understand was that landscape architecture and poetry are not one and the same.

After this, Delille proceeded to put the rest of the world in verse. His description of Lavoisier's discoveries is nothing short of grotesque:

> *Lavoisier, tu parais, et par toi l'univers*
> *Apprend que l'eau contient deux principes divers,*
> *L'oxygène propice aux facultés vitales*
> *L'hydrogène inflammable, en parts inégales. . . .*

> [Lavoisier, you appear, and the universe
> Learns that water contains two separate principles,
> Oxygen, helpful to the needs of life
> Flammable hydrogen, in unequal parts. . . .]

As for the other popular poet, Lebrun (born 1729), he was, because of semi-scientific odes on subjects like the Lisbon earthquake, dubbed the French Pindar. His most famous work, *La Nature, ou le bonheur philosophique et champêtre* (1760), is a paean to the poet of genius who, drawing his images from nature, can unite it with art; but, like Delille, his great poem is more pompous and didactic than passionate; and he frequently produces passages like this:

> *Heureux qui dans vos bras, filles de Mnémosine,*
> *Joint la fière Minerve à la tendre Euphrosine*
> *Et qui, même en ses vers, émule de Newton,*
> *Tente un vol ignoré du Tasse et de Milton!*

> [Happy the man who in your arms, daughters of Mnemosyne,[3]
> Joins the proud Minerva to the tender Euphrosyne
> And who, in his verse itself, a follower of Newton,
> Attempts a flight unknown to Tasso and Milton!]

In the theater, then considered a branch of poetry, we have at least one genius amidst a bunch of mediocrities who simply rewrote, badly, the plays of Corneille and Racine; some were briefly successful, others not; but one man managed to monopolize the attention of Versailles and Paris.

Pierre-Augustin Caron de Beaumarchais (born 1732) started out in life as

---

[3] Mnemosyne was the goddess of memory; her daughters were the muses. Euphrosyne was one of the three Graces.

a clockmaker and was so good at it that in 1753 he became clockmaker to the King; at the same time, he gained the favor of the King's daughters, whom he amused with his musical talents and his wit. By 1761 he had become noble, as a secretary to the King, that purely theoretical position. He should have had smooth sailing from there on, but in fact the rest of his life was a complicated, romantic hodgepodge of suits lost and won, inheritances stolen and regained, secret and ambiguous missions, first for Louis XV—he bought up a pamphlet attacking Madame du Barry and convinced the Chevalier d'Éon to start wearing skirts—then for Louis XVI, in the course of which he nearly killed himself.

The American rebellion was a godsend for Beaumarchais, since he could now make himself useful to Maurepas, Vergennes and the King. In no time a new corporation, Rodrigue Hortalez & Co., had been set up as a front through which the French government could send money and ammunition to the insurgents. From then on, everything went his way: he made a good deal of money trading, on his own account, with America; he recovered his lost inheritance and gained considerable prestige. And while working on a new play, *The Marriage of Figaro*,[4] he embarked on a campaign to establish authors' rights which was finally successful in 1790.

While *The Barber of Seville* is a wonderfully funny play and still, like the *Marriage*, often performed in France, it is no more than that; but the *Marriage* is no mere comedy: it is the first toll of the bell for the Ancien Régime. Louis XVI saw it so clearly that, after having it read to him privately by Madame Campan, he interrupted, saying: "This is detestable and will never be played. . . . That man makes fun of everything that must be respected in a government." The King, with his usual firmness, stuck to his guns for a little over a year; and, after public curiosity had been brought to white-hot pitch, the first night came on April 27, 1784. Even though Beaumarchais had removed some of the more objectionable lines, we can still well understand why Louis XVI was so upset.

The hero of the play, Figaro, is a valet who constantly shows himself cleverer than his master, Count Almaviva: in itself, this was subversive, as was the way in which Figaro resisted the count's pretensions. To the count, Figaro and his future wife are scarcely human, mere conveniences, really. When he refuses to give in, Figaro comes to represent the whole oppressed middle and lower classes. Then there are the lines themselves: "A great lord does good when he does no harm. . . . When you consider the qualities demanded of a servant, how many masters do you know who would be worthy of being servants?" This is bad enough, but there is still worse.

"Pretending to ignore what one knows, and to be aware of everything one does not know; to understand when one doesn't and not to hear when one does; especially to have more power than one really has; often having as one's great secret the fact that one has none; shutting oneself in carefully

4 An earlier play, *The Barber of Seville*, had been enthusiastically received in 1773.

just to sharpen one's pen and seeming deep when one is only, as they say, empty and shallow; pretending, more or less successfully, to be other than one is, spreading spies and giving pensions to traitors; softening seals [so as to open letters], intercepting letters, and trying to ennoble the poverty of the means by the nobility of the goals: I'll die if that isn't the whole of politics," says Figaro, accurately describing the French government, and the count, more damning still, answers: "Eh! but it's intrigue that you've just defined." There really was not much more to be said.

Still, the *Marriage* is not just a political play. The characters are real, often touching. The count is funny, but he's also hard and selfish; the saddened countess begins to fall in love with Cherubin, a ravishing young man just reaching puberty; and her attraction for him partakes of a complex mixture of mother and mistress. Susanne, the maid, who loves Figaro, is far more human than the stock repertory maid of the French theater. All in all, this is a richly textured play in which wit and political thrusts are allied with a fast-moving plot and a great deal of human truth.

With all this, Beaumarchais should have done well when the Revolution finally came; but it soon proved too much for him. He died in 1799, an impoverished exile in Hamburg. His plays, of course, endured as did the works of Jean-Jacques Rousseau and Bernardin de Saint-Pierre and even, for a while, those of the Abbé Delille. Once again, the arts showed themselves more lasting than the government, and survived when all else perished.

Chapter Nine

CHILDREN AND EDUCATION

In a world where the arts flourished, science prospered and there was a lot of gossip to keep up with, it is no wonder that children were sometimes forgotten. Anyone who remembered them and took a good look would have found that there were two different kinds of children: those of the aristocracy, and the others. The others were, on the whole, incomparably better off.

Middle-class children would one day be expected to earn money and further the family fortunes: they had to be educated accordingly. They lived in smaller apartments or houses than children of the nobility, so they were more visible and their parents often noticed them, sometimes even took care of them. They seemed quite real.

Aristocratic children, on the other hand, entered a limbo at birth; they reappeared again just in time to be sent away. They had their uses, of course: the name must go on; they served to keep the mother's dowry in the family; they were a way of holding onto honors and money: a child of three could be given the colonelcy of a regiment, an abbey, or the reversion of a governorship. They were sometimes necessary for family occasions—baptisms, weddings, funerals; but, apart from these brief appearances, they were largely ignored. Children didn't seem quite human, somehow.

The newborn baby's disappearance was quite literal: no upper-class mother breast-fed her own offspring. Within hours of the birth, the baby was taken off to the country outside Paris and left there for three or four years in the care of a wet nurse. Curiously, it never seems to have occurred to people who considered the lower classes as scarcely human that leaving their children with the creatures might have some effect on them. So the baby was whisked off and shared a peasant woman's milk with her own child. It was also treated just like the other children there—or worse if, as sometimes happened, the parents neglected to pay the wet nurse her salary.

Very little care was taken to ascertain the nurse's reliability, so she might be a drunk or careless. Sometimes there was an accident and the child died, no surprise to anyone, given the generally high rate of infant mortality. There were cases of a child, dropped carelessly, being crippled for life: Talleyrand's so-called clubfoot resulted from broken bones suffered when he was dropped by his nurse and left unattended afterward.

If the baby survived this exile, he was brought back to the parents' house at the age of three or four and turned over to a governor or governess who usually had more interesting things to do than look after a young child. There was no question of having one's offspring racing through one's salon or eating at one's table: they were kept upstairs, usually on the same floor as the servants, and safely out of the way. Some really devoted mothers might actually see their children almost every day for five minutes or so, but most were far too busy and would remember to ask after the little boy or girl at least once a month.

So the children wandered around the back parts of the house, upstairs in the attics, downstairs in the kitchens and pantries. They were seldom washed —the servants were busy too—or changed, so that their clothes were usually filthy and sometimes in rags. They were never served a meal but found what they could in the kitchen. They weren't even allowed out into the garden very often: their parents might be there, after all. As for an education, well, that, it seemed, could always wait. Their governor was probably writing verse to their mother or making himself agreeable to the visitors downstairs. However, when they were seven or eight they would have to be taught how to read, and a few elementary subjects; and since they might be reluctant to start learning after having been left to themselves so long, they were abundantly whipped.

Still, there were those family occasions when children were needed, and then they would be cleaned up and dressed exactly like miniature versions of their parents, the little girls in tight-fitting, décolleté bodices and hooped brocade skirts, with diamonds and feathers in their powdered hair, the little boys in embroidered velvet suits, swords at their sides, and their hair curled and powdered. Since the one thing they were always taught was how to bow or curtsy, they usually acquitted themselves honorably.

At the age of nine or ten little girls would be sent off to be educated in a convent, where they stayed until they were married. There they were taught little more than dancing, deportment and singing, and usually emerged from six or seven years' study in a state of almost complete ignorance. Of course they could never meet young men, but that was no problem: the families arranged the marriage. The bride would meet the groom either a few days before the marriage or at the ceremony itself, and would start deceiving him almost immediately afterward.

A little boy had more possibilities. He could be sent to Versailles and become a page; he would then attend a special school half the day, learning some French grammar, a little Latin, some arithmetic, history and geography; far more important, he would have dancing and deportment lessons, and be taught how to fence and ride. For the other half of his day, he would run errands for the royal family, look after ladies at balls and generally make himself useful. By the time he was sixteen he would have lovely manners, a thorough knowledge of the court and a good deal of sexual experience.

Alternately, he might be given a whole set of tutors who would teach him much the same thing as his brother the page, and become an officer at the age of sixteen or seventeen. He would then spend three months a year, at most, in the provincial town where his regiment was quartered and the rest of the year in Paris or at Versailles.

Finally he might, as a portionless younger son—girls had dowries, elder sons inherited the whole estate—be destined for the Church. He would then be sent, at the age of nine or ten, to a *collège* in Paris, like the Collège d'Harcourt, where he would live with his own tutor, attend classes in Latin, French, mathematics, history and geography, and visit his parents as often as once a week. Then at the age of sixteen or seventeen he would be sent to a *séminaire*, probably the Séminaire de Saint-Sulpice, where, along with other future priests, he would be taught some theology and how to say mass. He would also attend the Sorbonne's theology classes and eventually receive a bachelor's degree. He would then go to live with his uncle the bishop and become one of his *grands vicaires* (vicars-general) until, in short order, he received a bishopric of his own.

Royal children were brought up differently, but often no better. Of course, the Queen did not breast-feed, but the wet nurse at least came to live in the palace. Again, these children were generally less neglected than their aristocratic contemporaries; each had his own Household, consisting of at least a dozen persons and thirty or forty servants, all headed by the Governess of the Children of France; then, when the boys reached seven, they were given their own Households and tutors, headed by a governor who was either a great churchman or a duke with a reputation for culture.

There was no question of torn or dirty clothes, but there was no freedom, either. It can't be much fun for a little boy to be always curled and powdered and dressed in embroidered suits and knee breeches with white stockings, or to spend his life in public and without friends of his own age.

Royal children, especially the Dauphin, were supposed to be well educated, so they were tutored in the usual subjects, and also in political history. They were made to understand the complexities of etiquette early; they were accustomed to public appearances and the kind of behavior they called for.

That, at least, was the theory. In fact, Louis XVI's governor, the duc de La Vauguyon, was a bigoted, servile boor who managed to bring his charge to the age of sixteen in a state of almost total ignorance. A stupid man himself, he thought to assure himself of future favor by making it totally unnecessary for the Dauphin ever to do his homework. As it turned out, he made a mistake: Louis XVI always felt humiliated by his lack of knowledge and studied diligently on his own to catch up; but he developed real hatred for his governor and finally forbade him the court. As for Marie Antoinette, when she arrived in France in 1770, at barely fifteen, she could speak French and Italian, play the harp, dance and curtsy gracefully, but that was all, and it stayed all. She had her own library at Versailles, and her own librarian, whose job must have been very easy since she almost never opened a book.

—◦◦{   }◦◦—

All in all, this was a rather sad situation, but no one paid it much attention until Jean-Jacques Rousseau published his book on education.

Émile, ou de l'éducation came out in 1762, turned into a runaway best seller (it still makes fascinating reading) and revolutionized education, not just in France but all over Europe. In it, Rousseau, a brilliantly perceptive writer, pointed out, for the first time in centuries, that children were actually human. "People don't understand children," he wrote. "If they're very wise, they think about what men ought to know without worrying about what children are able to learn. . . . Start out by better studying your pupils."

In accordance with his theory of the good savage, Rousseau thought that something of nature could be preserved. "All is good as it comes out of its Maker's hands: everything degenerates in the hands of man," he warned, but went on to say that "mothers want their child to be happy, and to be so right now. In that, they are quite right." Here again was a shattering notion. No one had ever considered the possibility that a child had feelings, much less that he ought to be happy; and in an age when things ran according to rules and principles, he added: "True education should depend less on precepts than on exercises." In fact, the most startling aspect of *Émile* today is its modernity: one might almost be reading a livelier Bettelheim.

The innovations Rousseau recommended went to the heart of the matter. Babies had been tightly swathed for generations. Set them free, said Rousseau, they'll gain strength as they wriggle. Then too, he was horrified by the custom of sending one's baby to a village nurse where, he wrote, it was likely to spend its days suspended from a nail. "Let mothers deign to feed their children themselves," he urged. "Mores will be automatically improved, a feeling for nature will reawaken in every heart, the state will be repeopled," and besides, he added, the child is taught ingratitude when he sees his nurse being dismissed.

All this was startling enough, but Rousseau went much further. "As the true wet nurse is the mother, so the true tutor is the father," he told a world

11. This scene from Rousseau's Émile, designed by Moreau le Jeune, is captioned: "Each person respects the other's work." The boy learns the value of labor as he waters his own plot under his tutor's paternal gaze, much to the gardener's admiration. This was a radical new concept: an upper-class child is actually working with his own hands.

in which fathers were scarcely aware of their sons' existence. "What is this rich man, this busy father, doing? Paying another man to discharge those duties which are peculiarly his. Venal soul! Can you believe money will buy your son another father? . . . You are not even giving him a master, but a valet who will soon produce an image of himself."

Still, Jean-Jacques was a realist. He knew quite well that, no matter how convincing *Émile* may have been, no busy duke was going to raise his own son. So he at least tried to end the practice of putting a bored and bitter old man in charge of the child. "A child's tutor must be as young as possible while yet being wise." He went on to recommend gymnastics or at least exercise. "The weaker the body, the more it dominates; the stronger, the more it obeys," a precept many people today think they have discovered. And he added, "Hygiene is the only useful part of medicine," a revolutionary and at the time profoundly true statement (see Chapter Six).

Most children almost never left their parents' house; all wrong, said Rousseau, send them to the country where they can get fresh air. They had been left filthy; now they must take a bath every day and exercise freely. It doesn't matter if they fall and hurt themselves a little: it prepares them for the pain they will have to bear later in life.

This natural, healthy, physically strong child must be treated fairly and, above all, consistently. "Say yes with pleasure, be reluctant to say no; but let your refusals be unchangeable." He must be taught by experience, not speeches, and treated according to his nature: you cannot force a child to change but only make him a hypocrite and a liar. More than books, a child must learn how to live, and that entails facing him with the consequences of his acts. If he breaks a window, leave it broken for a while: discomfort is a good teacher. As for punishment, when, rarely, it becomes necessary, let it be the natural consequence of the fault, not the application of some abstract rule.

Again, he continued, let children lead natural lives: they should wear comfortable clothes, have easily managed hair, not pomade and powder; luxury is not good for them. Let their food be abundant but simple, and let them learn directly from nature: you can teach geometry more easily in a garden than in a schoolroom. Nor are collections of facts (of which education entirely consisted) important: teach the child to think clearly and logically. The facts will follow.

All this was startling enough, but Rousseau went a good deal further still. In an age when classes were rigidly defined, when no nobleman would work, when birth generally mattered more than achievement, Rousseau wanted to teach the rich how to be poor: while a poor man can always adapt to wealth, a rich man loses everything when he loses his money. What would he do then? On the other hand, "one can always live honestly and earn one's bread when one knows a trade." The child, therefore, must learn at least one handicraft—carpentry or masonry, how to make locks or watches. Many of the

French émigrés, a few years later, would have been happier men and women if they had been brought up according to these principles.

As for sex education, it was absolutely necessary. Openness was the guiding principle: tell the child the truth and conceal nothing from him—an idea which we have rediscovered only recently.

Rousseau, not content with just telling parents what they ought to do, also showed them what they must aim for. This is a description of Émile at the age of fifteen:

"Émile is hard-working, sober, patient, firm and very courageous. His imagination, which has not been overstimulated, never exaggerates dangers; he responds to a very few words and knows how to suffer without recrimination because he has not learned to fight against fate. As for death, he doesn't yet know just what it is, but, accustomed as he is to bear the laws of necessity, he will be prepared to die when he must without moans and without protests: that is the most nature allows in that moment we all dread. To live free and not be bound to human ambitions is the best way of learning how to die.

"In one word, Émile is virtuous in all that concerns him directly. To acquire social virtues as well, he will need only to find out about the relationships which call for them. He needs no more enlightenment than his mind is prepared to receive.

"He lives his life free of other people's prejudices and thinks it right that others feel the same. Demanding nothing of anyone, he does not feel he owes anything either: alone in the midst of society, he counts on himself only. . . . He makes no mistakes, except those that can't be avoided; he has no vices, or only those of which a man can't be free. He has a healthy body, strong limbs, a fair and open mind, a free, passionless heart. . . . Without disturbing anyone's rest, he has lived contented, free and happy as far as nature allows."

The self-sufficiency Rousseau prizes so highly may surprise us today, who live in an interdependent world; it was merely a corrective to the constant begging everyone relied on, from the pauper in the street to the courtier at Versailles. In a world where favor was everything, there was good reason to depend on no one and be self-reliant. Here again, Émile would have done well after 1789.

Curiously, although Rousseau's public led the kind of life of which he most disapproved, they took to *Émile* instantly. Instead of being shocked and indignant, they were thrilled and eager. In no time at all noble mothers were nursing their babies, children became visible, education was a fashionable topic. There was the hitch: while *Émile* certainly made many children's lives much nicer and their education more effective, it also created a fashion. Parents did pay more attention to their offspring, not because they wanted to but because it was the smart thing to do.

There was some real progress. By 1780 little boys were wearing sensible clothes—loose shirts, little open jackets and real trousers—and their hair hung loose and unpowdered. They were allowed to exercise more; they were fed better food more regularly. Most important, they were no longer treated as if they didn't really exist. But, since it was a fashion, the system was often distorted.

Rousseau had said that children ought to be hardened as a preparation for life, so they were awakened at six in winter and five in summer, made to wash in cold water and run out into the freezing rain. He said they should eat plain food, so they were never given sweets.

One example among many of a child subjected to this unpleasant regimen was the eldest son of the duc d'Orléans, the future King Louis Philippe. He was raised under the stern guidance of Madame de Genlis, who was a leading bluestocking, the author of sentimental novels, and his father's mistress. "She was a tough tutor, I can tell you," Louis Philippe confided to Victor Hugo many years later. "She brought us up with ferocity, my sister and I. We had to get up at six in the morning, winter and summer, we were fed milk, roast meats and bread; never a treat, never a dessert; hard work and no fun. It was she who got me used to sleeping on planks. She made me learn a great number of handicrafts; thanks to her, I am competent in almost any trade, including that of man of all work. I can bleed a man like Figaro. I can be a carpenter, a coachman, a plasterer, a blacksmith. She was systematic and demanding. When I was very young, she frightened me; I was a weak, lazy and cowardly boy; I was scared of mice! She made me into a rather bold man, a man of courage."

The contradictions between this system and *Émile* are obvious; by exaggerating, it distorts. Rousseau's happy child becomes an overworked little creature who never has any fun. Louis Philippe naturally thought well of himself, but impartial observers who complained about his interminable monologues often found him pompous, sententious and very governessy. Madame de Genlis had raised not so much a virtuous man as a male replica of herself. Still, in one respect the new system was a clear improvement: it had been the custom to whip children severely and often. Now they were just locked up in their bedrooms for a while; boring, perhaps, but not painful.

Neither the King nor the Queen ever read Rousseau. If asked about him, they might have remembered him as the author of a charming operetta, *Le Devin du village*, but his ideas on education caused a drastic change in the way royal children were raised. Marie Antoinette did not go quite so far as to breast-feed her children—etiquette would have made that impossible; but she insisted on hygiene, exercise and plain food. Her daughter, Madame Royale, and her two sons had impressive Households, but she insisted on their playing with ordinary children who were to be treated as equals. Whenever possible, she looked after her children and spent time with them;

she even tried to give them a sense of their duty to the people. During the very cold winter of 1783 she sent to Paris for all the newest toys and had them set up in a room at Versailles. Then she took her children in and explained that they could have none of these lovely things because the money she had planned to spend on them must go, instead, to relieve the sufferings of the poor.

That demonstration, when looked at closely, begins to reek of hypocrisy. The sufferings of the poor did not prevent Marie Antoinette from spending well over 300,000 livres on dresses that year—twice her allowance. She might have taken 500 or 600 livres from that particular budget and given her children toys; here again we see Rousseau misunderstood and misapplied.

As for those children who were sent to school instead of having a tutor, very little had changed. The boys were sent to a *collège* (there were several in Paris, and one in every provincial town of any size) where they were taught Greek, Latin, sometimes English, mathematics, drawing and fencing. Whipping was the main incentive and was still often savage. These *collèges* were relatively expensive: tuition ranged from 350 to 650 livres a year, to which were added 36 livres for laundry, 22 livres for heat, 18 for light, 6 for school supplies and 36 each to the servant and the doorman—a total of up to 800 livres a year; and this obviously included neither clothes nor outings.

The education dispensed was a little old-fashioned but solid: a boy of sixteen or seventeen, when he had completed the curriculum, knew a good deal more than his American counterpart today. The schedule was also tougher: no Sundays or holidays—school was open seven days a week, fifty-two weeks a year. On the other hand, each boy had his own fairly comfortable room and the food was excellent.

There was one major alternative to the *collèges* for boys of noble birth but small means: the École Militaire. It had been founded by Louis XV, who commissioned Gabriel to design the admirable buildings which still stand today right behind the Eiffel Tower. The students came mostly from the provinces: courtiers' children did not have to study, they were simply given appointments. At the École Militaire there was a stricter regimen than that of the *collèges*. The students received a thorough grounding in everything a competent officer needed to know, from mathematics and ballistics to the art of handling men. Its graduates soon demonstrated the efficacy of its teaching in battles from Madrid to Moscow under the leadership of its most famous alumnus who, even as Emperor, always remembered he had started in life as a sublieutenant fresh out of the École Militaire.

If you wanted to go into the navy, on the other hand, there was no special school: you learned mathematics and geometry in a *collège* and then, at the age of fifteen, took the yearly naval entrance examinations. Many young men did: in the late seventies and early eighties the navy had acquired a good deal of glamor through its part in the American Revolution.

For more peaceful students there were several possibilities. The University of Paris, which charged no tuition, was divided into four *facultés* (schools): theology, which you must attend if you hoped for a career in the Church; canon and civil law for would-be lawyers; medicine, which prided itself on its resistance to change and was actually teaching, in Latin, exactly the same things as in 1500; and arts, which, along with the Collège Royal, provided a liberal arts education.

A few specialized schools, all recently founded, dispensed a new, practical kind of education. There was the École des Ponts et Chaussées where engineers were trained in road and bridge building, and the École des Mines where, in this earliest dawn of the industrial age, new mining techniques were discovered and taught.

Finally, if you wanted to improve your riding, you could attend the Académie Royale d'Équitation in the Tuileries, where in 1789 horses would be replaced by members of the National Assembly. And if you craved education but weren't an adolescent, you could attend a number of free public lectures given every day by highly competent scientists and literary men; it was the fashion, all through the eighties, to spend an hour in the afternoon listening to the newest discoveries in science and the most recent achievements of poets and writers.

—◄◄{ }►►—

All these schools and *collèges* were for boys only. Girls could be educated at home or sent to a convent: in Paris alone there were one hundred and fifty-four. Convents really didn't teach much. They had two main purposes: the first was to keep girls out of trouble (you didn't have to worry about unsuitable young men), the second to teach them something about religion. They normally provided a year's preparation for the first communion, which took place at the age of ten. After that a little music, some pious reading, a smattering of history were considered perfectly adequate. When they reached fifteen or sixteen, the girls were taken out and married off.

Still, a few remained behind. Some of these felt a vocation and became nuns of their own free will, but they were in exceedingly small number. The convents were filled with girls whose dowries had been small or non-existent: there could be no question of marriage for them, and religious vows were a convenience for their families. The victims often minded; as a result, the atmosphere, in convents, was frequently neither peaceful nor holy.

While most girls of eighteen were appallingly ignorant, there were exceptions on every social level. The Neckers'[1] only child, Germaine, was taken in hand by her mother who, perhaps remembering her early days as a governess, stuffed her with knowledge of all kinds ranging from the Holy Scriptures to the plays of Racine. Germaine was made to study so hard, and allowed to play so seldom, that she literally began to wither away; then her

[1] Monsieur Necker, a very successful banker, was twice Minister of Finance.

mother, conscientious as ever, listened to her doctor and started the child on a new regimen of exercise and relaxation. Evidently it all worked: Mademoiselle Necker, better known as Madame de Staël, turned out to be a great writer.

Life was much easier for Manon Phlipon, the daughter of a Paris engraver. In her memoirs, started "in the prison of Sainte Pélagie, on August 9, 1793," the then Madame Roland, as she watched the Revolution she had greeted so enthusiastically, which was now going so very wrong,[2] remembered an elegiac childhood.

Her parents were typical Paris bourgeois, neither poor nor rich. Even in that relatively modest milieu babies were promptly sent away to a nurse; so little Manon spent her first two years in Arpajon, some twenty miles outside Paris. As soon as she came home, her mother, who seems to have been kind and affectionate, started teaching her the Bible; between the ages of seven and ten she was sent to catechism class every Sunday. Perhaps because her father, as an engraver, was in touch with artists and writers, there was a real attempt to educate Manon: tutors were hired and she was taught writing, history, geography, music and dance; and since this obviously bright child was dying to learn Latin, she was given lessons by one of her uncles. Then, at the age of eleven, she was taken to a convent so she could be prepared for first communion, but her mother visited her every week and, as soon as it was over, some nine months later, she came straight home again.

Once there, aside from sharing some domestic chores with her mother and being taught how to cook, she read her father's books: the *Lives of the Saints*, the Bible, Appius' *Civil Wars*, Scarron's *Roman comique*, the memoirs of Pontis, a seventeenth-century general, and of Mademoiselle de Montpensier, Louis XIV's cousin, as well as many books of travel, Plutarch, Fénelon, Tasso and some Voltaire; she started to draw, sang, and picked up the techniques of engraving from her father. Quite soon her old tutors were hired again, along with a new man to teach her arithmetic.

On Sunday everything stopped and the ladies got dressed to the teeth. A hairdresser came and built up a high, formal hair-do; they put on silk dresses with large hoop skirts and went for a walk in the Tuileries gardens or through the Jardin du Roi,[3] followed by dinner at the grandmother's. And even though the Phlipons lived quite modestly during the week, a lot of money would be spent on the Sunday clothes and coiffures of mother and daughter. On the whole, it was a happy life for Manon, all the more so since her father, after a brief and unsuccessful attempt at imposing his authority on her when she was only seven, seems to have left her quite free to live her own life. This was indeed the exception.

Normally fathers were absolute rulers, by law and by custom. Their authority over wife and children was complete; they, and they alone, in theory,

[2] It was Madame Roland who said on the scaffold: "Liberty, what crimes are committed in your name!"
[3] A zoo and botanical garden in one.

made all the decisions. If a son misbehaved, his father could have him imprisoned. The family fortune, which included the wife's dowry, was his to dispose of as he pleased. Children must have his consent to marry; conversely, he could force them to marry. This last case was the most common since, even among the very small bourgeoisie, marriages were arranged.

The wedding itself was a great occasion. The bride, of course, brought a dowry. It might be small: 1,000 to 2,000 livres for a hard-working seamstress, 4,000 livres for a girl at the very bottom of the middle class. The daughter of a baker, in the eighties, had 15,000 livres; that of a very prosperous shopkeeper might have 20,000. These sums were, however, generally not all in cash. Dresses, jewelry (if any), sheets and blankets, all went into the reckoning. There were many cases of a lower-class bride spending her all on a magnificent wedding gown; at least, since white was not yet *de rigueur*, it could be used again and again.

Then there was the wedding banquet. It lasted for hours, a whole day sometimes, and often cost far more than the father of the bride could really afford. In an age when there were no paid holidays and only the rich ever went beyond the suburbs, the wedding banquet was the one great occasion for spending. Service after service must appear on the table and be washed down by gallons of wine. There would be a band and dancing, then, finally, the father would solemnly bless the young couple, who would be escorted, amid many pointed jokes, to the bridal chamber. The bed was blessed by the priest who had solemnized the wedding, and the couple was installed in it. After a few more jokes the curtains were pulled shut and the two young people were at last left to themselves.

The cycle had started again. Children would soon be born, but not to be educated either like their parents or according to Rousseau's principles: the Revolution came and swept old habits away. By 1800 a whole new system of schools, run by the State, had come into being and very different principles obtained. Jean-Jacques's revolution had lasted but a single morning; still, his perceptions remain. Even today, *Émile* could do wonders for a complex and difficult world.

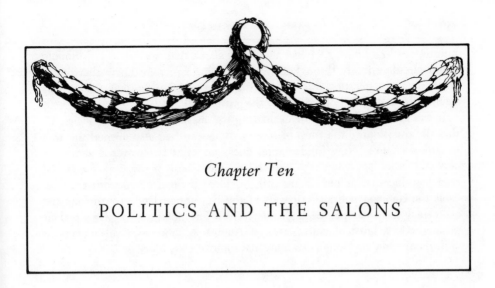

Chapter Ten

POLITICS AND THE SALONS

The press was censored; books could be banned. People were imprisoned at the whim of the King or his ministers. There were no representative institutions at all; yet politics were ever the subject of the day, and not just at court, where a well-conducted intrigue might change the ministry.

When the King really ruled, all power resided in his person; but poor, slow, well-intentioned Louis XVI was weakly trying to see his way to a policy which, as it improved the lot of his people, would keep the system unchanged. It wasn't just that he didn't know how to go about it: the "poor man," as Marie Antoinette called him, was subject to sudden and frequent cave-ins. Above all, he was utterly lacking in the ruthlessness without which reforms fail and even reaction gets nowhere. Quite often his principles were good; but then Maurepas, or the Queen, or Madame Adélaide, or practically anyone who came along and spoke loud enough could make him change his mind.

It was soon obvious that anything might happen. One day a particular policy might be implemented, the next day its opposite. Ministers came and went, for no particular reasons. Above all, the system had stopped working. The country itself was prosperous, many people were rich; never had so much luxury been seen in Paris; and the State was desperately poor. Successive Finance Ministers tried fending off bankruptcy all through the reign of Louis XVI, and their ultimate failure signaled the start of the Revolution. The bureaucracy had become unwieldy, irresponsible and inefficient.

Then there were the great political questions. Should France help the United States and fight England? Should the Austrian alliance be maintained? And what about reforms? Should the King continue to be an absolute monarch? (Louis XVI had no doubt about that answer. . . .) Should grains circulate freely throughout the kingdom? Everyone knew there must be changes; the question was which. And the answers were topics of burning interest, from the Hall of Mirrors to the gutters of Paris.

It wasn't just a question of evaluating the merits of different policies, either. By questioning the form of society, Rousseau had also opened the way to radical change. Now fundamental questions must be answered about the very nature of government. Only the people whose position was attacked read Jean-Jacques, or just about; still, his ideas trickled down until they became the common political currency of the Revolution; and even among the aristocracy his ideas proved highly effective. The nobles who gave up their privileges in a burst of enthusiasm on August 4, 1789, were all conversant with them: they had long been a favored topic of conversation.

--◈ ◈--

Like ancient Gaul, France, in the seventies and eighties, was divided into three parts: the court, Paris, and the people.

At court power was life (see Chapter Two). Politics had long since become pretexts for one faction or another, a way of replacing favorites and gaining the King's ear. This continued to be true: Maurepas, the accidental[1] Prime Minister, backed any policy if it kept him in favor and opposed it if it seemed to make another minister too powerful.

Maurepas, who died in office in 1781, was really the tired survivor of another reign. Calonne, a much younger man, who became Controller General of Finance in 1783, obeyed the Queen's every whim so as to keep his place. But now even the most frivolous courtiers found that policies were relevant: the financial crisis must be solved, and they were not at all anxious to give up pensions and stipends in the process.

Until the seventies, groups of courtiers had formed shifting alliances for pragmatic purposes. Great families who felt slighted, like the Noailles or the Rohans, might lead a cabal, and at first the Polignac coterie seemed only the latest of these. A group of hungry nobles had united around the favorite, the duchesse Jules, and used her to gain favors. This party grew quickly, however, as it came to realize it was up against an unprecedented problem: the possible disappearance of the system on which it relied for place or money. Under Louis XV the favorite was only worried that she might cease to attract; under Louis XVI the Polignacs, and many people like them, including the comte d'Artois, the King's brother, saw the abyss gaping before them. If the reformers had their way, court expenditure would be drastically reduced, pensions would be cut and useless functions abolished. Besides, there was no telling what a determined minister might do: if the day came when the King

[1] When Louis XVI came to the throne, he had meant to send for Monsieur de Machault, whom his father had admired. At the last moment his aunt, Madame Adélaide, convinced him to send for Maurepas instead. The King reluctantly agreed and the courier, who had already left, was hastily recalled.

ceased to be absolute, then all hope of power and riches would be gone. Clearly, the trend must be stopped.

The royal family itself split right down the middle. The King's next brother, the comte de Provence, thought fate most unfair: he was so much more intelligent than Louis XVI, he should really be on the throne. Like the duc d'Orléans, he hoped to become a French William III. On the other side were Madame Adélaide, to whom her nephew listened, the Queen and the comte d'Artois, who stood for the status quo. So Provence was left no choice: he became an ardent liberal.

In his mindless way, the comte d'Artois was a sort of leader for the conservatives. First of all, he liked the duchesse de Polignac and her set; then, his only income came from royal pensions. A reforming minister might think four million livres a year a little much for a perfectly idle prince; and, since he and Provence loathed each other, he had nothing to gain by a change in monarchs. Besides, Louis XVI was so weak, he could be relied on to finally say yes to any request Artois repeated often enough. As for a constitutional system, it would be clearly disastrous, since it was likely to diminish both status and income.

The Queen, of course, heartily agreed: she had every reason to want her husband to continue as absolute King. Her friends must be kept happy (and rich), she must be seen to be powerful; Provence hated her; and anyway, the people, in her view, had no rights at all. The monarch should be benevolent; but if he wasn't, that was just too bad. A true Habsburg, she knew that royal families were chosen by God to rule over other men; letting the people have a say was like letting your cook tell you what you should eat, both absurd and wrong. So she set herself firmly against any kind of reform; the only problem was that the people whom she convinced the King to appoint made a terrible mess of things and were unpopular, too. Still, she stuck firmly to the most reactionary policies.

The duc d'Orléans was an extreme liberal. A very rich man in his own right, he owned real estate in Paris and a great deal of land outside, so he was independent of royal subsidies. He was unpopular at court because of his unpleasant manner and his extreme debauchery, so he had nothing to lose if things changed, and possibly much to gain. He supported the idea of a limited revolution.[2]

This cool expectation of violent political change is a good measure of the evolution of the upper class: in 1740 the duc d'Orléans would have tried to find the King a mistress who, owing all to him, would bring him into favor. In 1780 he was quite ready to change the system altogether—and it also seemed the easiest course.

Of course there was also a government but, unfortunately, it was wholly dependent on the King. Maurepas was shrewd enough to realize he had been a mistake; it was therefore his one and only goal to keep the King's

[2] Like the King, for whose death he voted, he ended on the guillotine.

favor. At first, even though he opposed the Queen as a rival for the master's ear, he agreed with her in supporting the status quo, since he was incapable of reforming it. So he concentrated on successively getting rid of his two chief rivals, Turgot and Necker. In both cases he hid behind other people— the Queen, the Parlement, other ambitious men. Then he simply supported doing nothing, anywhere, except if it took too much effort to stop it, as was the case for the American war. As a result, nothing much changed until he died at the age of eighty-two. As it turned out, however, his was a costly triumph: either Turgot or Necker, if allowed to carry out their principles, might well have managed to avert a revolution.

The fight for power, until 1789, took place at court, but its echoes spread rapidly. Within a month of the new Queen's accession pamphlets attacking her could be found everywhere; and she could be blamed, it seemed, for just about everything. The first of these occasions came when all the elderly ladies who had long since retired from court came to pay their mourning visit. As the long file of curtsying dowagers passed before her, Marie Antoinette was seen to lift her fan to her face in an effort to hide a smile. The rumor quickly spread: the Queen was callously making fun of her elders, and in no time some verse was being recited all over Paris:

> Petite reine de vingt ans,
> Vous qui traitez si mal les gens,
> Vous repasserez la barrière. . . .

> [Little Queen of just twenty,
> You treat people so badly,
> We'll send you back across the border. . . .]

In fact what happened was that one of the ladies in waiting, who was even younger and who, like her mistress, had been standing there for hours, had seated herself on the ground and, hidden by the huge skirts of the other ladies, had been making faces. The Queen was innocent; no one doubted that she was guilty.

After that the pamphlet war went on. Court politics descended into the street. For the first time details of the royal couple's life became public knowledge and in the process were distorted maliciously. Often slanders were invented and they were believed, since they came from the very courtiers who were in a position to know. Soon it wasn't only in Versailles that politics formed the usual topic: they replaced the old preoccupation with the price of bread among the people.

It would, of course, be silly to claim that the Revolution was the result of these pamphlets, but they helped. People who were dissatisfied with their lives and who, with good reason, resented an overbearing, legally privileged aristocracy and a spendthrift court could focus on these pamphlets: then, as always, a good formula could replace a valid argument. When Marie Antoinette became *Madame Déficit*, little more needed to be said against her.

Then, too, Rousseau's ideas and those of the other Enlightenment philosophers were beginning to spread. Again, it was not so much that the shopkeepers were reading the *Discours sur l'inégalité,* but rather that new feelings were becoming generally accepted. All men, it seemed, were born equal; the rich were stealing from the poor. Feudal privileges were wrong and unfair. The people were overtaxed and the government was wasting money. Something must change. And all those pamphlets confirmed it.

Kings had been unpopular before, even hated: the people rejoiced openly when Louis XIV and Louis XV died. There had been revolts in the countryside, riots in Paris; but not since Étienne Marcel tried to impose parliamentary government on the young Charles V, in the fourteenth century, had there been a thought of actually changing the form of government. Now it had become a common topic of discussion among the people of Paris.

The Queen was the first target: she was a spendthrift, she was powerful, she was foreign; also, she had favorites, which no one could understand: what was she *doing* with them? And she stood for the system as it existed. She was one with those aristocrats whose carriages ran over the poor. She let the people starve while she heaped riches on the Polignacs. She even bought herself a palace, Saint Cloud, and you could tell the King had had nothing to do with it, since, for the first time in French history, the orders posted on the gate bore the Queen's name.

A number of hated ministers—Calonne, Loménie de Brienne—ran close seconds, especially since, as everyone knew, the Queen had put them in office. There was no talk, yet, of constitutions in the streets. "Faut que ça change [gotta change]," the people said, and burned the ministers in effigy. Through it all the King retained a kind of popularity: he was weak, he was dumb, but he wasn't wicked. If only evil influences around him could be dispelled, then all would be well. The Queen, court and ministers were at fault; take away their power, restrain their greed, that was what must be done.

Year after year the people became angrier. They listened to men who walked among them and told them what was wrong with the government, and how much better the duc d'Orléans would do. They heard the scurrilous songs and read the pamphlets. They understood men were born free and knew that, in America, people like them had put down the tyranny of an unjust King.

When, in 1789, there was a shortage of bread, and the Estates-General were conveniently assembled, it was a natural move for the people of Paris to rise and destroy the Bastille, that symbol of despotism, then, in October, march on Versailles and bring Louis XVI back to Paris. There, among his people, his natural goodness would flow unimpaired. Both he and the Queen, for a short while, became immensely popular: the golden age had come at last.

—◄{ }►—

In Versailles and in Paris, politics had to come after the two main preoccupations, intrigues and bread. The salons had no such restraints. Filled by a perfectly idle upper class, whose one consuming interest government had suddenly become, they were gaining enormous influence. "The power of French society in the years just before the Revolution was prodigious," wrote Talleyrand, who knew whereof he spoke. Never before or since has Paris had so many salons; never has their preoccupation been so completely political.

What was a salon? It was a gathering of people around a hostess, the people who, day after day, came and sat in her salon, her drawing room. Originally, salons had just been gatherings of friends; now they were centers of information where opinion was formed, where opposition grew.

A salon was always run despotically by one woman; birth and money helped to set one up, but they were not enough, nor were they absolutely necessary: Mademoiselle de Lespinasse, who ran one of the great literary salons of the century, had neither. You needed to know just who the right people were at any given time, then you must convince them to come to you. While helping to keep discussion free and open, you must make sure your salon had a point of view. Then its denizens must at all times be kept under control. Madame Necker, whose salon was one of the most successful in Paris, held that "no one person must take away too much of the other's space."

A good salon had a mixture of court nobility and *noblesse de robe,* of fashionable abbés and the very rich, with writers and philosophers and musicians added for good measure. An important foreigner was always an asset. So was anyone who had become the celebrity of the hour; but the middle class, actors, singers, and kept women were firmly rejected.

There were salons with themes. "Readings were then in fashion; they made the importance of a few houses. One could hardly have dinner at M. de Vaudreuil's, at M. de Liancourt's or at Mme de Vaines' without having to listen to them . . . but then, one would be counted among the distinguished men of the time." Mostly, however, people talked.

They talked of almost anything. There was court gossip and society gossip, and the theater and the newest paintings. Opera might just as well be the topic, and a very burning one it was when, in 1777, Gluck brought a new, modern kind of opera to Paris. There were funny stories, and a great deal of nasty comment. "Would you like to know what those three brothers are really like?" the Marquis de Créquy asked the Prince de Ligne, meaning Louis XVI, Provence and Artois. "A fat lockmaker, a wit from a provincial café and a dandy from the boulevard."

Almost more than what they said, it was how they said it that mattered. Conversation had become an art, the subject of much study. "Speaking is an liberal art which has neither goal nor result. . . . Conversation is not, for the French, a way of communicating ideas, feelings or business, but an instrument which one likes to play and which enlivens one's spirit," Madame de Staël wrote.

Conversation was everywhere, and always followed. "The tone of conversation [in Paris] is flowing and natural, it is neither weighty nor frivolous; it is knowledgeable but not pedantic, cheerful but not loud, polite but unaffected, gallant but not moony, ironic but not equivocal. You hear neither dissertations nor cast-away wit; there is discussion without argument; people joke without punning; wit and reason are artfully combined with definitive statements and sharp rejoinders, satire, clever flattery and austere morals"—and this paean to conversation comes from the savage and retiring Jean-Jacques Rousseau.

Everyone knew good conversation could be had only in Paris. "How I yearn for the gutter of the Rue du Bac," Madame de Staël would exclaim dolefully as she stared at the Alps from her window at Coppet. Conversation was such a well-known attraction that Mercier felt compelled to include a chapter on it in his *Tableau de Paris*.

"In a supper, how many judgments are given! We have boldly defined the basic truths in metaphysics, morals, literature and politics. It has been said of the same man, at the same table, on the right that he's an eagle, on the left, that he's a sparrow. The same principle has been considered on one side as fundamental, on the other as absurd; but, above all, with what ease we go from one topic to the next, and how great a number of subjects we cover in a few hours! You must admit that conversation in Paris has reached a degree of perfection which is unequaled anywhere in the world. Each remark is like the stroke of an oar, both light and deep. . . . [Conversation] is a delicate pleasure which belongs only to an extremely civilized society which has elaborated very subtle rules that are always obeyed."

Just as politeness must be easy and natural, so must conversation. "No one seemed to have in conversation a charm equal to [my mother's]. She was completely unpretentious; she spoke only in nuances. She never made a witty saying: that would have been far too well defined. Witty sayings are remembered, and she only wanted to please and have people forget what she said," Talleyrand wrote in his *Mémoires*.

By the eighties, the subjects of conversation were growing fewer as politics usurped all attention. The very nature of the government had become a normal topic: in the salons of the comtesse de Boufflers and the comtesse d'Egmont the theories of Montesquieu, Voltaire and Rousseau were daily topics along with the necessary reforms and even the desirability of a constitution. "Every aspirant to the ministry had at his disposal a few of the main houses in Paris, whose opinions and language they shaped. Madame de Montesson's house[3] belonged to the Archbishop of Toulouse,[4] who shared that of Ma-

---

[3] The morganatic wife of the previous duc d'Orléans.
[4] Étienne Loménie de Brienne, who was Finance Minister in 1787–88.

dame de Beauveau with Monsieur Necker. It was at Madame de Polignac's and at the Hôtel de Luynes that Monsieur de Calonne found his backers."

Madame Necker had her own salon where her husband was the focus of all praise; along with those of Mesdames d'Egmont, de Boufflers and de Brionne, it formed a center for all the liberal, pro-American young nobles who often followed La Fayette.

The American war was the great divider. The King and Vergennes helped to finance it (the first million livres came in 1775) and eventually joined it as a way of erasing the French defeat in 1763; but they had no sympathy for the ideas it represented. To most of the other French, at first anyway, the United States seemed both romantic—it was so far away, so primitive—and virtuous: Rousseau's theories about the patriarchal, rural man were current. It was fashionable to be pro-American: even the comtesse Diane de Polignac, sister-in-law of the Queen's favorite, joined the ranks of the Franklinophiles. Many young officers left France to join Washington because it was an adventure, or simply because life in Paris left something to be desired; this was the case with La Fayette, that awkward, gawky redhead, of whom the Queen made fun and who felt oppressed by his in-laws, the Noailles.

When the war was over, though, and its fighters returned home, they brought a new political point of view with them. The United States was the land of freedom and equality; it had just beaten a tyrannical monarch. Now to be pro-American was also to be a liberal. All this, along with La Fayette's real character, was quite apparent to Talleyrand's sharp eye: "Mediocre men sometimes play a role in great events for the single reason that they were there. M. de La Fayette had entered the world as a man of great wealth and had married into the House of Noailles. Had something extraordinary not distinguished him from the rank and file, he would have remained dull all his life. M. de La Fayette had in him only what it took to arrive in his turn. He is below the line where one is considered a man of intelligence. In his desire, in his way of distinguishing himself, there is something forced. His acts don't seem to belong to his nature; it feels as if he is following advice. . . .

"The example of M. de La Fayette had drawn the brilliant part of the nation after him. The young French nobles, after enlisting in the cause of independence, became attached to those principles they had gone to defend. They had seen the head of a great state come out of private life; they had seen the simple men who had helped him surrounded by the public's respect. It is a short step from this to believing that services given in the cause of liberty are the only true mark of distinction and glory. These ideas, transported back to France, grew all the faster that every sort of prestige, attacked as it was by the inferior men who had made their way into society, was growing dimmer every day . . .

"America became the only topic of conversation. Great nobles had that peculiarity that whenever something was new for them, they thought they had discovered it, and then, they grew all the more attached to it. Whatever would we be without America, is what everyone was saying."

The United States was thus an easy way to define your political position: if you were pro-American, you were for reforms in the government, and even a constitution. If you were anti-American, you were for the status quo, an absolute monarchy and the maintenance of feudal privileges.

Of course, within that framework the conversation was also shaped by daily political events. Turgot was a well-known writer, economist and philosopher when Louis XVI made him *Contrôleur Général des Finances*: he was therefore supported by all the philosophical salons, where his principles were understood and his innovations defended. Parties hadn't yet formed, however, and he failed to get the support he could have counted on two or three years later. When the King foolishly fired him in 1776, the outcry was restrained. The people who knew Turgot and his writings understood that a very great opportunity to reform the State had just been lost; but the interest in this change quickly died down. Turgot seemed, at the time, to be just one more minister disgraced, one more victim of court intrigue.

By the middle of Necker's ministry (1777–81), everything had changed. It wasn't just that people were more interested in politics: Necker, while he loudly and ceaselessly proclaimed himself a financial genius, was in fact a public relations whiz, and he had a competent assistant in his wife.

Until the Neckers came along, a salon might have a point of view; it might make its holder well known—this had been the case for Madame du Deffand and Madame d'Épinay; but none had ever been created with the sole purpose of advertising and furthering the career of its holder. In Madame Necker's salon, too, people talked about books, plays and philosophy; they exchanged gossip; but somehow the conversation had a way of coming back to the mutual admiration society organized by the hosts and enlarged, eventually, by the addition of their daughter Germaine. There were a few well-understood facts: Monsieur Necker was France's greatest economist and financier; after having accumulated a large fortune in banking, he had given up the pursuit of wealth to concentrate on helping his fellow men by reforming the finances of the State. And while it is, perhaps, easier to forget about money when you have more than you can ever use, still it is true that Monsieur Necker was as disinterested as his wife daily proclaimed him to be. When he achieved power, he refused both salary and perks, and eventually came out of office no richer—but no poorer—than he had entered it. In that, he was alone.

Madame Necker used her salon to make sure Monsieur Necker's theories, which he regularly expounded in timely pamphlets, were broadcast throughout society. She never tired of pointing out that he was the only disinterested person in a greedy court, the only statesman in an age of intrigues and cabals, the savior (if only the King would let him) of the State. When guests bemoaned the chronic budget deficit, she would shake her head impatiently: let them only call for Monsieur Necker and that insoluble problem would soon be no more. Then she would turn to Monsieur Necker, who would explain his newest idea to a well-conditioned audience. It is only fair to add that Monsieur Necker, that kind and uniquely faithful husband, did almost as much for his wife as she did for him. He never tired of pointing out to anyone within hearing that Madame Necker was a prodigy of intelligence and wit, a kind yet farseeing woman, a competent writer, especially on religious subjects (though to us she appears to have dipped her pen in lead instead of ink), an admirable mother, and altogether a pearl without price. When Germaine grew up, she added her voice to this chorus of praise.[5]

There was a presumption in Monsieur Necker's favor because he had, after all, made a large fortune virtually from scratch: it bespoke at least competence in the ways money is handled. It never seems to have occurred to anyone, least of all to Monsieur Necker himself, that reforming the State's finances was not the same thing as being a sharp businessman. And so, after much propaganda reached the King himself, Monsieur Necker in 1777 became Minister of Finances.

With that event, the output of propaganda in Madame Necker's salon reached unprecedented heights. It was based on two key ideas: one, Monsieur Necker was a highly competent and honest technician; two, by virtue of his being a Swiss and a Protestant, he was also opposed to the dreadful waste at court and to the Queen's spendthrift ways. People listened and were impressed. Monsieur Necker would tactfully allow people to infer that, only that very day, he had found himself forced to refuse the Queen's request for extra money (when he had, in fact, given her more than she had requested); then he would remind them that he was in the process of reorganizing the finances in such a way that the budget would soon be balanced and he would allow Madame Necker to point out that he had refused to accept the large salary that went with his office.

Along with the new interest in politics, people were also beginning to meet on a new, equal footing—a good thing for commoners like the Neckers. "Delille had dinner at Madame de Polignac's with the Queen.[6] . . . Gambling and wit had leveled everything. Careers, those great maintainers of hierarchy and order, were being destroyed. All the young men thought themselves able to govern. People criticized all the ministers' actions. The King's and Queen's own actions were discussed and generally blamed by the salons of Paris. Young women spoke, as if they understood it, of every part of the government."

Necker himself was quick to come up with new ways of extolling his own

---

[5] It is not, perhaps, the least curious fact about this extraordinary family that Germaine —Madame de Staël—turned out to be a great writer, political thinker and hostess, as well as, possibly, the first liberated woman.

[6] The previous Queen, Marie Leczinska, would never have dreamed of dining with anyone but the King or, rarely, an elderly and respected duke. To have a commoner sit down with the Queen was unprecedented and very shocking.

merits. In 1781 he surpassed himself and published his *Compte rendu au Roi* (*Accounting to the King*); this was the first published budget that France had ever seen. The very notion of a budget had, until Necker, remained vague. The controller himself hardly knew what was being spent or collected; he added up income and expenses at the end of the year in order to have some idea of what the new year would cost; but it never quite worked. For one thing, the King could decide at any time to spend more on anything; and he could, and did, give people money at whim: he just wrote a note, called an *acquis du comptant,* telling the Treasury to pay such and such a sum to so and so; and the Treasury did, in cash. Then there were court festivities; when the future Louis XVI was married to the Archduchess Marie Antoinette, for instance, his grandfather decided on the festivities (prolonged and expensive) quite without regard to what they would cost.[7] It was just up to the Treasury to find the money.

As for what was being spent, and on what or whom, that was a state secret. What the King chose to do with his money was nobody's business but his own. The Parlement might protest against a new tax, and the people resent the money spent on a favorite, but that was the end of it. Now, suddenly, Necker revealed all. The *Compte rendu* showed just where the money came from and where it went. People found out exactly what the King was doing with his money—or was it theirs?—and they didn't like it.

Before looking at the figures, it should be pointed out that Necker's *Compte rendu,* while quite straightforward when it came to State expenditures, was not quite as honest regarding its income. The whole point of this exercise, as far as Necker was concerned, was to show that he had done a superb job and ought to be made Prime Minister. So he made it look as if the budget had a slight surplus, an achievement no recent Finance Minister could claim. Unfortunately, the deficit for that year was around a hundred million livres out of a total budget of two hundred and sixty-four million; and it was all done with "anticipations."

An anticipation occurred when the *Contrôleur Général* anticipated next year's revenue by borrowing against it to cover current expenditures; thus, if he needed an extra hundred million in 1781, he would borrow at a high rate of interest against the revenues for 1782 and 1783. Of course, in those two years the problem would become a great deal worse since most of the revenue had already been spent. Eventually either taxes were raised drastically or the State defaulted, or both. Of course, that didn't look well. So, very simply, Necker didn't say most of the revenue for his balanced budget consisted of anticipations. He was promptly declared a genius since, after so many years of deficits, and right in the middle of a war, he had managed to balance the budget.

[7] When Louis XV asked his controller how he had found the festivities, the harried man replied with a pun: *"Sire, je les trouve impayables* [Sire, I find them inimitable/unpayable for]."

The *Compte rendu* was a master stroke of publicity. Within days of its publication people everywhere were singing Necker's praises. It wasn't just that he was so clever; in his comments he had pointed out that the King spent far too much on pensions ("probably more than all the other monarchies of Europe combined") and on running the court. People exploded with enthusiasm: they knew at last why it was so difficult to balance the budget. The need for reforms became plainer than ever and Necker was the darling of the liberal salons.

Like a few other masterpieces of publicity, however, this one backfired. Necker had, indeed, asked the King's permission before he published his *Compte rendu,* but poor Louis XVI had not understood what he was allowing. When he found out from the practically moribund Maurepas, he fired Necker.

The Neckers were outraged. Firmly ignoring the cause of the great man's dismissal, they howled about court influences and cabals of money-hungry place seekers. Their salon hastily shifted gears; praise of Monsieur Necker's achievements continued, but a new theme was added: he was the only man capable of so reordering the State's finances that they would remain on a permanently sound footing. Without him, catastrophe was on the way.

This proved a highly successful theme, so successful that it is still heard today, in slightly modified form: the Revolution need never have taken place if only Necker . . . etc. Even the King was taken in. When in 1788 the financial situation became really desperate, he reappointed the great man as Finance Minister to general applause. Madame de Staël was ecstatic: her father was vindicated; he would run the Estates-General and the country. As it happened, he failed dismally on both counts. Late in 1789, when the Revolution had taken politics out of the salons and into the streets, the frightened Neckers found it expedient to retire to their castle at Coppet, in Switzerland, safely out of the reach of the new authorities.

Necker's career is a perfect example of the power of the salons: he never would have been chosen by Louis XVI in the first place without the constant propaganda provided by Madame Necker and his other supporters, and he certainly wouldn't have been returned to power. La Fayette, who benefited from similar puffery, owed his role in the early part of the Revolution much less to his American exploits (such as they were) than to the way the salons took him up when he came home. For those last ten years of the Ancien Régime it really seemed as if the salons were as powerful as the King. They molded public opinion even outside their walls, made and unmade policy, and in fact banked on the kind of influence which is so often ascribed to the media today. In the end, of course, they collapsed with the rest of the power structure: by 1793 there was not a salon left in Paris.

The political history of the reign of Louis XVI, stripped of all adventitious material, is marked mainly by the successful fight against change conducted by the *privilégiés*. By 1774 it was clear that the system was not working well anymore. State finances, in disorder, really, ever since the 1690s, had grown unmanageable. The general rise in the level of prosperity had, as its consequence, raised the political expectations of the bourgeoisie. And while the peasants were undeniably better off than they had been when Louis XV came to the throne in 1715, they also felt more cheated by the feudal dues and other obligations exacted by the landlords, partly because they finally had time to think about more than just getting the day's food, partly because the *philosophes'* theories had filtered down to them.

Louis XVI, weak, slow and awkward as he was, came to the throne filled with good intentions. He wanted to preserve the Church and struggled, unsuccessfully on the whole, to appoint better bishops; he hoped to improve his people's lot; but he felt he must transfer his power unaltered to his successor and, like many indecisive men, he feared change. He was aware of the need for serious reforms, but would agree to them only so long as they left everything as it was. He wanted to spread happiness and, as a man of simple tastes himself, was even willing to retrench a little on court expenditure. He could be made to end abuses as long as they didn't affect his absolute power: thus, he freed the Protestants from all civil disabilities in 1787[8] and abolished the use of judicial torture in 1780. Most startling of all, he absolutely refused to use the army in 1789 because it would have meant shedding the blood of his people, and thus he delivered himself into the hands of the revolutionaries.

His very first major reform, the recall of the *parlements*, while it turned out to be a large step backward, was certainly well meant. He had, in fact, saddled himself with a body ready and able to cut short his halfhearted attempts at reform. After that it didn't matter much what efforts Louis XVI made: a combination of court cabals, the Queen and the parlements was always ready to stop him.

His appointment of Turgot as *Contrôleur Général,* for instance, was a step in the right direction. The new minister, a well-known physiocrat, had a comprehensive plan ready: he would make France into a modern state. He believed that in this pre-industrial country land and agriculture were the real wealth. Crops should be protected, their product allowed to circulate freely and go to the best markets. It all made a great deal of sense.

France, in 1774, was still a mosaic of provinces that had retained laws and customs often dating back to days before they were part of France. Among these were interior customs: as you passed from Burgundy to the Franche-Comté, or from Normandy to Brittany, you had to pay customs dues on any merchandise you carried. Obviously this raised costs and slowed down com-

[8] English Catholics had to wait another half century before theirs were lifted.

merce. Worse still, the free circulation of grain from province to province was strictly prohibited. That had made sense in the Middle Ages; by 1774 it was both absurd and harmful since it was possible for Normandy to experience literal starvation while Burgundy suffered from a glut. The free circulation of grain within France was, therefore, one of the physiocrat's basic tenets.

Famine, in the eighteenth century, was by no means uncommon. Louis XV had ordered the building of granaries outside Paris so that grain could be stored during good years and used when crops failed; but the people's fear was such that rumors immediately sprang up according to which the King was hoarding grain and causing artificial shortages so as to make a profit from his subjects' hunger. When Turgot convinced Louis XVI to order the free circulation of grain, he was going directly against those fears.

He was also going against the forces of privilege. The Parlement de Paris promptly refused to register the edict, not because it had so much to lose (though a few of its members probably feared a drop in the price of grain), but because it was a cheap and easy way of seeming to defend the people. It was also a good way of getting rid of Turgot.

Earlier that year Turgot, intent on freeing the economy from its medieval shackles, had produced another series of edicts for the King to sign: they abolished the *corvée* (see Chapter Four), the apprenticeship system and the rigid corporations which hampered the expansion of production and trade. It would now be possible for a tailor to cover a button with cloth and sew it onto a suit, or for an apprentice to become a master in less than eight years. The Parlement didn't hesitate: it refused to register, and, on March 12, 1776, the King had to hold a *lit de justice*. Of course the opposition claimed that the ancient rights and customs of the kingdom were being destroyed, when its real fear was that workers might be less grossly underpaid. That kind of argument found an audience, though. In a country where the King's right to absolute rule had long been recognized, the only claim that could stop him was that he was going against the ways of his predecessors. Thus, resistance to royal authority was founded, not on denial of its validity, but on immemorial rights that could not be breached.

On this, the Parlement took its stance, with the encouragement of Maurepas, who was anxious to get rid of a rival. And here is another paradox: the Prime Minister of an absolute King seldom hesitated to go behind his back to help the opposition and thus defeat any policy he didn't like. Of course, this attitude could be risky as the duc de Choiseul found out when he was fired. Still, Maurepas felt safe enough: after all, Louis XVI wasn't Louis XV.

The King was willing enough to back Turgot—up to a point. He didn't like having to hold *lits de justice*; they made him feel both shy and subtly in the wrong. It really seemed easier to forget about the controversial edicts, but

Turgot wouldn't let him. Six months passed and poor Louis XVI found himself forced to do it all over again (November 12, 1776), this time to ensure the free circulation of grain. It was too much.

Then there was Maurepas, whose only policy was to maintain himself in office. For him, Turgot was a dreadful nuisance. First, Maurepas was related to many Parlement families, and he didn't like the King to fight his relatives; then he realized that Turgot, if given his head, might well replace him; so every day Maurepas made sure the King heard something against that upstart.

He had a powerful ally. The Queen had yet to achieve complete power over her husband, but when she added her voice to the anti-Turgot faction it certainly helped. She had her own reasons, of course. Turgot was trying to retrench: obviously, he must go.

The King had assured Turgot of his complete and long-lasting support when he appointed him *Contrôleur Général;* no doubt he meant it. But he was far too weak to resist a combination of Marie Antoinette, Maurepas and the Parlement. He gave in, setting a fateful precedent, and fired Turgot.

Monsieur Necker was the King's next attempt. If you can't stand a reformer, then you can at least get a technician who will solve your financial problems. On August 22, 1777, Necker became *Directeur des Finances* under a shadow *Contrôleur.*[9] Louis XVI could hardly have made a worse mistake: instead of an expert, he got a man whose deep ignorance of public finance was hidden by a cloud of puffery.

The situation was serious: the State ran a deficit even in time of peace; when a war had to be fought—and France was now at war with England—the deficit naturally grew. There were several possible solutions. One was to cut down drastically on court expenditure and impose a temporary war tax; another, more drastic, would have entailed a complete change of the inefficient, inequitable tax collection system. As it was, taxes were collected by private men, the *fermiers généraux.* Every three years they submitted a bid: they would collect a specific sum and turn it over to the King. In return, they kept anything they received over the specified amount. It was obviously in their interest to collect as much as possible, and they did. The wealth of the *fermiers généraux* became legendary and they were among the first victims of the Revolution.

Finally, a farseeing minister, who had the complete backing of the King, might have widened the tax base by adding Church and nobility to the rolls. Necker did not even consider any of these possibilities. Instead, rather like New York City before the crisis, he borrowed. The deficit grew, year after year; the court became ever more costly, and Monsieur Necker borrowed.

As for lenders, he found them through a series of tricks. First he an-

[9] As a Protestant, Necker was not legally able to sit on the Council of State, so he was made the employee of a nonentity and ran everything anyway.

nounced he had balanced the budget and, being who he was, he was believed. Having thus been reassured, people were anxious to lend, since loans were no longer necessary.

Of course Necker also made his loans highly attractive; some of them were linked to a lottery: if your number came up, your capital was reimbursed with the full interest, just as if you had had to wait for the normal expiration of your bond. The rate of interest you collected was thus very high and made the whole transaction most desirable. It was not so convenient for the State, however, since it had to pay too much for the money it got, and reimburse some of the principal prematurely, too.

The other kind of loan was by annuity. You gave your capital to the King for good, you never got a penny of it back; but, on the other hand, you received an annuity for life. The rate of interest offered on these loans had to be unusually high—else why give up your capital? It could be as high as fifteen per cent; so, if you lived on for just ten years, you collected a hundred and fifty per cent of your original investment; if you lived on for twenty years, and you had originally invested a thousand livres, you would receive three thousand. This is obviously an appallingly expensive way of borrowing. As Talleyrand explained, these loans were "poorly conceived, costly and bad for public morals; poorly conceived since they didn't include an expiration date; expensive because the rate of government bonds didn't justify the high price at which [Necker] was borrowing; bad for public morals because his annuity loans gave rise to a kind of selfishness never seen in France before M. Necker." By selfishness he meant that you cheated your heirs of your capital so as to receive a larger income yourself.

When people asked Necker about this growing burden of public debt he answered that, since the national product would grow every year along with the population (and therefore the tax base), the loans could easily be repaid in the future. In the meantime, while still claiming to be balancing the budget, Monsieur Necker managed to borrow the fabulous sum of 530,000,000 livres over three years, and this at a time when the total yearly budget was 265,000,000 livres. It is exactly as if the federal budget were to borrow 2,000 *billion* dollars between 1980 and 1983.[10]

It is only fair to say that Monsieur Necker made some attempts at cutting court expenditure, though he went very carefully and, contrary to his oft-repeated boasts, almost never refused the Queen. Still, he managed to cut the cost of candles, for instance, by 400,000 livres a year. This was really quite simple. Versailles required a great many candles, and every morning, whether they had been used or not, they were taken away and became the perquisites of various court officials. The money was saved simply by announcing that, henceforth, only *used* candles were to be removed from the chandeliers.

Necker also tried to save money by abolishing a number of subordinate

10 The national debt of the United States is under 900 billion.

jobs about the court—there was no question of touching anyone important. This policy had a serious drawback, though: people who held these jobs had bought them from their predecessors, very much the way people today buy seats on the Stock Exchange. So, before they could be fired, they had to be compensated and a standard rate was established: 8,000 livres for a messenger, 60,000 livres for a washerman. As so often with Monsieur Necker, the theory was fine: cut down on yearly expenditure; but it also meant that a great deal of money had to be found to pay everyone off just at the time when cash was tightest.

In one case Monsieur Necker did save money, though he annoyed the Queen. The daughter of her friend the duc de Guines was engaged to marry the marquis de Castries; only the duke was quite unable to come up with the required 300,000 livres dowry. Naturally, he went straight to the Queen, who went straight to the King, who went straight to Monsieur Necker who courageously said no. The King told the Queen he couldn't afford to give Mademoiselle de Guines 300,000 livres; he was not well received. He went back to Monsieur Necker, who suggested an ingenious compromise: make the marquis de Castries a duke and forget the money. That time, it worked.

Incompetence aside, Monsieur Necker's task was almost impossible. Whenever he had a glimmer of what had to be done, he ran up against a solid wall of privilege and selfishness, just like Turgot. In 1781 he sent the King a memorandum suggesting the creation of provincial assemblies which, though purely consultative, could at least enlighten the government on local problems. It was a way of keeping in touch with public opinion; it might also have been the seed of a representative system. At first the King rather liked the idea, but the Parlement made it very plain it would oppose it to the death. The King began to waver, and the *Compte rendu* came just in time to relieve him. On May 19, 1781, Necker risked all and offered his resignation: it was immediately accepted.

If you ignore the first part of the *Compte rendu*, which lists revenues, and go on to the second part, which lists expenditures, it makes very interesting reading. In 1781 the American war was in full swing, and wars are notoriously expensive, so, alone, it cost 62,500,000 livres. To that must be added the unusually high navy budget—the war was also being fought at sea —which came to 29,200,000 livres. Then there was the artillery budget, again higher than usual: 9,000,000 livres. Altogether, they come to 103,400,000 livres. By comparison, the foreign affairs budget, including subsidies to client states, was limited to 8,525,000 livres. Even if you add this to the military budget, you still have only 111,925,000 livres. Where did the other 154,000,000 go?

One large item was 20,820,000 livres. It was tactfully listed as interest on the backlog budget. In fact it was interest on money the government owed but couldn't pay, so in the meantime it paid interest. Over 20,000,000 in interest suggests a capital of several hundred million livres—all due.

Then there were sumptuary expenses: the King's household troops, for instance, an elite troop in rich uniforms, cost 7,861,000 all by itself. This was nothing compared to the Households of the King, the Queen, Madame Élisabeth (the King's sister), Madame Royale (the King's two-year-old daughter) and the King's three old maiden aunts: together, they disposed of 25,700,000 livres a year—ten per cent of the national budget.[11] And there was a separate account for the King's two brothers: that came to a staggering 8,040,000 livres. So, in 1781, France was shelling out 43,421,000 livres on display alone—some seventeen per cent of the total budget.

To all this another huge sum must be added: the 28,000,000 livres paid out in pensions. A very small percentage of this total went to exceptionally brave or disabled soldiers and officers. The bulk of it consisted of pensions granted by the King to his courtiers, people who had considerable incomes of their own. As we have seen, the publication of this figure raised a tremendous outcry, as well it might. And when you add this to the sumptuary expenses, you get a grand total of 71,421,000 livres, almost a third of the budget, and rather more, by 6,000,000 livres, than was being spent on the war itself.

When, further, you realize that the real deficit for the year was over 100,000,000 livres, so that the real revenue was only about 150,000,000, this figure of over 70,000,000 is even more astounding: the King was spending half of his real revenue on totally unproductive and largely unnecessary display.

While the outcry would have been even greater if people in 1781 had seen through Monsieur Necker's little sleight of hand, there is one item that does not seem to have caught anyone's attention: a sum of 77,573,000 livres is not included in the budget at all; it is simply deducted from what the *fermiers généraux* owed the King. The reason is simple: it represents interest due on previous loans. Since the lenders worried about not being paid back on time, the sums due were simply assigned on the receipts of the *fermiers généraux*; they never entered the Treasury at all. So, out of a real budget of 342,573,000 livres, the King was paying out over 97,000,000 in interest. The only wonder is that the system lasted as long as it did.

After Necker's fall the process speeded up. Nonentities came and went, to be replaced by Monsieur de Calonne, who out-Neckered Necker: he, too, borrowed heavily, and then he spent even more heavily to show the King was well off. The Queen, egged on by Madame de Polignac, had been responsible for his appointment, and she found him an admirable *Contrôleur Général*. "How was I to know that money was scarce?" she exclaimed later. "Whenever I asked for 100,000 livres, Monsieur de Calonne would bring me 150,000!" When the money finally ran out, Calonne was succeeded by another of the Queen's protégés, Loménie de Brienne.

---

[11] Money comparisons tend to be very inexact. Budgets in pre-Revolutionary France represented a smaller share of the GNP than they do today in the United States. Still, imagine the President and his family spending 60 billion a year. . . .

In his turn, Loménie de Brienne was confronted with the now familiar impossible situation. He, too, tried to reform the system: in 1787 he proposed a new form of taxation, the *subvention territoriale,* based on land and payable by all. Naturally, the Parlement refused to register the edict. This time the King stood firm: he was too desperate not to. On August 15 he exiled the Parlement to Troyes, then, in another display of weakness, recalled it. The monarchy's last chance was gone.

The people might think the Parlement was defending popular liberties when it refused the *subvention;* in fact it was simply making sure that nobles (and all its members were noble) would continue to be exempt from taxation. In this last display of absolute selfishness, the Parlement proved the system's inability to change with the times. Holding on blindly in the face of mounting popular discontent, the *privilégiés* rushed to destruction. Rather than give up an inch, they lost the whole mile, and their lives as well.

Loménie de Brienne, along with his colleagues and some members of the salons, could see doom coming very close. Like Necker, he tried an end run around the Parlement and actually called an Assemblée des Notables. These notable men, who came from all over the country, might have been a real help if they had represented the general mood; but the government was so desperate for money that it selected only men who agreed with its financial policies. A story which made the rounds in Paris illustrates this fatal mistake. A lady had a parrot she prized extremely; one of her friends came in just in time to hear the bird shouting, "Long live the King." "Quick," said the visitor, "hide your parrot. If the government hears about him, they'll take him away from you and make him a notable."

On November 19, 1787, a frantic King held a *lit de justice* to force the Parlement to register an edict authorizing 480,000,000 livres in loans. During this stormy meeting one of the *conseillers,* Robert de Saint-Vincent, gave a preview of Revolutionary eloquence in his denunciation of the loans, and the duc d'Orléans, who saw his chance, promptly told the King to his face that this whole procedure was illegal. For once Louis XVI was stung into firmness. "It is, too, legal because it is my will," he mumbled back and exiled the duke to his castle at Villers-Coterêt.

Needless to say, this assertiveness didn't last. The duc d'Orléans was allowed to come back, the Estates-General were called and Loménie de Brienne was replaced by Monsieur Necker. Since, in the meantime, the Protestants' civil disabilities had been abolished, the great man, on August 27, 1788, became the new *Contrôleur Général.*

This time Necker was faced with a situation so extreme that no amount of juggling could hide the facts. Curiously, he also began to display the same indecisiveness which, until then, had plagued the King alone. It took only one speech at the opening of the Estates-General, in May 1789, for Monsieur Necker's vaunted talents to be seen for what they were: a public relations hype.

This story of French politics makes very sad telling; the foreign policy which accompanied them, with one shining exception, is equally depressing. In the 1760s the duc de Choiseul had consolidated two basic sets of alliances: one bound the several Bourbon monarchs (they ruled over Spain and the Indies, the Kingdom of the Two Sicilies, the Duchy of Parma and, of course, France) in the *Pacte de Famille;* the other, in a dramatic reversal of a centuries-old enmity, united France and Austria. These treaties endured throughout the reign of Louis XVI, but, in the case of Austria, thanks to Marie Antoinette's unceasing pressure, France got very much the worst of the bargain. Thus the second partition of Poland (1778) was allowed to occur without even a protest, though it was clearly contrary to France's interests. Then again, in 1785–86, the Emperor Joseph II, Marie Antoinette's brother, was faced with a rebellion in the Austrian Netherlands, today's Belgium.

It was clearly in France's interest to help the rebels, or at least receive a substantial compensation for failing to do so: after all, possession of this area had been an aim of French policy since the Middle Ages: it is all too easy, as two world wars were to prove, to come across that flat northern plain. At best, the Austrian Netherlands could have become French, as they did in 1795; at worst, they could have gained independence and served as a buffer between France and any possible invader. On the other hand, it was just as clearly in Austria's interest to retain this vital strategic and commercial area. The Emperor made that plain to his sister, who without a moment's hesitation put pressure on her husband. In spite of anything the Foreign Minister could do, Louis XVI gave in, and France covered itself with shame: it actually helped the Emperor put down the rebellion.

Still, there was that one shining exception, the American war. Here, too, France's interest was obvious. Vergennes saw it clearly and the Queen, luckily, didn't care. The peace with England, in 1763, had left France stripped of her colonies and humiliated; when the English colonies started to rebel, the King and Vergennes saw they might gain revenge. Secretly at first, they sent money and arms to the rebels; eventually they joined the insurgents. That story is too well known, and too long, to need retelling here; but the result of this policy, seen from a purely selfish point of view, was everything that could be wished. The English were beaten, France had its revenge and a new power, hostile to England, as the War of 1812 was to prove, had arisen in the West. France had called the New World into being to redress the balance of the Old.

--◃{ }▹--

It had become obvious, by the middle eighties, that the Ancien Régime was riding for a fall; when it would come, and in what form, nobody knew; that some drastic change must occur soon, however, was plain to see.

The Paris salons were full of well-informed, idle people; it is hardly surprising that they should have taken an interest in the coming crisis. What is more curious is that they should have felt so blithely secure. The warring reactionaries, Parlement vs. Queen's party, felt sure, on the other hand, that they could preserve the status quo forever. The liberals, who were equally sure that some change must come, never realized that a revolution was in the offing and that they stood to lose their property and their lives.

Catastrophe seemed out of the question. The current crisis, many people thought, was a blessing in disguise, since it would accelerate the necessary changes. As the eighties ran their fateful course, those bright young men, those smart young women thought that reality was limited to lively discussions held in an elegant salon full of furniture made by Jacob or Riesener. Politics, after all, was a fashion like any other—more serious, perhaps, than hats or hair-dos, but in the end no more dangerous. It was with exhilaration and confidence that they awaited the reconvening of the Estates-General: the world was theirs to play with; just a little more talk, just another little effort, and the new France would rise triumphant but amiable from the ashes of the old.

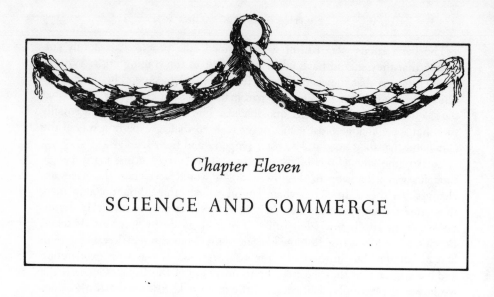

Chapter Eleven

SCIENCE AND COMMERCE

Nature, in 1770, was still a mystery. Chemistry and physics, as we think of them, had yet to be born. While Newton had published his *Principia Mathematica*, very little else was known about the universe. The most familiar animals were hardly understood; as for faraway countries, they were still widely held to house all kinds of mythical creatures. No one in France had ever seen a giraffe, a hippopotamus, a crocodile or an ostrich. There were no steam engines; electricity remained a dream in Franklin's eye. All in all, the sciences were almost as backward as the practice of medicine.

Still, attitudes had changed. Voltaire had translated and commented on Newton, so suddenly physics became fashionable; and, more crucial still, the *encyclopédistes* had shown conclusively that the world could be explored, observed, explained and understood. For the first time, almost, since Archimedes, intelligent men felt that no problem was too large or too complex: simple reason, coupled with careful observation, could solve any riddle. What man did not yet know, he would soon understand.

So scientists, philosophers and explorers looked about them. Bougainville sailed off to explore the unknown lands far to the west. Accurate maps appeared. Diderot, who was no physician, published his *Elements of Physiology* from 1774 to 1778. A few bold men even began to wonder why they shouldn't fly. Progress at long last became possible.

Georges-Louis Leclerc, comte de Buffon, was one of the stars of Madame Necker's salon. He was also France's greatest naturalist. Almost single-handedly he developed the Jardin du Roi which, though it belonged to the King, was hardly his garden. Situated in Paris, and well away from the royal palaces, it was a botanical compendium as well as a zoo and a gathering place for specimens (preferably alive) of exotic animals.

Buffon's *Histoire naturelle*, which he published over a period of eighteen years (1749–67), is a monumental attempt to understand our physical universe. Its fifteen volumes, divided into *The Theory of the Earth*, *The Natural History of Man* and the *Natural History of Quadrupeds*, established a new standard in the natural sciences. To this already impressive achievement he soon added nine volumes on *Birds* (1770–83), five on *Minerals* (1783–88) and seven of *Supplements* (1774–89) in which he tried, for instance, to outline a chronological and geological history of our planet.

This monument to the curiosity of man was published as a series of monographs and, unlike Rousseau, Buffon celebrated man as the king of nature and a triumph of the social instincts. But his greatest contribution was probably his methodology—many of his theories were wildly wrong. "The only true science," he wrote, "is the knowledge of facts," a startling departure from the old habit of trying to impose one's theory on a recalcitrant nature. Far from being subject to a restrictive and generalized principle, Buffon said, the world is infinitely diverse. "It seems that anything which can be, is," and he added, sensibly, that the object of science "is the how of things, not the why," thus eliminating all theological speculations.

That in itself was revolutionary. Nature was composed of phenomena which could be understood by mere observation; and since these had their own laws, they were valid in themselves and completely independent of God. Whenever possible, these phenomena, vegetable or mineral, must be observed in nature—and alive. Buffon would describe first the nature of, say, the lion, then its outward appearance, then its history: its habits, food, ways of hunting and using the product of its hunt.

"Physical truths," he wrote, "are never arbitrary and do not depend on us; instead of being founded on suppositions we had made, they are based only on facts; a succession of similar facts or, if you prefer, a frequent repetition and an uninterrupted succession of the same events constitute the essence of the physical truth, thus, what we call physical truth is only a probability so great that it is equal to a certitude. . . . All the facts of nature that we have observed or will observe are so many truths, and therefore we can multiply their numbers as much as we like simply by multiplying our observations; our science, here, is bounded only by the limits of the universe."

Even then, Buffon often let his feelings overrule his observations. "The noblest conquest that man has ever made," he enthused, "is that of [the horse], that proud and fiery animal . . ." and he thoroughly disagreed when Linnaeus classified it as a relative of the zebra; as a result, Buffon's classifications have not endured. However, he made many valid contributions to the natural sciences and wrote beautifully besides, a quality not to be disdained since it contributes to the spread of knowledge.

Unlike Buffon, Antoine-Laurent Lavoisier was a modern scientist whose work is still considered valid today. After studying botany, mineralogy and geology, he branched out to chemistry, which was the great love of his life.

Chemistry, it seems, was not as demanding a mistress in the eighteenth century as it has since become. Lavoisier married the daughter of a *fermier général* whose money was a great help. There were no foundations, no grants, no university laboratories, no chemical corporations then; if you wanted to do research you paid for it yourself. Since it had not yet been understood that scientists are men apart whose profession is all-consuming and to whom the rest of the world is as nothing, Lavoisier felt he could pursue two careers simultaneously. In 1768 he became a *fermier général* himself, and in 1776 he was appointed Director of Powders and Saltpeters by Turgot, who knew he was furthering science by providing Lavoisier with a free laboratory and space for experiments. When the Revolution came, though, the scientist disappeared behind the *fermier général*. In 1794, at the age of fifty-one, and despite much anguished protest, Lavoisier was sent to the guillotine.

Nature still comprised four elements—earth, air, fire and water—when Lavoisier started his work. Since no one quite understood what their components were, some were simply assumed. Thus a substance called phlogiston, which allowed fire to burn, had officially existed for a century; it was not Lavoisier's smallest achievement to prove that phlogiston was a figment of the imagination.

In the course of his study of the elements, along with metals and acids, Lavoisier, for the first time, isolated oxygen and hydrogen, and even recombined them to produce water. He also isolated sulphuric and phosphoric acids and thus revolutionized man's concept of the physical universe.

These discoveries were indeed far-reaching. They not only provided the foundation for all subsequent chemical research but also allowed Lavoisier to understand how and why we breathe by analyzing and describing the chemical process involved in the respiratory function. In two memoranda, one to the Académie des Sciences in 1777, and the other, in 1785, to the Annales de la Société de Médecine, Lavoisier proved that we breathe in oxygen which then passes into the blood, thus releasing carbon dioxide. He went even further. "Man's animal machine is principally governed by three main regulators," he wrote. "Breathing, which consumes hydrogen and carbon and helps to create warmth; transpiration, which grows or diminishes according to the necessity of expelling varying quantities of warmth; and, finally, digestion, which gives back to the blood everything it loses through breathing and transpiration."

Medicine, as we saw in Chapter Six, had scarcely left the Middle Ages—
and it was a chemist who provided a major surge forward. Once breathing
and the role played by chemicals in our body were understood, progress
could be made: within the next twenty years doctors were embarking on discoveries which have continued to this day.

Lavoisier's work was widely known and respected; it also had an unexpected side effect: chemistry became all the rage. Smart young women
flocked to Lavoisier's lectures, talked about chemistry and started a French
custom which still endures: some science has, ever since, been the topic of
the day. In 1900 it was Bergson's course that society attended; today the neo-
Freudian Dr. Lacan dazzles his audiences just as Lavoisier once did—though
his work may, perhaps, be less enduring.

Chemistry had practical uses as well. Berthollet, a pupil of Lavoisier's, isolated ammonia and worked out its method of fabrication. Soon a factory on
the island of Javel, in the Seine, was producing ammonia and chlorine,
which were put to good use for laundry and home cleaning, and laying the
foundation for the production of chemical fertilizers.

Another one of Lavoisier's students was to reach great fame, and in the
United States, too, though perhaps not for purely scientific reasons. A young
man named E. I. du Pont de Nemours, anxious to understand how gunpowder was made and what use saltpeter could be, naturally came to study with
the Director of Powders. When the Revolution came he emigrated to Delaware, started a gunpowder plant and founded the corporation and family
whose names are internationally famous today.

Since nature suddenly seemed so open to conquest, there was no reason
why an age-old dream should not come true: where Icarus failed, the Montgolfier brothers would succeed. Having noticed that hot air rises, they began
to wonder if it might take anything else up along with it. They experi-
mented, found that it would and, in 1783, built the first hot-air balloon. It
was made of waxed paper, powered by burning straw, and carried some
chickens in lieu of passengers. The straw was lit, the hot air rose and so did
the balloon. Soon a larger balloon was made, of canvas this time, lavishly
painted in blue and gold. As the King watched the first man to leave the soil
of his planet, the balloon bearing the brothers flew before an ecstatic crowd
(December 1); and soon imitators were flying everywhere, though it was not
until the new century that a balloon crossed the Channel.

Science also progressed in more modest, less spectacular ways. Urbanism
began to preoccupy some forward-looking architects like Ledoux (see Chapter Seven) and statesmen like Turgot. There was no up-to-date map of Paris;
Turgot had one made and it is still admired today, not just for the information it offers but also for the beauty of its presentation.

Cities, in 1770, were still largely medieval. Better lighting, better sanita-
tion, cleaner, wider streets, better public transportation may not seem very
scientific to us; yet they too were products of man's new belief in his power

to understand and organize nature. Life could be improved everywhere; so when new streets were built, they were wider, lighter and lined with trees. Roads, too, could be improved, and while not all French highways were paved, some were being shaped so that rain water would run off instead of forming ruts. Even intercity transportation was drastically modified. The *turgotine*, a new, faster kind of mail coach, began to link cities and villages faster, and on a regular schedule. For the first time you knew just when you would leave one city and arrive in the next. It made travel much easier. With better roads, speed became important. A new kind of carriage, the *dormeuse* (sleeper), had a fold-out bed so you could travel night and day in comfort. Soon people would think nothing of driving from Paris to Saint Petersburg in nine days; it had once taken almost six weeks: the modern age had come.

In one major respect, however, France continued to live in an earlier age: credit, the foundation of English commerce, was still scarcely understood. There was no Bank of France, though there had been a Bank of England for more than sixty years. There was no consolidated public debt. There were no real borrowing facilities; it could be very hard to expand a business.

All through the Ancien Régime, France suffered from a shortage of cash. Since there was no paper money, the economy was often slowed down by a scarcity of means of payment. The first effect of that scarcity was to keep prices artificially low, thus stopping expansion and investment.

England obviated this problem by having a central (though privately owned) bank which was allowed to print gold-backed paper money, thus making for faster, easier circulation. This encouraged both commerce and industry and helped, along with the British navy, to make England the world's first trading nation.

In France credit was ignored and trade largely disdained. The private banks, it is true, gave out their own paper backed by a hundred per cent gold cover. At least, if you had fifty thousand livres in Paris and you wanted to take it to Lyon, you didn't have to load a horse with gold: you could take a note drawn on a correspondent bank. Still, the method was slow and clumsy: the note was valid only in one place and for one person. The very notion of a joint stock company, in which a number of investors join together and provide capital for a new enterprise, was almost wholly foreign to the French. By 1789 there were fewer than ten such companies.

Investment, production and commerce were further slowed by the mercantilist tradition inherited from Colbert. He held that the wealth of a country was its gold; so, in order to diminish imports, he convinced Louis XIV to found a number of state-owned enterprises which produced mirrors, carpets, tapestries, even silk. This tradition continued in the eighteenth century. When the techniques of porcelain-making reached France, Louis XV promptly opened a state-owned factory at Sèvres. Since a number of other products, like tobacco and gunpowder, were also state owned, and since commerce was considered a demeaning occupation, there was no great incentive for enterprising young men to go into trade. On the other hand, French workers never had to suffer the appalling misery, filth and squalor which disgraced the Industrial Revolution in England.

French products went everywhere, but very few objects of foreign make came into France. The bulk of trade was in foodstuffs, tobacco and colonial products: sugar, spices, rice, tea, coffee. This allowed a number of businessmen, mostly from Bordeaux, to cash in on a highly profitable item of trade, referred to as *le bois d'ébène* (ebony wood): black slaves. Many French shipowners took part in the infamous triangular exchange of slaves, sugar and rum, and prospered. The city of Bordeaux was virtually rebuilt from scratch in the late eighteenth century and still looks glorious today. It was paid for in human flesh.

It seemed for a while as if the new connection with the United States might bring trade and profits, but old habits die hard. The newly independent Americans might not want to live under British rule, but they continued to buy British goods imported in British ships.

The picture changed dramatically when it came to exports. The French were famous for all their products, intellectual and commercial. There wasn't much trade in books: in that pre-copyright age foreign printers simply pirated the works; but the demand for just about every other French product was tremendous. French fashions were sent all over Europe; French silks from Lyon, famous for their quality and beauty, were frequently exported, along with Bordeaux wines and Champagne.

Then there was porcelain. Although Dresden provided competition, Sèvres was considered everywhere to be unrivaled. When Catherine the Great wanted a fine porcelain service, she ordered it from Sèvres. When Frederick the Great needed new coffee cups, he sent to Sèvres.

The same was true of French furniture: it was far and away the best, and recognized as such. The great cabinetmakers worked, whenever they had time, for foreign clients.

French exports took another, more curious form: maids, cooks and tutors. French ladies' maids were generally acknowledged to have the nimblest fingers, the liveliest sense of fashion and elegance; so many an English duchess or Russian princess was dressed by a Thérèse or Marie. And since France was already famous for its food, French chefs were to be found all over Europe.

As for tutors, they represent still another aspect of the taste for all things French. Culture was just as important as silks or food. Noble families everywhere spoke French; in Russia they often failed to learn their own language. And so tutors were brought in to teach language and literature, manners and taste. They left a deep impression in many countries.

Aside from international trade, there was, of course, the everyday commerce of shops and markets. Silk went from Lyon to Paris, the finished dress back to Lyon. Food must come to the cities, but usually from the surrounding countryside. Produce came into Paris every morning on carts, from thousands of little gardens; but seafood had to be sent all the way from the coast and was more reliable in the winter months. In an age without refrigeration and fast transportation, perishables couldn't go far, and special measures were sometimes taken: when fish in great quantity was needed for a royal banquet, special stages were set up along the road so it could travel with all possible speed.

Commerce, in its most visible form, was carried on in thousands of small specialty shops: there were neither supermarkets nor department stores. While this system had its drawbacks—you had to go to lots of different places—it also had its advantages. Comparison shopping was easy, as all the outlets for a particular kind of merchandise tended to be gathered along one or two streets; the merchants were personally involved in what they sold you and were personally responsible to you themselves: since they expected to see you again, face to face, they were more likely to sell you good quality at an honest price.

Many things, from suits to carriages, were made especially for you. If you needed a coat, you went to your tailor, and he knew you; we have seen earlier how this worked for furniture; the same was true of carriages and their decorations, or chimneypieces, or porcelain cups. Mass-produced goods didn't exist: it was a handmade world.

With the Revolution came war, and with it the interruption of all trade. With armies on all its borders, and the British navy patrolling its coasts, France no longer could export any of its products, and its commerce virtually ceased to exist. It would take Napoleon's armies to revive it.

II

NAPLES

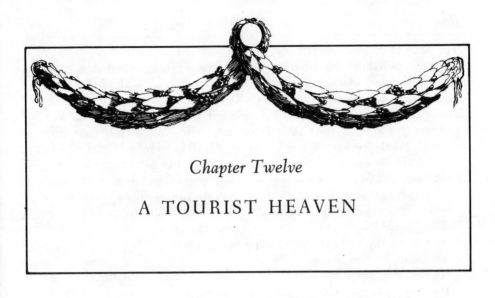

Chapter Twelve

A TOURIST HEAVEN

Throughout the seventies and eighties Europe looked to Paris and found its model there—for art, furniture, books, fashions. The English, the Germans came in flocks to see what it was all about; but, when they left, it was often not for home: along with their French acquaintances, they headed straight for Naples.

Why Naples? It might at first glance seem to have everything against it: it was very far away, down at the bottom of Italy, and reached only after traveling over miles of horrendous roads; it was hot, at a time when swimming and sun bathing were thought barbaric; it was the capital of a tiny, weak state, not a place that could matter in any way. But it had its attractions—attractions so potent, in fact, as to make it the birthplace of modern tourism.

First, every one of those drawbacks had a triumphant answer: yes, it was far away, but distance became almost negligible if it meant going through Venice, Florence and Rome; yes, it was hot—but the Bay of Naples was generally considered the most beautiful in the world, and the winter was balmy; yes, it was almost meaningless in terms of power politics—but its brilliant, decadent court gathered around a Bourbon King and a Habsburg Queen who, between them, were related to just about every royal family in Europe. And besides all that, there was a key reason for going to Naples: it allowed you to take a trip through time.

Some seventeen centuries before, Vesuvius, spewing up a torrent of mud and ashes, had obliterated Herculaneum and Pompeii from the face of the earth—or so it seemed. In fact, the hardened goo preserved them almost perfectly; and when, in the 1740s, they were dug up, they presented an amazed world with two unchanged Roman cities, forums, frescoes, temples and all.

The King of Naples watched over the digging and stored the many objects that came to light in his palace at Portici. First artists came, saw and, gasping, admired and imitated. Neo-classicism swept Europe, finding its French incarnation, prematurely,[1] in the Louis XVI style. Soon architecture and furniture were everywhere inspired by antique Roman standards. Roman temples sprang into being from Saint Petersburg to the Brandenburg gate, from the Paris Pantheon to the White House. And it all came from Naples.

Suddenly any curious, civilized person simply had to go and have a look at those vases and frescoes. Even the unconventional climate helped: the English discovered that they were spending their lives being cold and damp; the clear air, the sunshine, the warmth all became highly attractive, and they descended upon Naples in droves, so numerous, in fact, that the British Minister, Sir William Hamilton, was to write home in 1786: "It is really a serious consideration for our country the enormous sum of money being spent abroad by the subjects of Great Britain. . . . At Naples, this year . . . it is nearly £50,000." The great English trek to the sun, now stronger than ever, had begun; and the Germans soon joined in, led by two very different but equally powerful personalities: Emperor Joseph II and young Mr. Goethe. The French were slower to follow; at first they were represented only by their artists and a number of bold travelers. In a way, it was difficult for most Frenchmen to see why anyone would leave Paris, even for Naples.

Still, those who actually made the journey were dazzled, and promptly put their impressions down on paper so that everyone could share them. In no time at all Naples had become the first great tourist center, and a ubiquitous modern phenomenon was born.

Travel conditions, which seemed pretty rough in 1770, would strike us as unacceptable today. There were two ways to reach Naples: by sea, from Marseille or Genoa—but it wasn't entirely safe: the Barbary pirates still sailed the Mediterranean; or along appalling roads all the way down the Italian peninsula. It wasn't much fun to be bumping, day after day, along muddy or dusty rutted tracks; there was little food to be had, and what there was often turned out to be inedible; the inns were filthy caves, full of fleas and bedbugs; there was no place to wash, there was no place to rest. It would all have been quite impossible if you were in a hurry; but in those days people were perfectly content to leave home for months at a time and could interrupt the misery by stopping in all the beautiful cities along the way.

Curiously, Florence, Venice and Rome, all, then, the capitals of independent Italian states, seemed strangely provincial compared to Naples. Their populations too small, their palaces too large, those cities all seemed well past their peak. But while the Kingdom of the Two Sicilies, which was comprised of the bottom of the Italian boot and Sicily itself, was one of the poorest, most primitive of European states, its capital was a real city. "To me,

[1] Louis XVI came to the throne in 1774, but the style named after him had already been in existence for some ten years.

Naples is the only Italian city which feels like a capital," a French traveler, the Président de Brosses, had written as early as 1736. "The movement, the affluence of the people, the abundance and noise of the carriages, a proper and rather brilliant court, the dignity and magnificence of the great nobles: everything helps to give it that lively and animated exterior that one sees in Paris and London, but not at all in Rome."

The court mentioned by Président de Brosses was especially attractive in 1770. The sovereigns, Ferdinand IV and Maria Carolina, were young and fun-loving. There were hunts, picnics, balls, theater parties and midnight suppers. Foreigners were welcome at the palace, along with the Neapolitan nobles. Clothes and settings were almost as splendid as at Versailles, but the etiquette was a good deal more relaxed. Here too the courtiers spent most of their time intriguing, but nothing much was at stake, and everybody was far too good-natured and lazy to take any of it very seriously. For those twenty golden years before the French Revolution set Europe by the ears, the Neapolitan court seemed like part of an *opera buffa,* one of those charming musical fantasies composed by the local musicians, men like Piccinni, Paisiello and Cimarosa. Even that Eden, however, was not without its snakes.

That Naples was an Eden was plain to all. "To see Naples, say the Neapolitans, and die. Well, I say, to see Naples and then live," Dupati wrote in 1785; like all travelers, he had been stunned by the city's setting, that incomparable bay with its blue waters and blue sky, surrounded by hills where palaces hid in the lush vegetation and, ever and anon, a rumble came to remind you that Vesuvius was still active.

The French and the Italians raved; but it was an Englishman, John Moore, who came up with a cool description of the splendid site. "The bay is about thirty miles in circumference and twelve in diameter; it has been named crater from its supposed resemblance to a bowl.[2] This bowl is ornamented with the most beautiful foliage, with vines; with olive, mulberry and orange trees; with hills, dales, towns, villas and villages.

"At the bottom of the Bay of Naples, the town is built in the form of a vast amphitheatre, sloping from the hills towards the sea.

"If from the town you turn your eyes to the East, you see the rich plains leading to Mount Vesuvius and Portici; if you look to the West, you have the grotto of Pausilippo, the mountain on which Virgil's tomb is placed, and the fields leading to Pozzuoli and the coast of Baia. On the North are the fertile hills gradually rising from the shore to the *Campagna felice.* On the South is the Bay confined by the two promontories of Misena and Minerva, the view being terminated by the islands Procida, Ischia and Caprea."[3]

As for the weather, it might be hot in midsummer, but it was warm and mild in the spring, fall, and during part of the winter as well. It seldom rained, it was seldom cold, all in all, an ideal place for a holiday. And then

[2] Crater is the Latin word for bowl.
[3] Better known as Capri.

12. A Night Eruption of Vesuvius. *This plate was drawn by the Abbé de Saint-Non,
who also describes this spectacular event in this chapter.*

there was that golden light. "Even when everything has been depicted and described," wrote a traveler, "one still has to picture a magical effect which exists in the air, which colors every object, and which causes even those one knows in other climates to look different and new in this one."

After the first moment of rapture, all eighteenth-century travelers arriving in Naples had the same urgent goal: Mount Vesuvius. The volcano was old and famous; it had, after all, buried Pompeii and Herculaneum. It still erupted periodically and was always crowned, even when it was quiet, with a great plume of white smoke. Naples itself, though some twenty miles away, was not considered altogether safe—just unsafe enough, in fact, to give the traveler that delicious shiver. And the very first excursion out of the city was usually aimed straight at the volcano's slopes.

Of course these promenades quickly stopped whenever the first signs of a disturbance appeared. In the recent past there had been major eruptions, on March 18, 1766, and October 19, 1767, the last forcing the young King to flee his palace at Portici under a rain of hot ash, and with a river of lava only a mile and a half away. The most violent outburst, though, occurred over a twelve-day period, July 29 to August 9, 1779. "On the evening of the eighth," wrote the Abbé de Saint-Non, "people were able to judge the strength of the fire burning deep within the volcano; suddenly, there sprang out of it a mass of burning stones forming, in their flight, a mass of fire with the very crater of Vesuvius as its base; as it slowly rose, it formed a fiery cylinder of prodigious height. . . . This spectacle lasted for three quarters of an hour. At the same time, there came out of the top of the mountain a thick, black smoke which, because the air was so still, rose directly and reached an immeasurable height. . . . These [burning stones] were thrown up in so huge a number that the whole of Vesuvius, right down to the valley, seemed aflame. . . . Quickly, an unbearable stink of sulphur spread out over the environs. One could hear explosions that sounded like frequent artillery shots all the way to Naples." It must have been impressive but, as a tourist attraction, somewhat undependable.

Even when Vesuvius failed to perform, the court could be depended on. Nobody could have been more Neapolitan than young Ferdinand IV.[4] He was only nineteen in 1770 but had already been married for two years and displayed all the characteristics which, somewhat episodically, kept endearing him to his subjects. Naples was, in essence, a Spanish possession, but it was ruled as a separate state by the younger son of the King of Spain, himself a Bourbon and a first cousin of Louis XV. The King's father, Charles III, was far away in Madrid; and, prompted by his eighteen-year-old wife, the young King was trying to become independent of his father.

Ferdinand couldn't do much by himself. Left behind in Naples when his father moved to Spain, "his tutor, the Prince of San Nicandro, the stupidest man at court, [was] having him brought up in the deepest ignorance," ac-

---

[4] Better known to history as Ferdinand I, a regnal number he assumed as a result of later constitutional changes.

cording to a contemporary. In fact, the young King was almost illiterate and found it so difficult to sign his name that he had to have a stamp made. He was thoughtless and rough, but not unkind, and though he wasn't stupid he sometimes gave the impression of being an idiot through sheer lack of education. *"Er ist ein reicht guter Narr* [He is a right good fool]," his wife commented to her brother; and most agreed with her. Curiously, he shared certain characteristics with Louis XVI, his brother-in-law and cousin thrice removed. They both loved the hunt and physical exercise, indulged in coarse jokes, ate far too much, had good intentions and were weak and not too bright. There, however, the resemblance stopped: Ferdinand was lean and highly sexed.

"He must be five feet seven inches," the Emperor Joseph II wrote during his visit to Naples, ". . . very thin, gaunt and rawboned. . . . His knees are always bent and his back very supple, since at every step he bends and sways his whole body. The part below his waist is so limp and feeble that it does not seem to belong to the upper part, which is much stronger. He has muscular arms and wrists and his coarse brown hands are very dirty since he never wears gloves when he rides or hunts. His head is relatively small, surmounted by a forest of coffee-colored hair which he never powders, a nose which begins in his forehead and gradually swells in a straight line as far as his mouth, which is very large, with a jutting lower lip, filled with fairly good but irregular lower teeth. The rest of his features, his low brow, pig's eyes, flat cheek and long neck are not remarkable.

"Although an ugly prince, he is not absolutely repulsive; his skin is fairly smooth and firm, of a yellowish pallor; he is clean, except for his hands; and, at least, he does not stink."

Altogether, *il re nasone* (the big-nosed King) was hardly a prepossessing monarch; he usually shouted in high, unpleasant tones and was much given to bullying the courtiers around him; since he could not remember a time when he had not been King, he was absolutely uninhibited and always did exactly as he pleased, belching and farting freely; and, since he was used to the unceasing presence of courtiers and attendants, he developed a strong fear of being alone: even on the *chaise percée,* the contents of which were afterward passed around for inspection, he was surrounded by an admiring circle. And since he looked up to no one, his shortcomings seemed perfectly natural to him. He never tried to conceal his cowardice or ignorance. Indeed, rather like Dr. Pangloss, Ferdinand thought all was for the best in the best of all possible worlds. "He loves his country and admires it to excess, believing that all he has is excellent," according to the Emperor; in fact, he thought Naples unexcelled. Even the many reverses he had to suffer in the nineties and the first fifteen years of the next century failed to change his opinion. There was nothing wrong with Naples, it was just the outside world that was causing problems; and so, just like certain Italian beggars, he evolved a kind of low cunning in his dealings with powerful foreigners.

Still, Ferdinand was popular; *il re lazzarone*, he was also called, after the very lowest class of his subjects, whose tastes he shared. Like them, for instance, he loved to eat macaroni with his hands—only he did it in the royal box at the San Carlo theater; like them, he didn't mind shouts and noise and vulgarity. There has probably never been a more common monarch. His people loved it when, having been fishing, he personally sold his catch in the market and then gave away the money in alms; he was really one of them. Odd, ugly and uncouth though he was, this womanizer was also popular with the tourists: he was such a change from their own highly respectable sovereigns. And there was always the Queen.

Maria Carolina, who was only eighteen in 1770, started out as one of those model daughters through which the Empress Maria Theresa hoped to rule Europe. Like her sister Marie Antoinette, whom she soon came to envy (imagine the luck, being Queen of France), Maria Carolina was, and remained, thoroughly Austrian, and quickly became unpopular. She was almost a caricature of her sister, power-crazy, promiscuous, shrewish, hysterical. Still, none of these defects was yet apparent, and she did have her sister's charm.

As a young archduchess, she had been her brother Joseph's favorite and, despite her youth, was well educated, cultured and sophisticated—far more intelligent, in fact, than the lightheaded Marie Antoinette. In Vienna she had been told she was being sent off to a strong, handsome young King with whom she would rule over another garden of Eden. Instead, she found herself married to an ugly, illiterate oaf whose kingdom was among the most backward in Europe and was ruled, furthermore, by a Prime Minister, the Marquis Tanucci, who had been appointed years ago by the King of Spain, and who referred any problem directly to his old master.

What would happen to this young bride whose loud, vulgar husband drank too much and openly had mistresses? First, she tried unsuccessfully to educate him; then, when she failed, she started to become more like him. "She is beginning to take on the noisy Neapolitan manner," the French Minister wrote, "added to which, she speaks all the time because she is so lively; but she speaks thoughtlessly of each person to the others, when he is out of sight, and so is not liked." And then, in a court where sexual excess was open and constant, where ladies talked of nothing but their new lovers, it became difficult for an attractive young woman to remain faithful to her faithless spouse. Soon, like her subjects, she was taking lovers.

"Her Majesty is a beautiful woman," Lady Anne Miller wrote in 1770; "she has the finest and most transparent complexion I ever saw; her hair is of that glossy, light chestnut I so much admire; it is by no means red; her eyes are large, brilliant and of a dark blue, her eyebrows exact, and darker than her hair, her nose inclining to the aquiline, her mouth small, her lips very red (not of the Austrian thickness), her teeth beautifully white and even, and, when she smiles, she discovers two dimples which throw a finishing sweetness over her whole countenance; her shape is perfect; she is just plump enough not to appear lean; her neck is long, her deportment easy, her walk majestic, her attitude and action graceful."

Both sovereigns were young and pleasure-loving. Court balls often lasted until 7 A.M.; in 1774 masked balls, which had been forbidden by Charles III, were allowed again, and even the critical Joseph II thought that "the court has an air of grandeur and magnificence, the town palace and that of Portici are superb; among the copious nobility are several men and women of wit who could make life very agreeable." Still, it wasn't enough for the Queen. She loathed Tanucci for the simple and sufficient reason that he ruled instead of her; she loathed Spain and her father-in-law because Ferdinand still obeyed him. It was quite different from Versailles; there, Marie Antoinette ruled her husband because her coterie kept pushing her to it; Maria Carolina, on the other hand, dominated hers because she loved power more than anything in the world.

Luckily, as the Queen knew full well, her marriage contract was a long-term weapon: it included a clause specifying her right to sit on the Council of State as soon as she had given birth to a male heir. The happy event took place in 1775 and within a year Tanucci had been fired. The King of Spain was outraged, but he was too far away to do anything; after all, as Maria Carolina remarked, he was not likely to send an army all the way to Naples.

Even before gaining admittance to the Council, the Queen had tried to enforce her will by dint of dreadful scenes; after a while the weak Ferdinand would give in, partly through laziness, partly through cowardice, partly because his wife was so clearly superior to him. Yet while her demands, capricious and changing, might seem to make sense at the moment, they usually turned out to be mistakes and Ferdinand, who at any rate was not blind, was heard to comment: "The Queen knows everything. And yet she makes more errors than I do, although I'm just a stupid ass."

Even Maria Carolina realized she needed help; she found it, along with a new lover, in the rather dour person of an English visitor and ex-naval officer, Sir John Acton.

Actually his very dourness worked in his favor. The Queen was used to being courted; having to do the courting herself proved a refreshing change; and, since she could never be quite sure of Acton, she remained his devoted partner year after year. She started out by giving him the War Department, not a very considerable position since the Neapolitan army and navy were practically non-existent. When, a little later, Acton received the Finance Ministry as well, he became Prime Minister in all but name and proceeded to rule Naples with an iron hand. It was easy: whenever the King got suspicious, the Queen staged a violent disagreement with the Minister; satisfied that he was in control, Ferdinand would agree with Acton to spite his wife and all would be well.

Unlike earlier ministers, Acton had well-defined policies. Not unnaturally, he was strongly pro-English, which suited the Queen nicely since, as we have seen, she hated Spain. She didn't much like France either: she felt that, as the older sister, she should have wed the Dauphin while Marie Antoinette was sent off to Naples. The fact that her policy went against the King's natural affection for his father and the *Pacte de Famille,* the treaty linking all the Bourbon states, bothered only France and Spain. No one in Naples seemed to care very much.

The hitch, really, was that Acton tried to make Naples into something it wasn't: a major partner in the European game. In the process he spent far more than the kingdom could afford in order to build up the armed forces. This was very unpopular because it meant raising taxes—Maria Theresa's daughters seem to have had an inborn propensity for becoming Mesdames Déficit—and, worse, it was a complete waste: predictably, when the test came, despite their numbers and new weapons, the army and navy promptly collapsed, since no one could check the soldiers' urge to remove themselves from the proximity of any battlefield.

The Acton regime also had its good sides. A new atmosphere of freedom made itself felt: to Acton it came naturally; he was, after all, English; as for the Queen, she liked playing the enlightened despot. So in 1777 the university was modernized and had its income doubled; a new system of non-religious primary and secondary schools was established. New thought was encouraged, and a young man called Filangieri published *The Science of Legislation* in which he suggested reorganizing the State on a natural, rational basis which was defined in terms of both Rousseau's ideas and Montesquieu's work on laws and constitutions. It was quite competent, and serious enough to impress Goethe.

This liberal trend culminated in 1789 when the King—i.e., Acton—created the colony of San Leucio. This model village, built on the edge of the royal park at Caserta, was to be an embodiment of the society of the future. The paternal monarch, rather like his sister-in-law at the Hameau, had his own little house; but all the other inhabitants of the village were perfectly equal; not only was there no nobility, but the colony was self-governing and ruled by an Assembly of Elders elected by all the heads of family, who voted by secret ballot. Marriages were free: dowries were abolished and no one could be forced to wed against his or her will. In direct contradiction to the usual entail, all inheritances were divided equally among the children. Instruction and vaccination were compulsory. All in all, it was a remarkable institution; only that very year 1789 was also that of the beginning of the French Revolution. By 1790, while San Leucio went on, the rest of the kingdom was being ruled according to the most reactionary principles.

None of this mattered very much. There were no severe problems before 1790, no new ones, anyway. Nothing worked better than before, of course, but then it wasn't worse either. Acton actually turned back a shipful of French wheat sent to help the victims of a Calabrian earthquake in 1783, and everyone, except, presumably, the victims, thought it a fine gesture. Dupati might write home, in 1785, "The government is such, in this kingdom, that it is often only an added disorder," but it seemed as if it might all go on forever. That, too, was ideal for tourism: the foreigners could feel both superior and safe.

It might easily be awhile before a traveler was presented at court since it spent more time out of the city than in: there was the palace at Portici, with its Capodimonte "Chinese" porcelain room, various hunting lodges and, grandest of all, Caserta. Charles III had chosen the site for a double reason: it was safely away from Vesuvius, and as the area was quite desolate it was easy to purchase land. A new architect, Luigi Vanvitelli, was hired, and building proceeded apace.

Caserta was to be the Neapolitan Versailles; it was huge, sumptuously decorated with gold and marble, and surrounded by an immense formal park with geometric flower beds, a canal and fountains. In fact the building is nothing like its model; it looks both dull and endless. It is so large as to dwarf all architectural decoration; the eye wanders disconsolately over its grim gray façade. As for the garden, it must have looked less desolate under Ferdinand IV than it does today; presumably its greenery was kept watered and flowers bloomed; but nothing could ever have remedied the sadness of this flat, sterile plain, or the insufficiency, the narrowness of the waterways. Versailles did not take well to the climate of Naples. Still, visitors were dazzled by the rich interiors.

What Caserta may have lacked in animation, Naples more than made up. It was a densely populated city: with its half million inhabitants, it was larger than even such capitals as Vienna. And, thanks to the mild climate, it seemed as if every man, woman and child was out in its streets. Aside from the two main thoroughfares, the Toledo and the Chiaia, the city was a warren of narrow, winding streets opening onto little piazzas. Palaces and slums stood side by side, innumerable carriages, preceded by running footmen, dashed through the streets, vendors shouted their wares, chanting processions wound their way through the crowds, and the *lazzaroni*, lazy and satisfied, picked whatever pockets they could reach.

Naples, like every other city, had an aristocracy, a middle class and a proletariat, but it also boasted a unique, privileged group: the *lazzaroni*. Some thirty-five thousand in number, they were essentially a permanently unemployed mass of men and women for whom the city had no jobs and who liked it that way. To every visitor's shock, they made it plain: they didn't want to work. Unimpaired by such bourgeois necessities as rent (the climate helped), they would work just enough to eat, and happily stop working the moment they had earned a few pennies. They might go fishing for a while, or do some odd jobs, but their favorite occupation was fraud of one kind or another: fooling other people to get their money (*buscare*). They came in handy when you needed a false witness; and, given the complications of the legal system, who didn't? They sold damaged or stolen goods, they pretended to run errands, kept the money and sat down in the sun, and, if driven to real exertion, would do a bit of stealing. They were loud, vulgar, demanding and potentially dangerous: it was always one of the government's chief preoccupations to see that they were contented. No one had forgotten Masaniello's bloody revolt, some hundred years earlier, and in times of need the King had food distributed to them.

The *lazzaroni* had only one luxury: on every one of the innumerable feast days they appeared in rich clothes. Mrs. Piozzi describes men "panting for heat under a thick blue velvet coat; the females in a scarlet cloth petticoat with a broad gold lace at the bottom, a jacket open before, but charged with heavy ornaments and the head not unbecomingly dressed with an embroidered handkerchief from Turkey." Other visitors commented on the comic juxtaposition of a gold-embroidered silk coat with patched cotton trousers; but all that slightly soiled finery added greatly to the animation of the streets.

"One of the greatest delights in Naples is the universal gaiety," Goethe wrote during his visit there. ". . . The Neapolitan not only enjoys his food, but insists it be attractively displayed for sale. In Santa Lucia, the fish are placed on a layer of green leaves and each category—rock lobsters, oysters, clams and small mussels—has a clean, pretty basket to itself. But nothing is more carefully planned than the display of meat which, since their appetite is stimulated by the periodic fast days, is particularly coveted by the common people.

"In the butchers' stalls, quarters of beef, veal or mutton are never hung up without having the unfatty part of the legs or flank heavily gilded.

"[At Christmas and other holidays], the Toledo and other streets and squares are decorated most appetisingly; vegetables, raisins, melons and figs are piled high in their stalls; huge paternosters of gilded sausages, tied with red ribbons, and capons with little red flags stuck in their rumps, are suspended in festoons across the street overhead."

It was a mixed crowd who walked the streets. The first thing visitors noticed after the climate and the *lazzaroni* was the abundance of priests, monks and nuns; in Naples alone, there were over 15,000;[5] and, like the rest of the population, they always seemed to be out. Then came the seemingly innumerable lawyers in their black cloaks, and a flock of footmen in grand liveries. Middle-class women, accompanied by at least two maids and a retinue of eight to ten people, threaded their way through the multitude, avoiding the sedan chairs used by those who couldn't afford a carriage: the poorest noble would have considered himself dishonored if he had had to walk anywhere.

Naples wasn't exactly short of nobility, either. Titles had been granted

[5] And 109,000 in the whole kingdom.

freely, and sometimes sold, by the Austrian and Spanish viceroys alike; as a result, the kingdom could boast 119 princes, 156 dukes (by comparison, France had fewer than 50), 173 marquesses, 42 counts and 445 barons. As a class, the nobility numbered over 25,000 members.

Some were stone broke. Lady Anne Miller, writing home to say she had taken an apartment in the Marchesa di Grazze Reale's palace, went on to explain that it was just a high-class boardinghouse as the marchesa was quite penniless. And since she and her companion didn't stint themselves, they also hired a coach, horses and a coachman, two footmen, a maid, a cook, a scullion boy and a hairdresser, all by the month.

Many of the nobles, though, were rich and powerful. On their estates they still enjoyed all the perquisites of feudal lords and were quite independent of King and government. "The barons [i.e., the nobles] may still emprison their vassals by the use of an order bearing this clause: for reasons known to ourselves." And, like their French colleagues, they paid no tax.

More, perhaps, than any other aristocracy, the Neapolitans felt free to live any way they pleased. The Prince of Francavilla, who was famous for his collection of antiques, once invited a group of highborn English tourists to see it; and after lunch he showed them to a terrace outside his palace, where there was a magnificent pool. He clapped his hands, and twenty naked youths appeared, dived in, and performed a water ballet. Another clap, and they were out and available for use by the guests. When some of the Englishmen present asked the Prince if he didn't have some girls instead, he regretfully answered that he didn't, but asked them to come back the following week. They did and were greeted this time by ravishing—and naked—girls.

The Prince of Francavilla was more hospitable than most. "Luxury is considerable in the capital, and especially among the nobility," wrote the Abbé de Saint-Non. "But that magnificence is all on the outside. . . . One can see great huge palaces richly furnished but the three quarters of which remain uninhabited; people own the most magnificent plate, but it is never used. . . . The greatest lords, with their immense income, and the most brilliant households, sometimes lack for the most necessary things. They are preceded by four running footmen, are served by forty servants, have fifty horses in their stables, and yet, it has happened more than once that their butler has trouble getting their dinner served. This will only seem inconceivable to those who have not witnessed the disorder which prevails in the greatest Neapolitan houses. . . .

"One seldom eats there with a well-chosen company, but, from time to time, the principal nobles will have their *ricevimenti* [receptions] for three or four hundred people to whom a cookie will be the most solid food offered. Nothing could be more brilliant than those *ricevimenti*; you see pages in embroidered clothes, richly braided footmen, butlers whom one might be tempted to mistake for the master of the house, tables heavily laden with ices, sweets and *rinfreschi* [chilled drinks] of every kind; but it is all like fireworks; the next day, all this splendid luxury has vanished.

"The largest of these assemblies are usually in the houses of young women who have just given birth. . . . Neapolitan society is very pleasant and, especially among the courtiers, foreigners are treated with great kindness. . . .

"It is especially in the theaters that society people usually meet. The length of the shows, the size and comfort of the boxes allow their owners to have many guests, and they are, in fact, the gathering place for society, especially in winter. . . . The boxes [at the San Carlo theater] are so large and so deep that it is easy to receive many people in them. The custom calls for having ices and cold drinks served there: the result is that the show is what people care the least about."

San Carlo was the elegant theater, the court theater. Built by order of Charles III, for whom it was named, it was regularly attended by the King and Queen, and could be entered directly from the palace. People were expected to wear court dress, the ladies sparkled with diamonds, the actors and singers went about their business on the stage largely unheeded, except for an occasional aria—altogether, it was more like a huge, diverse salon than anything else. As a result, plays and operas went on for hours and hours, sometimes from seven at night to five in the morning, and it didn't matter since you could eat and chat there just as comfortably as if you were at home.

Visitors never failed to be impressed: San Carlo was famous throughout Europe. It was, Lady Anne Miller exclaimed, "amazingly vast . . . there are six ranges of boxes, the first consists of twenty-two, the others of twenty-four each. They contain from ten to twelve people conveniently.[6] . . . Armchairs are the only seats. The boxes are hung with silk, agreeable to the taste of their owner and well illuminated. The front of each range is faced with looking glass . . . [this produces] an effect which, at first view, persuades you that all is enchantment. The lights, the company, the stage are reflected from side to side and consequently so often multiplied that it confounds a spectator. The pillars that separate the boxes are decorated with large statues of genii, etc., finely gilt, they sustain wax candles of prodigious size and make a dazzling appearance reflected from the looking glass behind them. . . . Music is here in the highest perfection. . . . The royal box makes a superb appearance, particularly when the court is present, at which time the ladies belonging to the court and others are full dressed and covered with a profusion of jewels; but the Queen outshines them all, not only in magnificence of dress, but in a style of beauty and gracefulness of air peculiar to herself."

Part of that splendid music was sung by a very particular and immensely

[6] The theater could hold almost two thousand spectators.

popular kind of contralto: the castrati. Far more famous than sopranos or tenors, they were eunuchs who had been castrated at an early age so they might preserve those silvery children's tones. Many roles sung today by women were written specifically for the castrati. They were often grotesque, very fat or very withered, but they were sought after and kept just like opera girls.

Of course, there were other amusements, and the Corso was the chief of them. There the nobles paraded along the seashore in splendidly decorated carriages, painted and gilded on the outside, upholstered in brocade and gold braid on the inside, and with tall, wide windows so that the assembled crowd could look in. These coaches, accompanied by clouds of runners and footmen, all bearing torches as soon as it got dark, were pulled by six and often eight horses—a prerogative of royalty elsewhere in Europe. The owners, dressed to kill, would sit motionless as they were driven back and forth. This parade took place every Sunday, Tuesday and Thursday in summer and was an amphibious operation: parallel to the carriages, sumptuously decorated boats rowed back and forth, occupants on display. It was all very Neapolitan.

As so often in the eighteenth century, this glitter existed side by side with the utmost filth. The owners of those carriages, wearing their splendid clothes, thought nothing of getting out and relieving themselves right out on the street or on a palace stairs; and so of course the city stank abominably.

At night, while the smells lingered, the city assumed its most magic look. Although there were no street lights, everyone who walked about carried a torch; every carriage, every sedan chair was surrounded by torchbearers; the many processions which constantly wound their way through the city were a mass of burning wands; the very ships in the harbor—and all Naples was a harbor—were brightly lit. We have become accustomed to a kind of artificial light which is so bright that it dulls color, flattens form and makes the night a bleached-out parody of day. In Naples the velvety darkness formed a contrast, a setting for the bright, flaring but circumscribed glow of the torches which picked out color and glitter: it was a literally dazzling spectacle.

Still, in all that gaiety, a sober element could be seen making its way through the busy streets: the middle class. Unlike the rest of Europe, Naples failed to develop a real middle class, so there were few of these respectable, plain, hard-working people. They prospered mostly as intermediaries; they farmed the taxes, changed money—a profitable occupation in this tourist center—held export licenses, owned ships and were in charge of public works. Most often, though, they were lawyers.

The legal system in Naples was unbelievably complex. Each succeeding wave of conquest had left its laws behind, along with its courts, so there was almost no telling what was legal and what wasn't. Then, of course, the judges were corrupt, the legal processes maddeningly slow and the possible penalties most unpleasant. The fact that the city alone had over thirty thousand lawyers surprised no one except the foreigners. And, unlike the rest of the bourgeoisie, all those bickering attorneys seemed to fit right into the restless mood of Neapolitan life: they were, after all, a kind of legal *lazzaroni* and performed their part in the city's great baroque spectacle.

Aside from its ineradicable poverty, Naples has retained to this day a ceremony which has never failed to astonish the tourist: the liquefaction of San Gennaro's blood.

This patron saint of the city, whose very existence has recently been doubted, supposedly produced a biannual miracle: in May and in September a glass vial containing a little dry blood was displayed by the Cardinal-Archbishop of Naples. After the right amount of prayer from the frantic crowd, the dry blood was seen to liquefy and the faithful went into ecstasy. If the miracle failed to take place—a rare occurrence indeed—catastrophes were believed to be on the way.

Modern cynics have suggested several non-miraculous explanations of this scheduled demonstration of the saint's vigilance; in the eighteenth century everyone believed or was puzzled; but no foreigner found the ceremony inspiring. Even the Abbé de Saint-Non commented that it was "more frightening than curious to see; the women, especially, would speak directly to the saint, urge him on, and each attribute to herself the success of the miracle or the cause of its failure. . . . I have heard some, in their impatient frenzy, beg the saint in the most insulting way while others, sobbing, threw themselves flat on the ground." The whole crowd seemed to be possessed, shouting, "*Gennaro, fa dunque presto* [So hurry it up, Gennaro]!" Sometimes they berated the archbishop, especially if he happened to be new on the job, and they always looked around angrily for a scapegoat if the saint took a little too long to come through. One year the English consul, who had come to watch the ceremony, had to be quickly escorted out of the cathedral before the crowd tore him limb from limb: who could expect the miracle to take place when a heretic was present?

As for the tourists, they wavered between amusement—it was so typical—and disgust. "Religion here is mere superstition," a French traveler noted. "It is also extremely convenient: just say you are pious and you will be believed." The government, especially under Tanucci, viewed this with distaste but could do nothing; food and San Gennaro were the two subjects really close to the hearts of the *lazzaroni*.

It all seemed to be part of that ebullience so characteristic of the city. And while there were more priests and miracles than elsewhere, there were also more prostitutes of both sexes. Naples was famous for the abundance and charm of its endlessly virginal and willing young women and attractive, pliable young men who would perform with either men or women on request. Unfortunately—and that was why every whore claimed she was a virgin— syphilis was even more prevalent than the common cold in the tourist's

homeland; and since the only known cure involved taking fairly large doses
of mercury, with often unpleasant side effects, a sampling of local pleasures
could leave lasting and painful memories.

Some travelers were content just to look about them. Goethe, for one, was
enchanted with the permanent pageant of Neapolitan life. "Yesterday," he
recounts, "at the Molo, which is the noisiest corner of the city, I came across
a wooden stage on which Pulcinella was having a quarrel with a monkey.
On a balcony overhead, a pretty girl exposed her charms to all. Beside the
stage with the monkey stood a quack offering his nostrums against all ailments to a credulous crowd. . . . Today is the feast of Saint Joseph, the patron saint of all frittaruoli or pastry cooks. . . . Since, under the black, boiling oil they use for frying, there is a constant flare of flame, all fiery
torments are assigned to their mystery. Last night, they decorated their house
fronts with appropriate paintings: souls in Purgatory and Last Judgments
were blazing on all sides. In front of their doors, huge frying pans stood on
hastily erected stones. One apprentice kneaded the dough while another
shaped it into crullers and threw them into the boiling oil. A third stood beside the pan with a small skewer, picked out the crullers when they were
cooked and put them on another skewer, held by a fourth apprentice who
then offered them to the bystanders. The third and fourth apprentices were
boys wearing blond, elaborately curled wigs, which are regarded as the attributes of angels. To complete this group, there were some persons who
handed wine to the cooks, drank themselves and cried their wares. Angels,
cooks, everybody shouted at the top of their voices. They drew a great crowd
because, on this night, all pastry goods are sold at greatly reduced prices and
even a portion of the profits is given to the poor.

"One could go on forever describing similar scenes, each crazier than the
last, not to mention the infinite variety of costumes and.the hordes of people
you can see on the Toledo alone."

This scene, and many others like it, gave Naples an altogether misleading
look of prosperity. True, the climate and the fertile soil of the Vesuvian
plains made it easy to raise wheat, vegetables and fruit; the still unpolluted
sea was full of fish and shellfish; olives came in great quantities from the rest
of the kingdom; but the poor ate little more than macaroni with a little
cheese and oil, and they washed it down with lemonade. When meat was
given away by the government, the cheerful Neapolitans were suddenly
seized by a wild, frightening frenzy.

On each of four succeeding Sundays during carnival, a *cuccagna* would be
set up at the King's expense. This was a large, ornate wooden structure to
which live birds—chickens, geese, capons—were nailed by the wings, and
larger animals—pigs, calves, oxen—were tied by halters. A ring of troops
surrounded the *cuccagna,* and at a signal from the King they would allow
the impatient crowd to surge forward and frantically grab everything it

could. The Queen, who wasn't used to this kind of spectacle, and felt sick when she saw the live cattle torn to pieces, gave orders that henceforth only previously slaughtered animals would be tied to the wooden structure; but the birds were left alive and, in the crowd's desperate hands, they continued to be drawn and quartered in the same barbaric way. Curiously, travelers thought it all quite natural and watched with smiling curiosity.

At the opposite pole was a luncheon offered the Queen and court during her visit to a convent. As usual, many courses were set down before Her Majesty, fish, fowl, joints of meat, vegetables, salads, cakes—only they were all really ices, cunningly shaped and colored to look like all the dishes of a normal feast. The devotees of the *nouvelle cuisine* would have loved it, and Maria Carolina was delighted.

All this display of food, all this apparent prosperity, concealed the actual poverty of the kingdom. The national budget hovered around 40,000,000 livres,[7] and even then taxes often produced far less than had been expected. There was, of course, no industry, and outside the Naples area there wasn't much agriculture either. The chief manufactured articles were silk stockings, soap, tortoise-shell snuffboxes, marble tables and ornamental furniture; everything else, from books to carriages, had to be imported. To offset this, wheat, barley, hemp, flax, oil and wine were exported, but on a very small scale, and the economy was extremely fragile: a little bad weather always proved catastrophic. And while, in France, the government provided a framework embracing all economic activity, in Naples everything was left to chance. The one attempt at control through customs dues—which also provided the Treasury with a significant proportion of its income—was largely evaded by an army of smugglers. All in all, Naples was more like an operetta than anything else, as the French were to find out when they tried to govern it as if it were just a southern version of Piedmont.

A permanent spectacle, of course, was just what tourists liked. Neapolitans, it seemed, did everything differently, sometimes even backward. Throughout Italy and the rest of Europe the *piano nobile* was one flight up; in Naples it was on the top floor. As it happened there were two good reasons for this: it was quieter than the lower floors, and it was nearer the roof terrace. That, of course, was another one of those local eccentricities: instead of a proper roof where nobody ever went, Neapolitan palaces had flat terraces lavishly adorned with flowers and small trees. Once you got used to the idea of the garden being on the roof, it was both charming and convenient.

And then, the tourists thought, it wasn't really a proper city, since it lacked those public monuments and new houses to be found elsewhere. The Abbé de Saint-Non didn't mince words. "There isn't a single handsome palace in Naples. . . . The history of Neapolitan architecture will thus be very short since the best that can be said for it is that it doesn't exist." Not every-

---

[7] The French budget, by comparison, reached over 260,000,000 livres.

one was quite so severe; many visitors found the royal palace, designed by Domenico Fontana more than a century earlier, majestic and handsome; but, typically, while it was right by the sea, instead of having a garden sloping down to the shore it was separated from it by a small fishing harbor. Still, at least you could see the façade, while most other palaces were built along narrow, winding streets which precluded any view at all.

The other problem was that, so close to Pompeii, there was virtually no neo-classical architecture—and the baroque was going out of favor. Even Vanvitelli, whose vocabulary was essentially classical, was outmoded. The buildings he had designed earlier were only now being finished—Caserta, the size of which often impressed visitors, who deplored its immense, bland façade, and the Chiesa dell'Annunziata, which deserved better. Its interior, especially, was immensely seductive. "In a very soft white and grey harmony, the nave, from which little square chapels open, is adorned with fluted Corinthian columns between which ravishing rococo sculpture has been placed. The distribution of the light is exquisite, but the marvel is the cupola with its very high drum in which eight windows open; these are separated by groups of columns surmounted by sculpted figures bearing garlands."

Naples, as visitors often pointed out, couldn't boast much in the way of artists either: they were all German. The Hackert brothers produced mostly half-competent views while Tischbein painted stiff, porcelain-like portraits. Angelica Kauffmann, the Vigée-Lebrun of the North, came through Naples and stayed long enough to produce a highly flattering portrait of the royal family. Anton Raphael Mengs came to visit Pompeii and the Portici Museum; his visit convinced him of the beauty of the cold classical figures, apparently made of soap and clumsily arranged in the dullest compositions, with which he was to regale his compatriots. Still, mediocre as he was, Goethe thought the world of him.

There were two native art forms, however, which retain all their charm today: Naples porcelain and the *presepii*. Charles III had married a princess of Saxony who brought porcelain makers to Naples in her train; together, they had founded a porcelain factory at Capodimonte, then, selfishly, taken it to Spain when they moved on. Perhaps because he was miffed, Ferdinand started a new porcelain factory, right in the city this time. Using neo-classical forms, it was decorated with views of the city and bay, as well as genre scenes, and was best known for its large, dramatic bisque figure groups.

The *presepii* were elaborate Nativity displays. They could be as high as ten or twelve feet, or as small as two or three; starting as a purely popular form of display, they quickly became fashionable among the upper classes as well, so that the Christ child and his attendants were often transmuted from carved wood to gold lace and brocade-swathed porcelain. There might be as few as half a dozen figures—the child, Mary, Joseph, the Magi and the animals—or as many as a hundred, but even the simplest *presepio* was full of care, imagination and charm.

There was one major art form which dazzled everyone: the Opera. For a while the most famous Neapolitan composer was undoubtedly Niccolò Piccinni: his battle with Gluck had set Paris by the ears. To a modern ear, there can be no doubt about the relative merit of the two composers. Piccinni wrote pretty arias, as pleasing as they are devoid of feeling; Gluck's music expresses deep and direct emotion as it frees itself from antiquated forms. But it was just that light, tuneful aspect of Neapolitan music which assured its supremacy in its chosen field, the *opera buffa*. It was a genre which firmly rejected the serious, a kind of light, sentimental comedy put to music, and there Piccinni was unbeatable as were his two successors. Giovanni Paisiello quickly gained European fame for his output—he could write several operas a year—his naïveté and his charm. You could listen to his music and be amused and pleased; it was wonderful entertainment. As for Domenico Cimarosa, he headed straight for the most tremendous success in Naples and the rest of Europe. He traveled with his music, composing and conducting in just about every country west of the Niemen, and, after an initial success in 1772, scored a triumph at the age of twenty-five (in 1779) with his *L'Italiana in Londra*. After that he was endlessly successful, writing his masterpiece, *Il Matrimonio Segreto*, in 1792, and going on to be the apple of Napoleon's eye.

All the tourists agreed that music was one of the great attractions of Naples, and that the standard of musicianship for both instrumentalists and singers was exceptionally high. So they flocked to the opera, listened far more carefully than the local patrons and helped spread the fame of Neapolitan music all over Europe, just as they made the Bay of Naples a byword for scenic beauty. But more than music, or the bay, or the court, or even raging (with luck) Vesuvius, there was one attraction no tourist could miss: a visit to Herculaneum and Pompeii.

Ancient Rome was a good deal closer to people of culture in the eighteenth century than it is to us. All schools taught Latin, not just as a dead language but as one that still lived in medicine, the Church, law and poetry. Young boys saw their first verse when they read Virgil, learned about war in Caesar and decadence in Suetonius. They were expected to write Latin verse fluently and elegantly. What had happened to the might of Rome was still a subject of lively interest, soon to be rekindled by Gibbon's masterpiece. Ever since the Renaissance, Roman art had been sought, prized, collected; so of course when Herculaneum and Pompeii were dug up the impact was enormous.

The two cities were not just archaeological finds, either: there was something awesome and sensational about the sudden way they had been buried by the mud and ash of Vesuvius and, when they were dug up, they gave a horrifying picture of an entire population desperately fleeing: the cinder-coated figures of men, women and children, running, climbing, dying were far more dramatic than a hundred modern disaster movies. And, besides the

13. The Love Merchant. *This Pompeian fresco, here reproduced by the Abbé de Saint-Non, was much admired and copied. Blending charm and simplicity, it reappears as one of Vien's best efforts. (See Chapter Seven.)*

titillation of watching a seventeen-hundred-year-old disaster frozen by time, the visitor had the unique opportunity of revisiting a Roman city just as it had been when Virgil was writing.

"I feel quite amazed to be walking from house to house, from temple to temple, from street to street in a city built seventeen-hundred years ago and lived in by Romans," Dupati commented, and all the travelers felt the same. Of course, it was not Rome itself, and it took them awhile to adjust. "Pompeii surprises everyone by its compactness and its smallness of scale. The streets are narrow, though straight and provided with pavements, the houses small and windowless. . . . Their rooms, passages and arcades are gaily painted. The walls have plain surfaces with richly detailed frescoes painted on them . . . surrounded by amusing arabesques in admirable taste: from one, enchanting figures of children and nymphs evolve, in another, wild and tame animals emerge out of luxuriant floral wreaths. . . . [The city] bears witness to an artistic instinct and a love of art shared by a whole people," Goethe wrote after his first visit, and everyone agreed. The frescoes were beautiful and fascinating, so much so that Vien did not hesitate to copy them line for line (see illustration 13). The many objects—candelabra, vases, chairs, tables, jewelry—were, paradoxically, new, desirable, seductive. Even though they were all supposed to go straight into the royal museum at Portici, a number of these objects soon emerged in private collections.

The impact of this resurrection of Roman interiors was enormous. Pompeii and Herculaneum didn't attract only ordinary sightseers: English dukes, German writers, and all the artists in Europe made a beeline for them, and brought back book after book of sketches. When David wanted some antique chairs for a painting, all he had to do was to pass his drawings on to Jacob, who promptly made him a set of authentic Roman furniture. Of course designers hadn't waited for David, and as early as 1770 we find replicas of Roman objects all over Europe. The rococo, in any event, had run its course, especially in France, by the late sixties, and the latent classicism of the French temperament would have surfaced sooner or later—it had, in fact, always been present; but the form taken by the classical revival was directly shaped by the finds in southern Italy. Marie Antoinette, always aware of current trends, had her library in Versailles done up in the Pompeian style and was surrounded by antique-looking tables and objects. By 1792, thanks in part to Jacques-Louis David's influence, the Roman revival was completely dominant; furniture, architecture, clothes (women's, at least), all were taken from the antique; and when General Bonaparte came to power, it was as First Consul, a title borrowed directly from ancient Rome.

The museum, which occupied a wing of the royal palace at Portici, right over the site of Herculaneum, contained all the objects gathered (and not stolen) by the diggers, and was part of the visit; if visitors yearned for more modern paintings, they went to another palace just outside the city, Capodimonte, where they could see works by Titian, Guido, Correggio and

14. Roman table, chairs and candelabra *found in Herculaneum. These objects, among many such reproduced by the Abbé de Saint-Non, provoked immediate and widespread admiration; they influenced contemporary design everywhere and reappeared almost unchanged as part of the Empire style (1795–1815).*

many other Renaissance painters, since Charles III had inherited the famous Farnese collection, as well as gold and copper medals, cameos and rare books. Surprisingly, though, the enchanting porcelain room made in the Chinese-rococo style right at Capodimonte had been moved to Portici. It has now been restored to its original location and is well worth seeing. Finally, everyone made a pilgrimage to Virgil's tomb, high on a hill astride the city. It was a strong man—or woman—who could resist committing his emotions to paper in the form of a Virgilian elegy when he got back to town.

There was more antique beauty in Naples than was to be found in museums and buried cities, however. It lived again, everybody agreed, in every feature and every movement of that charming Mrs. Harte, old Sir William Hamilton's companion.

Sir William, the English consul, was one of those Englishmen who establish themselves abroad, stay there, and become one of the sights themselves. A born courtier, he managed to please and amuse both Ferdinand and Maria Carolina, and was thus always the best informed of foreign envoys; it also didn't hurt that the Prime Minister, Sir John Acton, was a compatriot. But

Sir William was far more than an efficient ambassador: he was also the chief guide, the chief party giver, almost the chief attraction of the city.

His parties were famous. "There is an assembly once a week at the house of the British Minister; no assembly in Naples is more numerous or brilliant than this . . . [in part because of the] high favor in which he stands with the sovereigns. Sir William's house is open to strangers of every country who come to Naples properly recommended, as well as the English; he has a private concert almost every evening; Lady Hamilton[8] understands music perfectly and performs in such a manner as to command the admiration of even the Neapolitans."

Sir William had also been up to the crater of Vesuvius more times than anybody could remember; indeed, no illustrious visitor would have considered going up without him. He knew and understood Pompeii and Herculaneum better than anyone else and could explain them in the most illuminating way. Of course, he collected himself, and Goethe was invited to see the collection. "Sir William Hamilton and his Fair One continue to be very friendly," the great writer noted. "I dined at their house and, in the evening, Miss Harte gave a demonstration of her musical and melic talents. . . . Sir William showed us his secret treasure vault, which was crammed with works of art and junk, all in the greatest confusion. Oddments from every period, busts, torsos, bronzes, decorative implements of all kinds made of Sicilian agate, carvings, paintings and chance bargains of every kind lay about all higgledy-piggledy; there was even a small chapel. Out of curiosity, I lifted the lid of a long case which lay on the floor and in it were two magnificent candelabra"—which, it quickly became evident, Sir William had illegally bought from one of the workers digging at Pompeii.

Still, other ministers have had interesting collections and hospitable houses. Sir William could boast of a unique treasure: the beautiful Emma Harte. This spectacular-looking young woman had, after a rather checkered career in England, been bought by the aging Sir William from his nephew and brought to Naples; even before she gained European fame, as Lady Hamilton, for her affairs with the Queen of Naples and Lord Nelson, she was a local star because of her great beauty, her dazzling if somewhat plump figure, and her supposedly classical dances and poses in tableaux vivants. She must, in fact, have been something like our modern sex goddesses, a Jean Harlow or a Marilyn Monroe, since everyone was automatically seduced, and no one became aware of her extreme stupidity and lack of education. We can gauge the effectiveness of her appeal when we read what Goethe, not usually a man to disregard intellect, wrote about her: "The old knight has had a Greek costume made for her, which becomes her extremely. Dressed in this, letting her hair loose, and taking a couple of shawls, she exhibits every variety of posture, expression and look, so that, at last, the spec-

[8] Sir William had married Mrs. Harte in 1791; this was written two years later.

tator almost fancies it is a dream. One beholds there in perfection, in movement, in ravishing variety, all that the greatest artists have rejoiced at being
able to produce. Standing, kneeling, sitting, lying down, grave or sad,
playful, exulting, repentant, menacing, wanton, anxious, all mental states follow rapidly after one another. With wonderful taste, she suits the folding of
her veil to each expression, and, with the same handkerchief, makes every
kind of headdress." Soon, no visit to Naples was complete if you hadn't seen
Emma perform.

—◦◖ ◗◦—

There was no reason, it seemed, why it shouldn't all go on forever. Under
its bumbling, ineffective but amiable government the Kingdom of the Two
Sicilies would continue to be the great European resort, the obligatory aim
for the English doing the grand tour, and for all the other travelers who
liked a mixture of exoticism and ancient Rome. It was safe, too—not large
enough, or powerful enough, to be a significant element in European politics, and therefore unlikely to be involved in war: it would be, in fact, the
Monte Carlo of the eighteenth century.

Like all other contemporary predictions of the future, however, this one
was quickly invalidated by the French Revolution. By the turn of the century a French army under General Championnet was occupying Naples;
soon Napoleon made it into another Bonaparte fief and put his sister
Caroline on the throne while Ferdinand and Maria Carolina stayed in Sicily
under the protection of the British navy. When, in 1815, Ferdinand returned to his mainland possessions, he found a changed world. Naples' day
as the great European tourist paradise had lasted a bare thirty years, but in
that time it offered a wonderful illustration of the eighteenth century—on a
tiny scale, and with a frivolousness spectacular even by the standards of the
age.

Caserta was no Versailles, Naples was no Paris, but, in its small, rather
backward way, the Two Sicilies embodied much that was attractive and amiable in the century. It seems somehow exemplary that it was ruled by
members of Europe's two grandest dynasties, the Bourbons and the Habs-
burgs; its splendid court, its quarrelsome but easygoing people, its spectacular
landscapes, all united to make it an especially attractive, if unreal, part of a
world still quite unaware of its impending death. Everyone thought that,
under its golden sun, the *opera buffa* would go on forever, but Naples lived
and died with the Ancien Régime. And already in the eighties there was a
perceptible shift. A few avant-garde tourists began looking for farther horizons; true, most of those who reached them had a good reason to go; but
when they returned, it was evident to all that interest and the future lay to
the west, not the south, in the newly United States.

III

AMERICA

Chapter Thirteen

ROUSSEAU'S AMERICA

It seemed almost too good to be true, and yet there it was, plainly visible: a new country, held together and governed under the terms of a freely accepted social contract. Nor was that all. Its people were good, virtuous, hardworking, tolerant and welcoming. There was no crime, no corruption, no overweening court or aristocracy. On this new continent, still largely unexplored, still mostly uninhabited, lived the men of Rousseau's dreams—not quite good savages, perhaps, but at any rate good primitives. The many French who came to fight the war had expected adventure; they found political and social revelation.

Bored young aristocrats, in the late seventies and early eighties, had many good reasons for going to America: nothing much was happening in Europe and it was one way of finding excitement; then, too, many people still felt the humiliation of 1763: here was finally a chance of getting back at the English. If you had a military career, as most of the volunteers from La Fayette on down actually did, it was a handy way of deserving advancement, which might otherwise not come for years; if you just liked exotic journeys, strange, unexplored lands and their peculiar customs, this was the perfect time to go and have a look. And by 1779 it was also the fashion: when you returned to Paris, after spending six months or a year in America, you could be sure of a general welcome. As La Fayette was later to confess, women who wouldn't have looked twice at you before now competed to become your mistresses. And so they went, braving the forty days' crossing, with its often dreadful weather, the discomfort and the expense.

The later in the war they came, the easier it was for them. The French gradually became popular, so few of them had to face the same difficulties as La Fayette on his first trip. Still, the military situation being what it was, they tended to arrive in small, out-of-the-way places—most often the still unglamorous Newport. And liberty or no, it could be rough.

"You know the French, my dear father, and the people of the court well enough to realize the despair felt by young men of that class who find themselves forced to spend the winter quietly in Newport, far from their mistresses and the pleasures of Paris; no suppers, no plays, no balls, they are quite desperate and can only be consoled by being ordered to march against the enemy," Count Axel Fersen, that handsome Swede who was to catch Marie Antoinette's fancy, commented in a letter home. And you could see his point. Newport, in 1780, was barely more than a village, and its women were infinitely virtuous.

There was, in fact, every reason for the French to dislike what they found. They went from the most sophisticated country in the known world to a primitive wilderness. They who hated to leave Paris and Versailles now wintered three thousand miles away from their pomp and glitter. There were no palaces and no parks, no fashionable clothes, no fashion at all, in fact. People walked or rode; there were practically no carriages. Food, though abundant, was cooked very plainly. There was no opera, no theater, no music, no elegant promenades, no salons. Women, chaste until they married, remained faithful to their husbands. And then, most of the French officers belonged to noble and powerful families, and here was a country in which all men were equal. It really shouldn't do.

And yet it did. They came, they observed, they raved. They were so used to sophistication that they delighted in simplicity; but, more important, they had read Jean-Jacques Rousseau: they knew all about men being good, kind and virtuous as long as they weren't corrupted by civilization. Here at last was a state of nature. They were young, after all, and open to new experiences, so they looked, and they saw the future.

This French view of America was based more on contrast than reality, more on manners than substance. The very presence of a French army and Spanish subsidies was proof of the political leaders' great sophistication, and the new Constitution, soon to be written, attests to anything but a state of nature. Again, the establishment of religious tolerance, a goal still unreached in Europe, hinted at the existence of a consensus society, something not to be found in a primitive environment. The American population, between 1770 and 1790, was still mostly Anglo-Saxon; its ancestors may have fled England, but they adapted its sophisticated political traditions to a new environment. In a real sense, the emigrants merely accelerated an existing process and created in America the England of the future.

The smart young men who came in 1780, however, saw what they ex-

15. Clipping the Admiral's Wings (*1778*). *This contemporary caricature shows an English admiral adorned with a vulture's claws and wings. The American Congress clips his talons while a Frenchman and a Spaniard cut off his wings. On the right, a Dutchman reopens trade while, far left, a Frenchman makes off with bales of tobacco. The point of view is clear: the end of the English domination means, first and foremost, freedom of trade for France, Spain and Holland—the other three maritime powers.*

pected to see. Rousseau had prepared them for societies simpler than their own and, sure enough, there it was, a funny new country which embodied all the principles expounded in the *Discours sur l'inégalité, Émile, La Nouvelle Héloïse* and *Du contrat social.* And then there was liberty. Anyone with any feeling for fashion knew liberty was wonderful in every way; everybody, from Rousseau and the *encyclopédistes* to Mademoiselle Bertin[1] and the Necker salon said so. Of course you couldn't have it at home, since the King was an absolute monarch, but here was a new country, a new edition of the early Roman Republic,[2] where liberty could flourish unimpaired. Even La Fayette, regarded as a nitwit back home, could see that it was won-

[1] Her *pouf à la liberté* was a momentous creation.
[2] Comparing George Washington to Cincinnatus, for instance, soon became obligatory.

derful; and, if fighting for the cause of liberty helped make you the man of the hour when you returned home, well, that was just an added benefit.

The very simplicity of the Americans' life style was an extra attraction. It would never have occurred to young Count Fersen, for instance, to live simply himself. Like all the other French officers, he was accompanied by several servants and a great deal of luggage; similarly, while extolling the republican virtues of homespun and cotton stockings, he never considered giving up lace, powder or gold braid. Discovering America, in fact, was very much like looking at Greuze's paintings: you loved it, you were touched, you might even shed a few tears, but you would hardly move in with those deserving peasants.

The extraordinary thing is that, in spite of these limitations, the French proved remarkably accurate observers. There was indeed a great deal to be said for the way the Americans conducted their lives; and while the picture may be a little rosy at first, it is not because the positives were exaggerated; simply, the negatives had a way of vanishing. Even this, however, soon stopped being true. By the late eighties, observers like Brissot, the future French revolutionary leader, reported on corruption in state legislatures in a thoroughly modern way.

—◆{ }◆—

Newport was the first sight of the new continent for many of those young men: it provided a convenient and safe harbor for the French fleet which had brought them across; and it was a fitting introduction, since America was still a country of small towns and open spaces.

It looked very good. "We have seen the most beautiful country in the world," Fersen reported admiringly, "well farmed, full of charming landscapes and comfortable inhabitants, but all without pomp and luxury; they are satisfied with the bare necessities which, in other countries, are reserved strictly for the lower classes; their dress is simple but good and their customs have not yet been spoiled by European luxury." This, interestingly, is not unlike contemporary descriptions of the way English farmers lived; another vignette, left to us by Claude Blanchard, confirms this aspect of the United States as a better England. In Newport, he tells us, "I chanced to enter a school. The master seemed to me a very worthy man; he was teaching some children of both sexes; all were neatly clad; the room in which the school was kept was also very clean. I saw the writing of these children, it appeared to me to be handsome, among others that of a young girl of nine or ten years old, very pretty and very modest and such as I would like my own daughter to be when she is as old; she was called Abigail Earl as I perceived upon her copy-book where her name was written. I wrote it myself, adding to it, 'very pretty.' . . . The master had the tone of a father of the family." We could be reading Rousseau—or Dickens.

And Fersen went even further: he actually extolled the simplicity of the social setup. "There is little society in Newport; there are six or seven houses where people are invited; I only frequent two of these where I go in the evenings to relax and speak English. In one of these houses, at Mrs. Hunter's, there is a pretty, cheerful, amiable eighteen-year-old girl who is also a very good musician. I go there every night and like her a great deal, but without its meaning anything."

That in itself was as clear a proof as you could want that Fersen had reached the good society Rousseau yearned for. In France, upper-class young girls left the convent only to be married, flirtations were not innocent, and no sensible parent would have allowed his daughter any real freedom. Here, on the contrary, girls came and went as they pleased; they saw young men quite alone; and yet they remained chaste until their wedding night. Indeed, it seemed that trust was general: doors were left unlocked, daughters and wives unguarded. Even the chests containing the household's most precious objects were quite devoid of lock and key, and you could travel along the loneliest roads without fear of being robbed.

This however, may have been a sign less of a righteous society than a consequence of life in very small social units: you are hardly likely to steal from a neighbor, since your theft will quickly become evident; and, similarly, if you seduced an eighteen-year-old girl, the whole village was likely to find out pretty fast, and to retaliate. Of course, religion also had something to do with it: people still dreaded sin and behaved accordingly. This might well have annoyed the French. If you're used to easy women, it can be unpleasant and frustrating to come up against universal virtue; but, much as the young officers might miss their mistresses, one wonders whether it wasn't actually restful not to have to affirm one's ability to please woman after woman: it was surcease from the usual competition.

The general morality also implied that people mostly told the truth: this, too, came as immense relief after the deceit and intrigues of Versailles. "The lack of virtue is so foreign to the Americans that relationships with unmarried girls are without consequence and that freedom itself assumes a tone of modesty," the marquis de Chastellux commented, and the vicomte de Ségur, the son of that Minister for War whose appointment was discussed earlier (see Chapter Two), raved about this. The United States, he wrote, is "a country where people are sincere and free. Private interests are all subsumed in the general interest; people live for themselves; they dress according to convenience and not fashion. . . . The laws protect your will against all others. Nothing forces you to be false, or cringing or flattering. . . . The only reign there is is that of a small number of just laws which apply equally to all. . . . Unmarried girls are mildly coquettish so as to find husbands, married women are virtuous so as to keep theirs, and the disorder called galanterie which entertains us so much in Paris here revolts people under its name of adultery." And the best part of all this was that young Monsieur de

Ségur felt quite free to discard American habits as soon as he left the continent: virtue is definitely easier if practiced only—and briefly—on foreign shores.

There is nothing quite like having the best of both worlds: the French came to America, admired, and went home to preach what they had practiced only for a few months. Still, there is no doubt that when the French aristocracy in a body renounced all its feudal privileges on August 4, 1789, it was in large part because it had seen equality at work in the United States: it was possible, it was practicable, it was right.

It would be difficult to overestimate the importance of America's contribution in this respect. Equality existed nowhere in Europe, not even in Switzerland where an entrenched upper class oppressed the remainder of the population. Altogether, the French could not get over it: everyone in America was absolutely the same. There were no lords, no bishops, no figures of hereditary authority. One man was as good as another—and, most amazing, many women were as good as their men.

Some of the sharper observers noticed that money made a difference; while this may have been a little less true during and right after the war, it was quite obvious by 1790. Talleyrand, who had no great sympathy for either equality or the United States but took refuge there for a year during the French Revolution, tells the story of a farmer whom he, Talleyrand, had asked whether he would not like to go to Philadelphia and meet Washington. After a little thought the farmer answered that, if he went to Philadelphia, he would much rather meet Mr. Bingham; and when Talleyrand asked who Mr. Bingham was, the farmer answered in a matter-of-fact way that he was the richest man in the city.

"I have found all through America," Talleyrand goes on, "this same admiration for money, and it was often expressed in just as vulgar a way. Luxury has come there too quickly. When man's basic needs are barely being met, luxury shocks. I remember seeing, in Mr. Robert Morris' parlor, the locally made hat of the master of the house resting on an elegant porcelain table. . . . It was such that a European peasant would have scarcely consented to wear it." There is little doubt that respect for money has always been a characteristic trait in America; but in 1796, when Talleyrand was staying here, there were still very few rich men; in 1780 there cannot have been more than fifty between Maine and Virginia. And, of course, wealth carried no feudal rights.

All over Europe the nobility had special rights; even in England a peer could be judged only by the House of Lords, and his property, if entailed, was free from seizure. In America, to everyone's amazement, the laws applied to everyone equally—even the rich. And titles made no difference.

Of course there were no titles of nobility; but there were military titles which their holders greatly prized. Yet, though a colonel, a captain or a major would have been most offended if addressed as plain "Mr.," his (new) exalted position in no way prevented him from carrying out his business as usual. It could be quite startling for European visitors, stopping at an inn, to hear the innkeeper called Colonel Smith; he really had been a colonel in the American army but obviously did not think of it as a career—hardly anyone did—and didn't consider running an inn beneath him because he had once commanded soldiers. Work, in fact, was never deprecated: only idleness was shameful. It was the very reverse of the French viewpoint.

Our colonel had good reason to be proud: his inn was most likely an excellent one. While American roads were notoriously bad, the inns more than made up for the discomforts of travel. They were clean, new, in good repair; the rooms had good beds with fresh sheets and no vermin; the food was plain but good; and the prices were reasonable: you generally paid two shillings for bed and board.[3] In fact travel itself, which was usually expensive in Europe, here turned out to be quite reasonable. Thus, if you took a stagecoach from Boston to New York, you had to plan on spending four days traveling. You left, in a well-suspended coach, at four in the morning and paid 64 shillings (about 192 of our dollars). You had to add another 8 shillings for four nights at the various inns and 8 to 10 shillings for the ferries—they were extra.

If, from New York, you went on to Philadelphia, it would set you back a further 26 shillings, plus 8 shillings for the ferries. South (and west) of Philadelphia scheduled service became extremely rare. There were a few other small cities—Richmond, Virginia, was one—but the traffic dwindled greatly.

Most of the road between Boston and Philadelphia went through large areas of still unsettled country. As late as 1788, one third of the state of Massachusetts was untouched wilderness. Connecticut, a traveler wrote, was the paradise of the United States; with its charming houses and abundance of every kind of supplies, it seemed like an unending town all the way to the New York border, and was obviously the first manifestation of our megalopolis.

In other ways, too, enduring patterns were beginning to appear. A village store, for instance, was generally established in a building all its own (in Europe it occupied the ground floor of the owner's house) and was well kept and attractive. In many places the general store, stocked with everything from molasses to hoes, had come into being, much to the wonder of passing Europeans. People traveled often, and as if it were the most normal activity in the world. It was surprising to see all kinds of men riding from one town to another on the flimsiest of pretexts, but altogether flabbergasting when it was a woman—a proper, virtuous, middle-class woman—riding alone and fearless.

This, too, was a shock to the French. Virtuous women may have been scarce in Paris, but they were theoretically conceivable. The idea of women

3 The monetary system in the thirteen states was complex enough to confuse a computer. The value of any given sign, shilling or dollar, varied from state to state. In this case, a shilling is equal to one French livre, or three 1980 dollars.

of business was quite another thing. And yet in the seventies and eighties (truer, perhaps, than would be the case a hundred and fifty years later) American women enjoyed the same freedoms as men and assumed the same responsibilities. On Nantucket, where the men were at sea for weeks at a time, it was the women who took care of business, and they continued to do so even when their husbands returned. Many shops all over the United States were kept by women; and while not every statesman's wife had the wit, intelligence and authority of an Abigail Adams, many women had great political influence. Victorian men may have thought of their wives and mothers as fragile, dumb and inconsequential creatures; the men who gained independence for their country made no such mistake.

The status of American women surprised the French, who were used to feminine power of a very different sort. Still more astonishing was the presence everywhere of an exotic sect whose principles were as stern as they were moral, whose dress set them apart, who abhorred violence yet managed to prosper in an unsettled world: the Brethren, also called, derisively at first, the Quakers.

Not every traveler liked them: people who unite an aggressive simplicity of life and high-sounding principles to a successful taste for making money can, of course, end up looking like hypocrites. That was Chastellux' view. "They are sparing of blood, it is true, especially their own; but they cheat both parties out of their money, with a complete lack of shame and without restraint. It is a generally accepted opinion in trade that you have to be careful of them, and that opinion is sound."

The Quakers obviously presented a challenge by their very being. The sect, which settled mostly in Pennsylvania, had at first been severely persecuted; now that, finally, tolerance prevailed, they had spread and were to be found all over the Eastern seacoast. They could be very disconcerting to a European visitor, if only because of their habit of using the second person singular—thee, thou—which, in France, was only applied, and then sparingly, to one's nearest and dearest. That they practiced the simplicity they preached, however, was undeniable. St. John de Crèvecoeur, a Frenchman who settled in America well before the war, was fascinated by them. "The manners of the *Friends* are entirely founded on that simplicity which is their boast and their most distinguished characteristic," he wrote, "and those manners have acquired the authority of laws. Here they are strongly attached to plainness of dress as well as of language. . . . They are so tenacious of their ancient habits of industry and frugality that if any one of them were to be seen with a long coat made of English cloth on any other than the *first day* (Sunday), he would be greatly ridiculed and censored; he would be looked upon as a careless spendthrift whom it would be unsafe to trust, and in vain to relieve. A few years ago, two single-horse chairs were imported from Boston, to the great offense of these prudent citizens; nothing appeared to them more culpable than the use of such gaudy, painted vehicles, in contempt of the more useful and more simple single-horse carts of their fathers. This piece of extravagant and unknown luxury almost caused a schism and set every tongue a-going. . . . One of the possessors of these profane chairs, filled with repentance, wisely sent it back."

There is, obviously, much to be said for a sect so intent on evangelical simplicity and so averse to bloodshed; the very people who would not have considered living this way for a second could see it. The vicomte de Ségur, whose way of life represented everything the Friends hated, commented that "this sect . . . lives on as the monument of the only society which ever, perhaps, has preached and practiced, without any admixture or prejudice, the morals of the Evangels and Christian charity in all their purity and simplicity. The very need to defend themselves could not force them to shed blood, and that of preserving their fortune could not force them to take the name of God in an oath."

That the Quakers prospered was obvious. Many of the richest merchants and bankers belonged to the Friends, as did some of the biggest farmers, whose clean and simple establishments nonetheless admitted of substantial wealth. Evangelical simplicity is one thing, and admirable if that's what you like; but wasn't there a strange contradiction between so much apparent plainness and the real and efficacious greed that went with it? Is it really morally better to make a lot of money and hoard it than to make a lot of money and spend it? The point at least bears discussion.

In their very simplicity, the Quakers brought a picturesque if sober element to the American scene. The men all wore round hats, most often white, and a coat of fine, though simple, cloth, usually black or dark gray; and their American-made stockings were of cotton or wool according to the season, with the winter change-over always coming on September 15, quite regardless of the weather. They wore their hair straight, free of curl or powder, and eschewed lace and silver shoe buckles: they could hardly help standing out in a crowd. Their wives, though, were apparently in closer touch with the century and were sometimes seen sporting such abominations as silk hats or fans.

All this plainness did not extend to food. The Friends ate quite as well as anyone else with the means to do so; they simply replaced wines and liquor with porter or hard cider. But to the Europeans the most extraordinary Quaker custom was that of the *meeting*. These gatherings of the sect took place every Sunday, when they were open to all, monthly and every three months for members in good standing; then there was a yearly assembly which ruled supreme and set policy, and the conditions of membership for the rest of the year. It was hard enough for the Europeans to understand a church without bishops; a church without priests or ministers was well-nigh incomprehensible.

Even the most austere of Protestant sects had a proper, if plain, church and altar. The Friends came together in large, square meetinghouses where

only a slightly higher bench marked the placement of the preachers who, in
every other respect, were simply members of the congregation: there was no
clergy of any kind. After a deep silence, which lasted as long as an hour,
preachers would hold forth in slow, toneless voices, breaking their speech
with long periods in which they waited for further inspiration. After a while
all joined in prayer, the preacher kneeling and the men standing up. It all
seemed both grim and strange.

The French, of course, instantly related to this very oddness: to them, it
was all just another exotic form of behavior in this strange land where you
might expect almost anything; when confronted directly with it, they responded in a good-natured spirit. The vicomte de Ségur, for instance, ran
into a Quaker's daughter, one Polly Leighton, in Newport; his account of
the encounter is especially entertaining, mixing, as it does, scrupulous report-
ing with a style more appropriate to a contemporary love novel than to the
subject.

"Her dress was as white as her skin; the muslin of her ample shawl, the
envious baptist scarf which scarcely allowed me to guess at her fair hair, the
simple dress of a pious virgin, all seemed to be trying in vain to conceal the
slenderest waist and to veil the most seductive attractions.

"Her eyes, like twin mirrors, seemed to reflect the sweetness of a pure and
tender soul. She greeted us with a trusting naïveté which enchanted me, and
the use of 'thou' which her affiliation caused her to use gave our new acquaintance the feel of an old friendship.

"During our conversations, she always surprised me by the virginal candor
of her questions.

"'Hast thou not in Europe,' she asked me, 'either wife or children since
thou leavest thy country to come so far and practice the wicked profession of
a warrior?'

"'But it is in your own interest,' I answered.

"'The English,' she continued, 'they have not done thee any harm, and
what carest thou about our freedom? It is wrong to interfere in other people's
business, unless it be to reconcile them and prevent them from shedding
blood.'

"'But,' I answered, 'my King has ordered me to bear his arms against your
enemies and his.'

"'Well,' she said, 'thy King orders thee to do an unjust, inhuman thing
which goes against God's orders. Thou must obey thy God and disobey thy
King. I am quite sure that thy wife, if she be a good woman, would agree
with me.'" One can sense Ségur's delight: he had come across Rousseau's
good savage, and she was ravishing, too.

Life in America answered to Jean-Jacques's description of the primitive
state in other ways as well. Every day men were claiming and enclosing new,
virgin land. Homesteaders were at work all over the Eastern states. The
United States was still a country of farmers, and even the immigrants

couldn't wait to get out of the cities. Of course they needed a little capital, since in most places you actually had to buy the land you were settling; but "little" is the key word here. In Vermont you could buy a hundred acres for $20 (100 livres); at three of our dollars an acre, it was not too hard to become a landowner. In the more settled states, Massachusetts, Connecticut, Pennsylvania, you might have to go all the way up to a dollar an acre ($15 of 1980); this was only if you were settling new land. A rich man who fancied a country house near Philadelphia would have to pay up to $42 (210 livres) an acre; at that price, even President Washington was unable to buy himself the farm he wanted for relaxation.

Once you had acquired your land with a partial down payment, you still needed food; so you took along a milch cow, a pregnant sow and two of the cheapest horses you could find to pull your wagon in which you had stowed away a good provision of flour and cider, along with some tools. Altogether, it might set you back some four to five hundred livres. Assuming you had bought yourself fifty acres, your total investment came to some 750 livres— not a huge sum—part of which could be paid in installments.

As for the land itself, it was exactly the way nature had made it. So if you were homesteading you started out by chopping down a few trees; then, in the clearing, you put up a one-room turf house with the help of your neighbors: it was a universal practice for all the families of the area to come and assist in building a settler's house.

It wasn't a very difficult process: large slabs were cut out of the turf and put together to form walls—often without windows—and a roof, which was supported by rough crossbeams hewn out of the newly felled trees. The chimney was a hole in the roof, the bathroom a pail of water, the kitchen a fire built on two stones. And there, in the dirt and discomfort, the settlers spent the first year.

As soon as the house was up, the rest of the land had to be cleared and the trees used for fences; then the crops must be sown early enough to have a harvest the following summer. By the time a year had passed you would have several pigs, grain and vegetables and you could start paying off your debt. Within two or three years the sod house would come down or be used for a barn, to be replaced by a proper wood home with at least two rooms and often more. Prosperity was on the way.

That farming paid, and paid well, even without price supports, is undeniable. America seemed to all the visitors a country without poverty. It was always possible to find land and grow food; anyone could earn a living, so there was a conspicuous absence of mendicancy. A happy norm prevailed, with almost everyone comfortable, though hard-working, and very few people at either end of the economic scale.

We owe the best description of this happy state once again to a Frenchman, the naturalized Pennsylvanian St. John de Crèvecoeur, whose book, *Letters from an American Farmer,* describes a new-found paradise and actually waxes lyrical in its descriptions of the American farm. "Here," he says, "everything is modern, peaceful and benign. . . . Our religion does not oppress the cultivators: we are strangers to those feudal institutions which have enslaved so many. Here nature opens her broad lap to receive the perpetual accession of newcomers and to supply them with food. . . . Here he might contemplate the very beginning and outline of society, which can be traced nowhere now but in this part of the world. . . . Misguided religion, tyranny and absurd laws everywhere depossess and afflict mankind. Here we have in some measure regained the ancient dignity of our species; our laws are simple and just, we are a race of cultivators, our cultivation is unrestrained and therefore everything is prosperous and flourishing.

"Here are no aristocratical families, no courts, no kings, no bishops, no ecclesiastical dominion, no invisible power giving to a few a very visible one; no great manufacturer employing thousands, no great refinement of luxury. The rich and the poor are not so far removed from each other as they are in Europe. . . . We are a people of cultivators, scattered over an immense territory, communicating with each other by means of good roads and navigable rivers, united by the silken bands of mild government, all respecting the laws without dreading their power, because they are equitable. We are animated with the spirit of an industry which is unfettered and unrestrained because each person works for himself. . . . A pleasing uniformity of decent competence appears throughout our habitations. . . . We have no princes for whom we starve, toil or bleed: we are the most perfect society now existing in the world. Here man is free as he ought to be."

Of course Crèvecoeur was beating his own drum. His good roads and navigable rivers were more often rutted tracks and rapids; as for being "the most perfect society existing in the world," the breadth of that claim is such as to be self-defeating; yet it was partly true. The feeling that America represents the *ne plus ultra* of human affairs may sound a little strange at this early date, but it is a feeling that has continued to manifest itself from that day to this. The "silken bands of mild government" have given way to "the world's best Constitution"; the feeling is still very much the same; here, it is, typically, expressed by a successful immigrant. Crèvecoeur has a curious way of embodying, at its very beginning, an enduring American myth; it sometimes seems to endow him with prophetic powers. A hundred years at least before the melting pot became a cliché he wrote that "here individuals of all nations are melted into a new race of men whose labours and posterity will one day cause great changes in the world." He was quite alone, and uniquely right, in having thought so.

He was right, too, when he described the farmer's condition. His tone may be somewhat lyrical, yet it is truthful. Taxes were very low; there were neither church nor feudal dues; no man was better than any other; and there was plenty of land to go around. That in itself was perhaps the most significant difference of all. In Europe the peasant was tied to his land as much by scarcity as by feudal custom: he knew full well that, if he left, he would not find another field to till. In America, on the contrary, all you had to do was move a little farther on. In a very short time—Ohio was the wild, unexplored West—you would come to a wilderness where you could find your own domain. It was always easy to resettle, so there was no way for a great landowner to establish dominion over you. If he bothered you, you left.

Crèvecoeur claimed a good deal more. If America was so perfect, it was by conscious design. "Because a man works," he wrote indignantly, "is he not to think? And if he thinks usefully, why should he not, in his leisure hours, set down his thoughts?" The application to himself was obvious, and rooted in a firm tradition: the French physiocrats advocated precisely such a life, such a combination of farming, thinking and writing. The marquis de Mirabeau, the father of the great revolutionary, had won fame as *l'Ami des Hommes* (the Friend of Man) for just such a blend of activities. And Thomas Jefferson would soon add his name to the list.

Perhaps because of his relatively easy life, and because the country was so sparsely settled, the American farmer proved to be both hospitable—and sensible. Unless you were traveling along one of the few established roads, there were no inns, and you had no choice but to ask the hospitality of a local householder. It was always granted, and you soon found yourself in a plain but charming house with a room all to yourself and a bed with fresh sheets; your host would stable and feed your horses; you would have dinner with the family and spend a thoroughly pleasant evening; and the next morning, when you were ready to leave, you would be presented with a bill roughly equivalent to that of an inn. There was no awkwardness, no embarrassment; it was understood that you would pay for the hospitality you had received.

It took the Europeans awhile to get over that: either the man received you in his house and you treated him as an equal, or he was an innkeeper whom you paid, that is, someone inferior to yourself. The notion that you could pay someone who remained your equal was hard to accept. Even harder was the fact that nothing was ever locked, and that you were trusted not to run away with the man's wife—she was often quite alone with you—or with his silver. Even the chest where he kept his most precious belongings lacked both lock and key. Many travelers who had read Crèvecoeur concluded that he was right after all.

Not everyone was a farmer. Unlike that of Naples, the American population was (already) largely middle class; commercial activities flourished and multiplied; and, of course, there were the fishermen and whalers: the United States was a coastal nation. Specialized fishing communities had evolved in a number of ports, and they functioned quite differently from their farming equivalents.

Nantucket, for instance, owed its considerable prosperity to whale and cod fishing. Its only town, Sherborn, consisted of some five hundred and fifty frame houses, lathed and plastered within, handsomely boarded and painted without, but all very plain and devoid of ornaments. There were two places of worship, one a meeting hall for the Friends, the other a Presbyterian church. In the center of town the county courthouse stood near the market place, and, while the three docks had room for as many as three hundred vessels, the streets were unpaved and there wasn't a single carriage.

Except when the ships were in port, Sherborn was a town of women and children, and it was the women who ran it. They were shopkeepers and business persons; they arranged for the sale of the catch and the repairs to the boats; and now and again they welcomed the men home. In many ways it was a typical New England community. Everyone dressed simply and without variations; they all looked the same, just as the houses did on the outside. There was no drinking, no music, no dancing; so people made up for it by copious and prolonged meals. There was nothing much to do, and no loose women, so they married early. They didn't read much: except for the Bible, there were practically no books around. They were a sober, practical people, with a reputation for being industrious, just and merciful. Still, the men got away to the high seas; the women who stayed home were apparently not busy enough to avoid boredom: in a startling preview of later habits, "a singular custom prevail[ed] here among the women . . . the Asiatic custom of taking a dose of opium every morning. . . . They would rather be deprived of any necessary than forgo this luxury."

And then, there was one totally disparate group. Still around, and fairly well treated, especially since they often joined in the fight against the English, they would appear now and again, much to the Europeans' amusement: they were, after all, real savages.

It was a moment of truce with the Indians; as a result, they were treated almost as if they were human. It would not last, of course, but in the meantime they would come and visit even in small towns. In 1781 "a score of savages arrived at Newport; part of them were Iroquois. . . . The only clothing they had was a blanket in which they wrapped themselves; they had no breeches. Their complexion is olive, they have their ears gashed and their faces daubed with red. There were some handsome men among them, and some tall old men of respectable appearance; we also remarked two young persons of at least five foot ten inches high and one of them with a remarkable physiognomy; some of them, nevertheless, were small. These savages, for a long time friendly to the French . . . complimented M. de Rochambeau.

"In the evening, they were persuaded to dance; their singing is monotonous, they interrupted it with sharp and disagreeable cries. In singing, they beat time with two little bits of wood. In dancing, they content themselves with bending the hams without taking any steps; there is no jumping, no springing." Clearly, the Indians had yet to learn the minuet.

It was all very picturesque, but aside from all these exotic characters, the French came to recognize underlying political and ethical principles which impressed them so highly that they tried to apply them at home. That they should have been ready to admire is perhaps not surprising in itself: people do tend to think well of their allies, even if that admiration does not outlast the war; the American attitude toward the Soviet Union during World War II is a good case in point. Then, too, there was the old view of England as the hereditary enemy; in that sense, the American War for Independence was merely a new episode in an old and continuing rivalry. What really made the difference was that the United States seemed to embody everything the *philosophes* had been yearning for. Suddenly liberty and equality were not just theories but the reality of a new, friendly country.

In France, in 1780, there was only one legal church; and since it kept birth and death registers, it was impossible to have a legal existence unless you were a Catholic. This had, of course, been deplored by a long line of French thinkers, all of whom preached religious toleration; and now, here in America, you could see, in a city like Boston, dozens of spires reaching to the sky—a non-denominational sky. Those many churches belonged to a wide variety of Protestant sects—Episcopalians, Presbyterians, Calvinists, Lutherans, Unitarians, Anabaptists, Methodists and the spireless Quakers— without, *ipso facto,* excluding the Catholics. There was no religious persecution, and the new Constitution would soon embody the separation of Church and State.

And all were free: free to speak and to write anything they pleased; free to choose their own government and their own head of state; free to decide on their taxes and other obligations. More than that, they were equal, before the law and each other. There were no privileged castes, no feudal rights, no arbitrary imprisonment. No one was better than anyone else. And, clearly, all prospered.

As for the scarcely visible government, it had to represent the general will since it was expressed only through the actions of elected representatives. The general will, as Rousseau had predicted, overcame private concerns: after all, the war made life expensive and sometimes dangerous. Many people were ruined by it, yet they made sacrifices in order to achieve justice for all. The French found it all the more thrilling that it wasn't quite new: what they witnessed was simply the enactment of principles discovered in their own country. So, naturally, they tended to disregard whatever might not fit their rose-colored view of this new, real utopia.

No taxation without representation is obviously a noble ideal: people should consent to their own government, and, clearly, they had not consented, for instance, to the Stamp Act. Still, many Americans were motivated less by principle than by cheapness and bad temper: there can be little argument that the British government spent more on America than it received from it. To the French, however, used as they were to arbitrary and sometimes excessive taxes, there was no doubt: the vicomte de Ségur, *inter alia,* carries on at great length about the iniquitous British taxes and the virtuous, principled American resistance to them. There could be no question: it was a fight between Good (freedom, equality) and Evil (despotism).

The Americans themselves did not see the situation so simply. For one thing, there was a substantial group of Tories who were bitterly opposed to the war and its goals. They liked things the way they were and wanted to stay British for a variety of reasons: some found great prosperity in trading with England and had no wish to see commercial exchanges interrupted; some were linked to and helped by the colonial government; some simply liked tradition and feared change; some, finally, felt they owed their superior social status to their connection with some titled British family; these last were numerous and influential. One of the richest merchants in Boston, for instance, Mr. Russell, took great pride in his remote connection to the Duke of Bedford's family.

By the time the French came to America (1780), however, many Tories had either moved away or confined themselves to their own houses. They were seen as a tiny body of mean-spirited men, no more, really, than an ordinary, unimportant reactionary element.

There was another complicating factor that seems to have by-passed the French entirely: the differences between the states. The ambiguity inherent in a confederation of sovereign states, none of which could achieve independence without the others, was obvious to all Americans, and Franklin, for one, exerted considerable ingenuity and eloquence in trying to resolve the problem. It was quite clear that the Americans' original preference was for the very loosest kind of confederation; it took the drift and disorders of the years between 1783 and 1787 to convince them of the need for a real federal government.

The disunity between the states on a number of basic issues was equally obvious. The Commonwealth of Massachusetts, for instance, gave itself a constitution which prohibited slavery; Pennsylvania declared that any slave entering its borders would, *ipso facto,* become a free man. The Southern states, on the other hand, held fast to their slaves and even continued to import them—a trade regarded by the Northerners with horror. The European visitors, of course, sided with the North and simply assumed that, with time, the South would see the light. Then, when it became necessary, a kind of blindness seemed to intervene: endless praise was heaped on George Washington, but it apparently never upset anyone that the great man owned slaves.

Again, the unevenness, the frequent unreliability, of the American fighting man never seems to have struck French observers. The high rate of desertion, for instance, or the often poor discipline among the troops completely escaped otherwise stern and fussy French officers who simply saw virtuous citizen soldiers ready to return to the plow as soon as victory was achieved. The only problem they did notice was the lack of money in general and of cash in particular; but they were so used to appealing to their King for supplies that they simply pitied the Americans and grumbled at their government's slowness in sending over funds. It never occurred to them that, while there was a genuine insufficiency of metal currency (see Chapter Sixteen), there were also many Americans who simply hoarded their gold.

Another reason for this ideal—but inaccurate—view of America was that so many of its leaders seemed to have a native genius for propaganda. Ségur, Chastellux, Fersen and the others had met Franklin in Paris; now they came to Washington's camp, where they were received with a mixture of friendship and politeness which went straight to their hearts. The great man himself behaved like a cordial king (he had enormous presence and dignity) who was also your friend: the response was immediate. And then there were the intellectuals who, to the delight of the French, also turned out to be politicians, men like Tom Paine, Samuel Adams and Jefferson. This mixture of Rousseau-like virtue and Platonized philosopher-kings who were democratic leaders instead of monarchs proved altogether irresistible. The United States, that new, disunited and troubled confederation, had become, in French eyes, the land of the Free and the home of the Good.

There were a few observers who thought that France ought to benefit from the help it had given the Revolution. Brissot, for instance, prints endless lists of the goods French merchants could be selling to the Americans; and Beaumarchais, hardly an idealist, looked for large profits in the cargoes he accompanied to New York. But, on the whole, what the French brought back from America was a political and social vision all the more attractive for being partly unreal.

There can be no doubt that a large part of the theoretical substructure of the independence movement was English: the founding fathers had read Locke and believed in a parliamentary tradition. The French, however, did not always see this clearly: the country, its fight for freedom, its political life, were too close to what they had been reading in Paris before they came over. And so they took back with them a vision, tinted by their own foreknowledge, which they believed they could apply successfully in their own country. Blithely unaware of the different nature of French society, they thought they could make France into an older, more sophisticated United States. The extent of their mistake had become obvious to most of them by 1792; in horror, a large majority veered to the opposite political position. Still, the result is undeniable: probably for the only time in its history, America, unknowingly, had exported revolution.

Its influence was all the more effective because all those brilliant young officers had political connections in Paris and Versailles, money and friends. Then, too, they wrote, and their books about the United States made exciting, lively reading. They were very popular, allying as they did just the kind of romantic exoticism then in fashion with a liberal political content. The Americans, it seemed, were picturesque, virtuous and free. Now it was up to the French to equal their achievements.

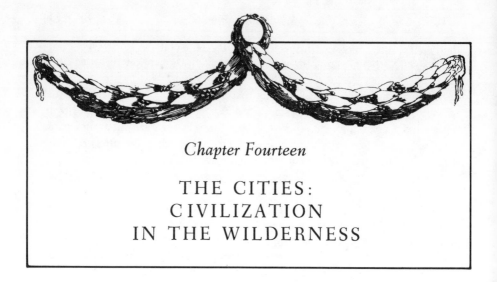

Chapter Fourteen

THE CITIES:
CIVILIZATION
IN THE WILDERNESS

The French sometimes looked away from that ideal society on which their gaze often seemed to be fixed; and when they did, what they were likely to see was an army camp or one of the three major cities in the United States: Boston, Philadelphia, New York. There were good reasons for this; supplies were easier to find in the cities, their social life was immensely livelier than that of a small town like Newport, and, in a country without a center, they were all capitals—Boston of a major state, Philadelphia and New York, successively, of the new nation. Political decisions were made and appointments in the army given out there: already by 1780 they were the places that mattered.

Their houses were larger and more comfortable; their markets sold a wider, more luxurious variety of goods; influential newspapers were published there; you could meet fashionable women and powerful men. They had banks, where you could cash your draft, and tailors and bootmakers and horse dealers. They even had entertainment of a sort. So if you weren't fighting the English—and most of the war, rather like a baseball game, was spent sitting and waiting—the cities were where you wanted to be.

Each of the three major cities had its distinguishing characteristic. Boston was a great trading, fishing and whaling center with strong ties to England; Philadelphia was the political center all through the Revolution; New York, unimportant at first, but beginning to catch up in the eighties, was the most sophisticated, luxurious, European of the three. Far behind came Providence, a thriving smaller city which owed its animation to its strategic position between Newport, where the French fleet was at anchor, and the rest of the country.

The thirteen colonies' entire population, in 1770, hovered around four million people, so the cities were large only by comparison: Philadelphia had some forty thousand inhabitants and Boston probably fifty thousand. As for New York, it was still mostly contained in the area below Canal Street. Still, the cities were diverse. Boston had its huge, protected harbor from which a forest of spires could be seen towering over the city. The most English metropolis in America by choice and habit, it was described as "well-built; it displays an indescribable cleanliness which is pleasing; most of the houses are of wood painted grey; some are of stone and brick. The people seemed to be in easy circumstances. Nevertheless, the shops were poorly stocked with goods and everything was very dear, which resulted from the war. Their bookstores had hardly anything but prayer books; an English and French dictionary cost eight louis [192 livres]."

It was a lively city, with its heavy maritime traffic; except for the war years, most goods imported into the United States came through Boston, though New York began to catch up in the late eighties. The news from Europe also came there first, and it had an intellectual tradition to defend. The Boston Latin School, with its seven-year curriculum emphasizing Latin, was probably the best in the country, and Harvard College was famous for both the quality of its faculty and the excellence of its library. It also boasted a collection of physical science apparatus which had been recently replenished by British gifts after a fire.

It was a busy city with endless carts, but very few carriages, rumbling down its well-paved streets. A new system of street lighting was installed in 1774, so people coming out of its numerous but expensive taverns no longer had to stumble home in the dark. Still, by European standards, it was a little stodgy: it had no cafés, a traveler noted with dismay, or theaters, or opera, or concerts. Churchgoing was the only public entertainment. Then, too, the Puritan spirit lived on; people dressed plainly, in dark wool suits if they were men, simple linen dresses if they were women. Only the men wore their hair powdered, and, even then, not everyone did. The ladies, on the other hand, were fond of bleached blond hair. It was a city for making money, a city of solid, slightly dull culture; it was, in fact, just beginning to be something of a backwater, all the more so since it had lost an unusually high proportion of its richer citizens, who had left with the English.

Philadelphia was altogether livelier. It was considered the metropolis of the new United States, the handsomest, best planned, best built of its cities. It was wealthier—in 1772 it numbered eighty-four carriages; but its wealth was not yet flaunted; it was also more news-oriented, more scientific, more political. Unlike Boston, it was a really modern city: its streets were straight and wide, as they followed the grid pattern originally laid down by William Penn. All the travelers were impressed. "Philadelphia is a very extensive city, and regularly built," wrote Claude Blanchard. "The houses are of brick and pretty high, the streets straight, broad and pretty long; there are sidewalks for persons on foot. Some public buildings are also to be seen there which are worthy of a great city, such as the house where the Congress meets, the hospital and the prison. The absence of quays upon the Delaware[1] deprives it of a great convenience and a great beauty." And not only were there side-walks: they were lined with gutters on either side and bordered by a low palisade so as to keep carriages away.

Everyone agreed. Boston was all right, and very clean, but Philadelphia was a real city. Its brick houses were plain but they had lovely proportions and were adorned with painted window sills and doors. Its longest street, Front Street, which ran parallel to the river, was over three miles long. Its harbor had room for three hundred ships—fewer than Boston's five hundred —but it had a large central market, more books, more luxury. True, many of its inhabitants were Quakers who lived very simply; but there were carriages in the streets, and women in silk dresses. Most important, during most of twenty years it was the seat of the Congress. So, if you wanted to meet Tom· Paine, or Samuel Adams, or Thomas Jefferson, you went to Philadelphia.

Aside from its hospital, model prison and modern, humane insane asylum, there was the former Statehouse where both the Congress and the legislature now met. It was plain enough, brick with white trim, decorated only at the door, but with an arcade between the two chimneys which rose at either end of the building. The inside was just as simple but you could sit in on the debates which were freeing a continent—and that was worth watching.

Still, Philadelphia was no Paris. The streets had no names and the houses no numbers, which made finding your way extremely difficult. It had an abundance of public fountains but no public promenades, except for the small park behind the Statehouse; the French complained bitterly about the lack of exercise. And here too there was an absence of public entertainments. With an obvious sigh of relief, however, we are told that here at last was a city where prostitutes flourished.

Besides frequenting these ladies, there was a fair amount of other things to do in Philadelphia. For one thing, it had the most forward-looking public institutions: its model prison was the first to practice solitary confinement in all its rigor, and it was thought a great step since it entailed clean cells, as opposed to the old, filthy common rooms, and prevented one criminal from corrupting another. It was all most interesting, as was the one and only school for black children, where they were treated as well, and taught the same things, as if they had been white. Unlike Boston, Philadelphia had a fairly large black population. Slavery was outlawed, so most of the blacks were free servants, who were indeed paid salaries, though at a slightly lower rate than their white counterparts. And after you had been properly edified by all this, there were several salons where you could go for tea and conversation. It wouldn't do to stay too late, though. By eleven the streets would be empty, save for the patrolling night watchmen.

[1] In derogation of Penn's plan.

For all its political importance, however, Philadelphia still fitted into a traditional American pattern. The Quakers looked much like the Puritans; simplicity, plainness, modesty were still highly prized. New York, on the other hand, was hard at work earning its reputation as a Jezebel among cities.

Boston had started the Revolution, Philadelphia had sheltered its political arm: New York was happily occupied by English troops during most of the war. It wasn't even so much that all its inhabitants were Tories, though many were; simply, New Yorkers liked the good life, and the English, after all, were Europeans. You could rely on them for sophistication and elegance.

Few of the French went to New York. Before 1783 it was enemy territory, and after, it remained somehow off the beaten track. When Brissot finally got there in 1788 he agreed with everybody else: by American standards, it was luxurious. Even here there were not yet many carriages in the streets, but those you saw were really elegant. Of course, it may have helped that the only carriage maker in America was established right across the East River, in a little town called Brooklyn. Then, too, people were dressed just like Europeans—or at least just like Europeans of two years ago—in silk, velvet, lace and gauze. They all wore their hair curled and powdered, and the women worked just as hard at looking chic as if they had lived on the other side of the Atlantic.

Elsewhere in the United States the food was abundant but plain. In New York it was abundant but complicated and expensive. Fine, costly wines were imported and consumed, as was a new delicacy that the men smoked, the cigar. Physically, the city looked like a cross between Boston and Philadelphia—crooked streets but brick houses—and great, almost feudal estates survived just a little way to the north.

New York was altogether more modern: coal was used for fuel instead of wood, and with good reason, since a cord of wood cost 48 livres. Labor was already expensive: workers earned 4 to 6 livres a day, double what they were paid in Philadelphia. Doctors' fees were reasonable, but lawyers were—already—ruinous. Food was terribly dear: you had to pay 6 livres a pound for beef and 40 for tea; milk went as high as 8 livres a pint, and bread 6 livres for four pounds. It makes today's prices look cheap, but the circumstances were exceptional: in 1785 the federal Congress, with all its attendant crowds, had moved in, causing a great scarcity of supplies in this city with a population of less than forty thousand people.

It suddenly became almost impossible to find a room in any of the inns or hotels; if you did, room and board would cost something between 21 and 32 livres a week, about double the national average, and the same was true of other essential expenses. The man who combed your wig charged 12 livres a month, and laundry was outrageously high: you had to fork out 2½ livres per dozen pieces. New York had already become a rich man's town.

Providence came a very poor fourth: it was a large town rather than a real city. "It only has one street," Chastellux wrote, "but that street is very long;

the suburb, which is quite extensive, is across the river. This town is attractive, the houses are small but well built, and well arranged inside." And, though the population hovered around three thousand, Providence managed to be hospitable even by American standards, helped on by the prosperity based on its exports of wood and smoked meats. Then, too, it had its own college. One traveler noted that his innkeeper's son, who had a job as a tutor there, owned fifty books in Greek, Latin and English, thus combining upward mobility with the possession of a veritable treasure trove.

Providence soon gained another, different reputation for immorality. It was a well-known fact that in America, unlike in France, women were virtuous. What was Chastellux' surprise when he found his innkeeper's daughter pregnant and unwed! It was, to be sure, the usual story: the young man had promised marriage, taken advantage of the girl, then gone on a short trip and never returned. The girl felt her shame, the parents were kindness itself to her, but there was no getting around it: immorality had reared its ugly head in the New World.

This unfortunate case was much discussed in Paris, so much so, in fact, that when Brissot arrived in Providence he felt compelled to make a beeline for the inn to see if indeed the ugly story were true. Sure enough, he reported with great satisfaction, it wasn't! If only that cynical aristocrat Chastellux had stayed around another year or two, he would have been there to witness the return of the young man, held back by nothing more than a long and severe illness, so severe, in fact, that he had been unable to send word, especially since remorse and anxiety had further weakened his already undermined constitution. All was well, however, the young couple was now reunited, married and living in a bliss all the more intense for having been so long suspended. Who said Providence was immoral now? Brissot demanded in triumph. There is no reason to suppose he lied, but the story does have all the flavor of a Greuze composition—*The Wedding of the Seduced and Deserted Fiancée*—and seems almost too good to be true. . . .

When its daughters were not heedlessly surrendering themselves to seductive young men, Providence, like the other cities, played a quadruple role, political, commercial, financial and educational. It was the place where men came to find out about the latest events, especially during the war, to discuss them and to decide what measures were to be taken, how much money was to be raised and what was to be done about the rising inflation (see Chapter Sixteen). Power was still diffuse: it really mattered what the men of Providence (or the other cities) decided; and while there was, of course, a legislature, it was still very close to the small population and reflected its wishes far more directly than at any later time.

A city's mood had a way of spreading into the countryside. It was the place where the news came first and people reacted before anyone else. Since most judicial and commercial institutions were also located there, people would come in to transact business and find out what was going on and the state of public opinion. While the press was already thriving—the theoretical underpinnings of the Revolution can be largely found in John Adams' Novanglius articles for the *Massachusetts Spy*—the cities took on some of the role frequently attributed to the media today: they presented the news and sometimes slanted it.

Then, the cities were religious centers: the diverse sects, each competing for a following, made it impossible to have a preacher of every denomination out in the countryside. The city was thus the fountainhead of ecclesiastical activity, the place where you could find just that shade of worship closest to your heart, the place also where new attitudes were evolved. It was in Boston, for instance, that, despite grave misgivings, the first Catholic church in the state was built. Most people had strong feelings about the Whore of Babylon. When the Abbé Robin came to Boston he stayed in the house of a known Catholic, only slightly redeemed by the fact that he was French. Soon after the abbé's arrival the house caught fire. The neighbors came to watch but didn't help: a Catholic was really outside the pale, and the poor householder was lucky it was only a minor fire.

The cities were also commercial and trading centers. There were general stores in the country, of course, but they could play only a limited role: if you needed to sell your crop or buy a horse, you went to market in the city, or to a merchant there. Market places were centrally important to the life of the city; it was greatly to Philadelphia's credit that its central market was unique in size, cleanliness and convenience. All imports came through the cities, and that covered just about every manufactured product, from snuffboxes to house paint: the United States, before 1790, was not a manufacturing nation.

Last and decidedly least, the cities were centers for fashion and learning. Elegance did not have a very good press during our period: fashion, supposedly, was just what the United States was not about, and writers like Franklin thundered away at people so weak and so corrupt as to waste the nation's resources on importing fine clothes, carriages and wines. Learning was respected, at least within the cities, each of which had a college and sometimes even a library; but, for the pioneers opening up the wilderness, it must have seemed like a lot of unnecessary fuss.

In spite of the fact that the cities were local or even national capitals, they were not smaller replicas of Paris. Although, just as in France, most of the population was rural, here it was the rural masses that counted, not the fashionable center. In France the country followed the capital; in America the cities were really little more than extensions of the country.

—◄ ►—

Nothing could be simpler than life on a farm. The houses were clean and new, but plain and often small, although the conveniences were already prized. One traveler noticed with admiration that the outdoor privies had not only two isolated seats but a third, smaller one for children as well. It was all very different from France, of course: cleaner, newer, more prosperous; but still there was room and money only for the barest necessities.

The cities, on the other hand, boasted of wealth and tradition. This was all relative: there were few, if any stone houses, no boiseries, no tapestries, no Sèvres porcelain, no sculptured motifs. Houses were usually made of wood or brick, two or three stories high, but not very large, with, at best, a kitchen, dining room, entrance hall and parlor downstairs and three to six bedrooms upstairs. And elegance meant English furnishings, not French, although the war began to change all that.

English, or English-looking, furniture was highly desirable, as was silver (instead of pewter or even tin) tableware; but the most essential object was the carpet. A good carpet was very expensive, so the less prosperous had to do without and look for substitutes: in Boston they used an inch of sand. But in the grander houses the rarest, richest oriental carpets could be seen, not just on the floors but sometimes draped over the tables as well. Then there was that old English standby, the highly polished mahogany dining-room table, with its sideboard and chairs. This was all for show; bedrooms were often simpler, although four-poster beds were not infrequent.

Even when the houses did not belong to the rich, their "cleanliness and simple elegance always look[ed] pleasant." There wasn't much exterior difference between those of the rich and those of the merely comfortable; even size did not vary greatly; inside, wealth was judged by the quality of the carpets, the amount of mahogany furniture and table silver, along with the presence of precious objects from the East: the United States had started to trade with China.

The rich also lived better. If they didn't mind showing off, they might even own a carriage or a country house. Madame de la Tour du Pin, whose presentation at Versailles we have read about, found herself forced by the French Revolution to move to America. After commenting on the comfort and the solidly pleasant look of the interiors she had seen in Boston, she goes on to describe an expedition to a country house in Wrentham. "The location," she notes, "was delicious because of its situation, its coolness, its fertility. There were lakes with scattered, tree-covered little islands which looked like gardens floating on the water, and woods as old as the world bathed their hoary trunks and their young shoots in a water as pure as crystal: it was an enchanting landscape." Significantly, Madame de la Tour du Pin ignores the house; we may gather it was small and simple.

In Philadelphia and New York the look was less English. There, as the eighties progressed, French furniture, silver and porcelain made their appearance. By the early nineties a few Americans were even taking advantage of the numberless auctions through which the revolutionaries were dispersing aristocratic belongings; they acquired some first-rate pieces: that Sèvresincrusted table of Mr. Morris' is a good example of this trend. Still and all, by French standards, American interiors remained very simple.

Food wasn't much more complicated. Quantity and repetition, along with simplicity of preparation, were its most striking features. To the French, scarcely an abstemious people, it seemed as if the Americans never stopped eating; it is true that, in the absence of all entertainment and widespread amorous intrigues, there wasn't much else to do.

Breakfast was abundant, and very close, still, to the English breakfast, with its courses of fish, sausage, ham, kidneys, smoked fish and eggs. Dinner didn't come until four in Boston or five in Philadelphia, but it was a large meal. Four or five different kinds of roast or boiled meats—lamb, veal, beef, pork—would all be put down on the table at the same time, along with a dozen different vegetable dishes; the French never ceased to be amazed at the American consumption of vegetables. It was all good, plain, solid fare, there was lots of it, and it was very English. No one, of course, knew anything about the French *nouvelle cuisine* nor would it have been possible to produce its essences; there was, in fact, very little effort at preparing interesting dishes, no sauces, no pastry cases, almost no stews. And in contrast to the many services recommended in the *Cuisinière bourgeoise*, in America there were only two: the meat and vegetables, and the desserts. These consisted of a great variety of puddings and pies, all put on the table together and served —things never change—with weak coffee. Afterward fruit and nuts appeared, wine was passed around and toasts were offered, to the King of France, General Washington, the host, the guests, and so on, endlessly.

Around eight everyone would leave the table; good strong tea would be served in the parlor. More guests might come in then. At nine there was more to come. Supper was served and it, too, was a substantial, though often cold, meal consisting of salads and cold meats, followed by more puddings, pies, fruit, nuts, and wine, so that eating went on almost uninterruptedly from four to ten. It is no wonder that travelers were struck by the number of overweight Americans.

The consumption of liquor kept up with that of food. The two-martini lunch had yet to be invented, but the multi-punch dinner was a salient feature of life, especially in Boston. There a huge silver bowl full of rum, lemon juice, spices, sugar and hot water would be passed around as soon as the guests entered the house; everyone drank straight from the bowl and it was often replenished before the company sat down to dinner. Wine was not much in evidence during the meal, but quantities of it were drunk when the fruit and nuts were served: it might be claret, port or madeira, and would often be followed by more punch; only very grand houses and New Yorkers served brandy or liqueurs. Because of the triangular trade (slaves, sugar, rum), rum was abundant and cheap, so it was naturally drunk most often. And in taverns and lesser households porter, a kind of beer, was highly popular; it could generally be bought for a shilling a bottle whereas madeira varied from four to six shillings, depending on where you bought it, a liquor store or a tavern.

On the whole, and with the exception of expensive New York, food was cheap and plentiful. You could buy meat for half a shilling a pound, a loaf of bread for a quarter of a shilling, butter for under a shilling a pound; vegetables were fresh, tasty and cheap. By comparison, a cord of wood cost seven shillings, and a load of coal twelve shillings.

With very few exceptions—the siege of Boston was one—food remained plentiful all through the war and, in terms of metallic money, prices rose only moderately. The meal described here by Claude Blanchard was absolutely typical: "I dined at Providence with Dr. Bowen, a physician and a respectable old man," he wrote. "He said grace before sitting down to table. . . . They do not eat soups and do not serve ragouts [stews] at these dinners; but boiled and roast meat and much vegetables. The dessert is composed of preserved quinces or pickled sorrel. The Americans eat the latter with the meat. They do not take coffee immediately after dinner,[2] but it is served three or four hours afterwards with the tea; their coffee is weak and four to five cups are not equal to one of ours, so that they take many of them. The tea, on the contrary, is very strong. This use of coffee and tea is universal in America. The people who live in the country, tilling the ground and driving their oxen, take it as well as the inhabitants of the cities. Breakfast is an important affair with them. Besides tea and coffee, they put on the table roasted meats, with butter, pies and hams; nevertheless, they sup, and, in the afternoon, again take tea. Thus, the Americans are almost always at table; and, as they have little to occupy them, as they go out little in winter and spend whole days alongside of their fires and their wives, without reading and without doing anything, going so often to the table is a relief and a preventative [sic] of ennui, yet, they are not great eaters.

"They are very choice in cups and vases for holding tea and coffee, in glasses, decanters and other matters of this kind in habitual use. . . . Burning a great quantity of wood is one of their luxuries. It is common." Thus, it seems, in at least two respects, people here haven't changed much: they still eat right through the day, even if snacks have sometimes replaced sit-down meals, and they like to keep their houses very warm. Another perennial habit had also become established: the picnic. Blanchard describes this one with some awe.

"I was invited," he says, "to a party in the country. It was a sort of picnic given by a score of men to a company of ladies. The purpose of this party was to eat a turtle weighing four hundred pounds. . . . This meat did not seem to me to be very palatable; it is true that it was very badly cooked. There were some quite handsome women; before dinner, they kept themselves in a different room from the men, they also placed themselves at table

2 They did elsewhere.

all on the same side, and the men on the other. They danced after dinner. . . . Neither the men nor the women dance well; all stretch out and
lengthen their arms in a way far from agreeable. . . . During dinner, we
drank different healths as usual, we to those of the Americans, and they to
the health of the King of France. This extended to everybody; for, on passing through an anteroom where some Negro servants were drinking, I heard
them drinking together the health of the King of France." The picnic, in
this case, appears to have been inside a country house rather than outside on
the grass; but then, even in America, people preferred comfort to the joys
and discomforts of nature.

While most foods were home-grown, and therefore readily available, the
war caused limited shortages. Tea, for instance, had until then come from
English merchants in English ships: all of a sudden the price of a pound of
tea skyrocketed to forty shillings, the same as a not very good horse. Imported European wines went through similar variations, as did some manufactured products. The colonies had relied on England completely for most
industrial items, from sewing thread to nails, from house paint and tools to
good furniture and carriages. The immediate consequence of the war was to
make all these goods scarce, then altogether unavailable, and it was some time
before factories were started to produce them. By the late eighties nails,
paints, paper, glass, and wallpaper were all going into production. France
took up a very small portion of the slack during the war, and trade with
England resumed afterward, so that most of the missing goods were again
available, and cheap, after 1790. In a very short time however, those new
factories would start to dominate the market.

As for the cost of living, it varied immensely, and not just from city to
city: obviously a scarcity of, say, nails, would send the price rushing up.
Then the war and its costs created severe economic distortions; taxes fluctuated and so did the currency. In essence, the years from 1772 to 1787 were
marked by a slow inflation which appeared much more drastic than it really
was because of the wild gyrations of the paper money (see Chapter Sixteen)
printed by the states and the federal government. All the prices given here
have been gold and silver currency prices so as to avoid confusion.

Some constant figures do emerge. Laborers, for instance, were paid an average of 800 livres a year, and on the whole they lived better than their European colleagues. A prosperous farmer, with a capital of 8,000 to 10,000
livres invested in his land, might have very little money income—some 400
to 500 livres a year, but that was because he was largely self-sufficient. Servants were paid 60 to 72 livres a month and were given board and lodging.
A wigmaker would charge you 14 livres a month to take care of your wigs; if
you wanted a real luxury and rented a horse and gig, it cost 20 livres a day.

Rents could vary enormously. In Chester, Pennsylvania, you could lease a
fully furnished inn with 150 acres of land for 1,400 livres a year; in Philadelphia you could rent a small house for as little as 300 livres a year, or a

large, splendid, centrally located one for 2,500 livres. For 46,000 livres you could buy a large stone house there, with three gardens, 250 acres of land and fishing rights in the Schuylkill.

The people who lived in the nicer houses had proportionate incomes. Lawyers (good ones) charged 24 livres per consultation, and extra for writs and deeds; they could easily make 9,000 to 12,000 livres a year. Doctors didn't do quite so well, but even on 5,000 livres a year you could be comfortable. And, of course, even in the eighteenth century there were millionaires. Mr. Morris of Philadelphia, he of the Sèvres table, had a fortune of a million and a quarter—or over seven million livres. By comparison, the governor of Massachusetts was paid $3,800 a year (22,800 livres), and the President of the United States (after 1788, of course) $25,000 a year (150,000 livres), while the Chief Justice of the United States had $4,000 (24,000 livres) and a circuit judge $1,200 (7,200 livres).

As for land, John Adams expected it to return six per cent on the capital invested. And all through our period lower salaries had a tendency to rise, in real terms, much faster than the others, thus beginning a trend which proved long lasting. By 1792 a workingman was making as much as 2,000 livres a year. There was no shortage of workers or servants: the blacks and some of the new immigrants supplied those needs, but not in great abundance: unemployment was virtually unknown. And it was all very decent; the lumpenproletariat of the nineteenth century, composed mostly of Irish and a mass of middle Europeans, would have shocked and horrified people a century earlier. On the whole, the population was spread along a very narrow economic fan: there were very few really rich people, and almost equally few very poor men; most of the population lived comfortably, either on the farms or in the cities.

—◦◦{   }◦◦—

The war made life difficult in some respects but it was a great boost to the social life of the cities which the French visited. In staid Boston there were dinners and balls every night; Philadelphia boasted salons where the visitors might meet the local lights, and the Chevalier de la Luzerne, the French envoy, kept a permanently open house. There might be no theater, no opera, no concerts, no ballet, no court festivities; but all through the seventies and eighties no presentable person ever had to spend an evening in solitude.

Philadelphia, as the capital, had the most glamorous parties. When the marquis de Chastellux arrived there he found himself, suddenly and surprisingly, in the midst of the most intense social life. The very day he arrived he attended a grand dinner given by La Luzerne, from which, exhausted as he was by traveling, he excused himself at midnight; the next day he heard that it had gone on until 3 A.M. The following afternoon he went to Mr. Reed's house, which was arranged and furnished in the English manner, to meet Mrs. Washington, who was on her way to the front to see her husband; then he was taken to see Mrs. Beech, Franklin's daughter, who, with other ladies, was busy making shirts for the soldiers from cloth she had purchased herself; on that day in 1781 they had already sent off more than two thousand.

After that it was off to Mr. Morris; the millionaire, who had made his fortune in trade and shipping, was a friend of Franklin's and had been a member of Congress in 1776. He lived well but without undue luxury—he obviously hadn't bought his Sèvres table yet—in an English-looking house, was a great supporter of the new Republic and an epicurean philosopher who, like the rest of his compatriots, never seemed to stop eating.

And it wasn't just millionaires. There was Samuel Adams, "a man wholly given to his purpose, who spoke only to give me a better opinion of his cause and a greater idea of his nation. His simple, cheap appearance seemed to exist as a contrast with the strength and breadth of his thoughts; they were all turned towards the Republic and lost none of their heat though they were expressed precisely and methodically." After this conversation, full of his enthusiasm for the new nation, Chastellux was off to see the Congress in session, which gave him a chance to marvel at the way an assembly of free men, freely chosen, seemed able to control the executive branch of government.

Philadelphia wasn't all politics and serious talks. While, in the afternoon, you might visit a learned anatomist or a man who had made a machine faithfully representing the orbits of the various planets around the sun, at night there were gay dinners and balls, though of course they didn't conform to French usages. Indeed, pleasure was highly organized. All dances were prearranged, and each lady given a partner with whom she must dance all night —there was no question of choice. Luckily for Chastellux, foreigners were complimented with the handsomest ladies for dancing partners; and, in the dances themselves, precedence went to the richest guests, a startling notion for a European whose social life had always been governed by the primacy of rank. Supper was always served at midnight, the ball always ended at two.

There was no trifling with proper amusement. " 'Come, miss, have a care what you are doing,' shouted the master of ceremonies to a damsel who was permitting a bit of gossip to interrupt her turn in a contradance. 'Do you think you are here for your own pleasure?'

"A manager, or master of ceremonies, presides at each of these amusements," Chastellux continues. "He [sometimes] gives to each dancer a folded ticket which is numbered and thus it is chance which decides the partner you are to have and must keep the whole evening. All the dances are arranged in advance and are called out in order. These dances, like the toasts they drink at the table, have a certain political flavor. One is called 'The Success of the Campaign,' another, 'The Defeat of Burgoyne,' a third, 'The Retreat of Clinton.' The managers are generally chosen from the most distinguished officers of the army. . . . Sometimes a young man who has come alone to a ball is unable to dance at all because no one is willing to accept his invitation."

Still, organization had its virtues, and so did the looks of the American ladies. "I do not remember," the vicomte de Ségur wrote in Providence, "to have ever seen more gaiety and less confusion, more pretty women, well dressed, full of grace and with less coquetry." Each of the cities had its stars. In Boston, for instance, the two Misses Jarvis, Miss Betsey Brown and Mrs. Whitemore were generally acknowledged to be the most attractive women and the best dancers. In Philadelphia, there was the tactfully unnamed Miss V., who was "famous for her coquetry, her wit and her nastiness: she is thirty years old and does not seem ready to get married. In the meantime, she wears rouge, white, blue and every other color of make-up, has extraordinary clothes and hair-dos and, a thorough Whig in every respect, she sets no limit to her freedom."

There were evening teas and music parties. Many American women were good musicians in an age when one either played an instrument and sang or heard no music. Boston, though, was still too puritanical. Its young ladies were kept firmly away from this heathen distraction. And last but not least, there were cards: whist, an early form of bridge, was the most popular game, played for very high stakes, except during the war, when it was considered unpatriotic to spend one's money this way. Only then did people play just for fun.

All these cheerful goings-on were naturally restricted to the Whigs. Tories were firmly boycotted socially and even, in some cases, found it expedient to leave the country. Since they were often the richest people, the houses visited by the French had, until recently, been second best, and their hosts were highly exhilarated to have thus reached the top of the heap. Even when they returned, the ex-Tories, who tended to stay apart, were no menace to the new society. That they were important and numerous, though, cannot be doubted. Madame de la Tour du Pin, who met them, gives an accurate picture of their position. "Mr. Geyer is one of the richest landowners in Boston. . . . He had been numbered among the partisans of Great Britain and . . . had even taken his family to England. . . . Mr. Geyer speaks rather good French. . . . The city still looked like an English colony. The richest and most distinguished citizens, though they obeyed the new government, regretted, without any longer opposing it, the separation from the mother country. They still had ties of affection and family with England. They kept its customs unchanged and several of them, having taken refuge there, had only returned after the signing of the peace. People called them loyalists. Among them were Mr. Jeffreys, the brother of the famous editor of the *Edinburgh Review,* and a Russell family which made sure you were aware of its close relationship with the Duke of Bedford."

Another feature of Boston's social life was the club. A number of families, usually from twelve to twenty, would belong to one of these and gather once a week, each time in a different member's house. Supper was served between nine and ten and was composed of two meat dishes, lots of vegetables, pies and wine. Everyone behaved very freely and the evening, apart from the supper, was spent playing cards, chatting, reading the newspapers and singing drinking songs.

Of course none of this happened on Sunday. Boston was stricter, but everywhere in the United States Sunday was the day of the Lord and neither work nor fun was permitted. This rather gloomy observance had its good side: at least, laborers were allowed to rest one day a week; on the other hand, that was about all they could do. A Frenchman who was caught playing the flute, one Sunday in Boston, was almost lynched. Sundays were for being bored.

If, during the other six days, you wanted to do something more intellectually stimulating than eating or dancing, there were a variety of young but promising institutions. In Philadelphia the Franklin Library had already opened its doors and provided the well-to-do public with books it could not readily find elsewhere; but it cost seventy livres to join it. In Boston there was the Harvard College library, which was accessible to outsiders. And everywhere learned societies worked to expand the bounds of knowledge while making it more easily available than before. In Philadelphia, Chastellux, who was a member of the French Academy, was received as an honorary member of the Pennsylvania Academy; that day he heard a report on a singular indigenous plant—he fails to tell us which—then the reports received from other American learned societies and finally a debate to settle whether local societies should be allowed affiliation with the Pennsylvania Academy. They were rejected with great scorn, since it was felt they would lower the standards of which the Academy was so proud. And there was an Agricultural Society, busy improving methods of cultivation and finding ways to control the most destructive pests. Even after Franklin's death his spirit lived on in these groups of often competent men anxious to increase the sum of available knowledge.

More frivolous people always had fashion as a last resort; but America was too new, vigorous and simple a country for fashion to rule as it did in France. Of course luxury became increasingly important. All through the war Franklin was complaining about the money wasted on imports of luxury goods when it should have been buying weapons. Increasingly through the eighties people were spending large sums on wines, clothes, furniture, carriages and porcelain. Women made great efforts to keep up with Continental fashions, and sometimes succeeded despite unavoidable delay: even in New York the very newest fashion was at least a year old. Still, fashion went no further than that: the Puritan ethic was still too strong, and it was shameful to be idle. A thorough devotion to fashion requires every hour of every day; no one in America was willing to give up the time.

Observant and sympathetic as they were, the French tactfully ignored another great gap in their favorite foreign country: the arts. Perhaps because the simplicity of life precluded energy being spent on apparently unnecessary activities, perhaps because the Puritans didn't think much of graven images, the arts failed to develop on any level other than the primitive. True, the Shakers, who had settled in New York State, had started to make their starkly simple furniture. A plain style of wood architecture had evolved of itself, so the American cities looked simple but attractive. But as late as 1790, with one or two exceptions, there were neither painters nor sculptors nor architects nor composers nor great cabinetmakers on the new continent. This was so obvious that Houdon had to be sent for when a statue of George Washington was required. L'Enfant, another Frenchman, was asked to make the plans for the new federal capital. Unlike the ancient cities of Greece, where democracy had been invented, and whose history was well known to the founding fathers, in American cities the arts did not keep up with politics. And even in the one field, the printed word, where America left a lasting mark, it is to political philosophy, or even applied politics, that we must turn in the absence of novels, poems and plays. It may be said that the men who wrote the Declaration of Independence, the Constitution and the various essays that accompanied them had done enough; it still remains a fact that, in every other field of artistic endeavor, the new country did not yet have much to offer.

In several other respects, however, it was already ahead of its time. American medicine had not yet made any great discoveries, but all the major cities had modern, clean, airy hospitals where the sick were, at any rate, kept warm and comfortable. Smallpox had already been eradicated thanks to the widespread practice of inoculation; tuberculosis was now the greatest killer (no one knew how to treat it), closely followed by a deadly "sore throat," probably a form of diphtheria, and a violent, often fatal strain of flu. And then there were the fevers or agues to be caught in marshy country, varieties of malaria and yellow fever, probably, which began to recede with the draining of the swamps.

The cities, too, partly because they were new and not very large, followed standards of cleanliness quite unknown in Europe. City planning, soon to triumph on the banks of the Potomac, had already made its mark in Philadelphia. The slums were yet to come; in the meantime American cities were indeed nice places in which to live; and, as cultural centers, they really represented civilization in the wilderness. Slowly but surely a new mixture of imported and home-grown knowledge was accumulating, then making its way out into the countryside. The bulk of the population, between 1770 and 1790, was made up of farmers; but from their faraway, primitive settlements they looked to the cities for other values and found there the link between their past and their future.

Chapter Fifteen

LIVING
THROUGH THE WAR

Daily life, in France and Naples, proceeded on a fairly even tenor through most of the seventies and eighties. In America, on the contrary, a widespread war caused physical and moral disruption while it lasted, and enormous political and economic change when it ended. It was a singularly meaningful conflict: not only a new nation, with a new form of government, but also a new (if temporary) European order in which the power of England was singularly diminished emerged from it. It was in some ways a civil war; as such, it divided the population sharply and gave rise to new forms of intolerance and persecution. More than that, and even before Asia and Africa had really begun to feel the weight of colonization, it was the first of the wars of national liberation: England could no more hold onto its American colonies than, almost two hundred years later, could France to Algeria or the United States to Vietnam.

The American people emerged from the war with a new identity born in part from its new experiences. Politics could never be the same, of course; and while the roots of self-government may have reached deep into the Anglo-Saxon past, the thirteen colonies did manage to evolve, after a good deal of bickering, a form of government which the French instantly recognized as freer and fairer than any other on the face of the earth. The magnitude of the achievement is awesome: wars of national liberation, in every other case, have given rise to dictatorships, not democracy; and the lack of active hatred shown the Tories once the war was over is absolutely mindboggling.

All in all, the war served as a sort of incubation period after which many traditional patterns of American life were modified or reversed. Jefferson was extolling a nation of farmers at the very moment when the United States was transforming itself into a nation of industrialized cities. Economically, the period ending in 1790 represents the swan song of the old order. Commerce with England resumed at the end of the war, of course, and continued far into the next century as a mainstay of the economy; but, slowly, the focus was shifting, and the East—China, then Japan—was catching up to the West. Then, too, the very presence of the French armies and their officers, young men, most of them, who belonged to the trendiest circles at home, opened up the American vision. Until 1770 the colonies had really been little Englands, less sophisticated, more egalitarian, but sharing the same cultural and political viewpoint. The French presence brought the rest of the world into focus; the colonial mentality began finally to be discarded.

Few Americans were untouched by the war: its very nature made it ubiquitous. It was a rare city which, like New York, could bask in the comfort of long-term British occupation. Boston and Philadelphia were besieged and taken: each felt the horrors of the war directly. Troops moved across most of the new nation, towns changed hands, sometimes more than once; there really was no completely safe area. Thus the whole country was involved in the conflict, directly, physically. It wasn't just that trade was disrupted or the currency fluctuated madly, but you were likely to find troops at your doorstep tomorrow. Like it or not, the war was an essential element of everyday life.

War was still, luckily, a good deal more civilized than it was to become later. One may wonder what America would be like today if the British had had B-52s, "protected villages" and concentration camps; as it was, both sides —it was the custom—showed great restraint. The difficulties of the occupied Bostonians, for instance, look like absolute bliss compared to the treatment inflicted on modern victims of guerrilla warfare. Then, too, food was always fairly easily available; there was no serious interruption of the farmers' labors; so there was no famine and none of its attendant dislocations.

Even when a battle didn't take place right outside your door, the war made itself felt in a variety of other ways. A drastic scarcity of manufactured objects—all heretofore imported—became plain: Mrs. Adams' letters are a catalogue of complaints because she couldn't find needles or thread, or nails or tools. And whenever you could get your hands on them, they were likely to cost a great deal more than before. Then there were the taxes.

The Revolution had been started precisely because people didn't want to pay taxes, but the war had to be financed. The reluctance to do so was extreme and widespread. Even when Louis XVI started to subsidize the insurgents there was never enough money. Troops went unpaid, unarmed, unprovided. The states did not contribute enough, the Congress could not (and sometimes would not) raise the sums needed today, tomorrow, next month. The load of the public debts kept growing and there was only one remedy: more taxes. So people suddenly found themselves paying a variety of new and unpleasant taxes.

As if to add confusion to imposition, prices which, until now, had been steady began to fluctuate. It all depended on where the armies were: if they were somewhere near, you could be sure that scarcity would drive the prices up; on the other hand, you could always try to take advantage of all those foreigners, friend or foe, who were fighting it out on American soil. After all, the Hessians and the French needed exactly the same things and could be made to pay dearly for them, in hard cash. "Everything here is extremely expensive," Fersen wrote to his father in despair, "it costs twice as much as in Europe. . . . I have to pay twelve sols[1] to get a shirt washed and it costs nine livres to get my horse shod." It was even worse when it came to buying that essential necessity, the horse itself. Fersen couldn't get a decent one for under 1,400 livres, an enormous price. And things in Newport soon got worse, since it sheltered an entire French army. Fersen was moaning that "this country is ruined, there is no more money, there are no more men," and sending his father this monthly budget:

Wages for two servants:	120 livres
Wages for a valet:	100 "
Food for four horses:	90 "
Washing:	40 "
Miscellaneous:	60 "
	420 livres

This does not include food or lodging, both of which were provided by the army; it also says something for the greed of Newport washerwomen that it cost as much to do one man's laundry as it did to feed two horses. As for Fersen's staff, it was not unusually large. Most French officers took servants with them: war was all very well, but it was no reason to be uncomfortable.

Fersen's complaints ring out with self-pity. He had, after all, come as a volunteer to join a war and ought not to have expected peace and plenty. For other people, ardent though they might be in the cause of independence, life could be singularly difficult. When John Adams went off to Philadelphia he left his wife behind and did us a great favor. Abigail Adams, who wrote fully and often, was a born reporter. Her letters make fascinating reading and give us a good idea of just what it was like to be a Bostonian at the beginning of the war.

Mrs. Adams knew just where she stood: for the war and against the English. In fact she saw herself very much as the Roman matron, running her family as her husband goes off to fight, and she let him know it. On August

[1] There were 20 sols to a livre. Fersen was paying 1.80 of our dollars per laundered shirt.

19, 1774, she wrote him: " 'They ought to have reflected,' says Polybius, that 'as there is nothing more advantageous or desirable than peace, when founded in justice and honor, so there is nothing more shameful, and at the same time more pernicious when attained by bad measures and purchased at the price of liberty.'" The sentiment is as noble as the erudition is impressive. Of course it was the fashion to refer to classical examples. The French Revolution was rife with them, and the quotation was very timely; but Mrs. Adams, like a number of Americans of both sexes, was well read and intelligent. The French might think they had come across good savages; Mrs. Adams, and others like her, took pride in their classical heritage.

Soon, however, exhortation gave way to description. "Great commotions have arisen in consequence of a traitorous plot of Colonel Battle's," she wrote on September 2, and related the seizure by the English of the province's stock of gunpowder, along with the coming of a new atmosphere of general tension and suspicion. By September 14 she was able to add with satisfaction that "not a Tory but hides his head," and soon many were leaving the city, either for safe, faithful Canada or for England itself.

Exhortation was never forgotten, though. Abigail was horrified by what she considered unbridled luxury. "If we expect to inherit the blessings of our fathers," she scolded, "we should return a little more to their primitive simplicity of manners. . . . I have spent one Sabbath in town since you left. I saw no difference in respect to ornament, etc. . . . As for me, I will seek wool and flax and work willingly with my hands" (October 15, 1774).

By the spring of 1775 the British held Boston and the situation was rapidly deteriorating. Mrs. Adams, who was running her farm at Braintree, looking after the family's interests and raising her children as well, wrote: "Our house has been, upon this alarm, in the same state of confusion that it was upon the former. Soldiers coming in for a lodging, for breakfast, for supper, for drink, etc. Sometimes, refugees from Boston, tired and fatigued, seek an asylum for a day, a night, a week" (May 24, 1775). Soon the colonies were proclaimed to be in a state of rebellion; the blockade followed, and life, in the smallest particulars, became very difficult. "The cry for pins is so great that what I used to buy for 7/6 are now 20/–[2] and not to be had for that," Abigail complained on June 15.

By July, under the British occupation, Boston was in a state of alarm and despondency. Unlike New York, the city felt it was in enemy hands, and the English knew it. "The present state of the inhabitants of Boston is that of the most abject slaves, under the most cruel and despotic of tyrants," Abigail moaned on July 5; this may have been a slight exaggeration, but in fact the British authorities were imposing strict new rules: the citizens were forbidden to go on top of their houses or to any other point of eminence on

[2] Seven shillings and six pence and twenty shillings respectively. One shilling was worth one livre.

pain of death, for instance, lest they signal the American sympathizers outside the city and reveal military secrets. Then, too, the harbor had been
closed. This spelled ruin for a city which relied on trade for its income. The
once bustling port fell silent: Boston was dying. Even worse, fishing vessels
were forbidden to go out, and the city depended on fish for its daily food.
The situation was so clearly impossible that the authorities inaugurated a system of passes allowing fishing vessels to come and go—only, they were so expensive that almost no one could afford them, and the scarcity grew worse.

There were arbitrary arrests, greatly multiplied by public rumor. "It is reported and believed, that they have taken up a number of persons and committed them to jail, we know not what for in particular."

On July 16, Mrs. Adams wrote further of the Bostonians: "Their distress
increased upon them fast. Their beef is all spent, their malt and cider all
gone. All the fresh provision they can procure, they are obliged to give to the
sick and wounded. . . . They were obliged to be within every evening at
ten o'clock, according to martial law. . . . [General Gage] has ordered up all
the molasses to be distilled up into rum for the soldiers; taken away all licenses and given out others, obliging to a forfeiture of £10 [200 livres] if
any rum is sold without written orders from the General."

Life had indeed become difficult; people were left without sufficient food
or income, and treated like the enemy they really were; of course, this was
still the civilized eighteenth century, and we have seen a good deal worse in
the last fifty years; but, if Mrs. Adams' letters ring with indignation, it is not
just because she was a patriot and wished America free, it is also because
basic standards of human dignity were ignored. "An order has been given
out in town that no person shall be seen to wipe his face with a white handkerchief. The reason I hear is, that it is a signal of mutiny," she reported indignantly on July 20.

In October Boston was sick; dysentery was taking a heavy toll from both
the population and troops. By the time the British left the city in March
1776 it had really suffered and would take some years to recover. The disruption inflicted by the war took many forms. Education at Harvard, for instance, all but came to a standstill because the college buildings were used by
the American troops as barracks. It then had to face severe financial problems caused by the rapid depreciation of the public securities and paper
money in which much of its funds had been invested. And it was not only
Harvard that suffered this way.

Even when the British army evacuated Boston, supplies were kept low by
the blockade. A few privateers and occasional French ships managed to get
through, but on the whole supplies just didn't come in; nor were the maneuvers of the rival armies up and down the Eastern seacoast good for agriculture. Food grew scarcer and more expensive while the currency was apparently losing all value, and the unusually cold winter of 1778 didn't help

either. By March 1779, Abigail Adams was complaining to her husband about prices—and well she might: butter had risen to 12 shillings a pound,[3] as had sugar; potatoes were 10 shillings a bushel; butcher's meat 8 to 10 shillings a pound, flour 400 shillings per hundredweight. And the worst of it was, Mrs. Adams lamented, that you now had to pay a man 6 to 8 shillings a day: how was she to run the farm when, not so long ago, wages had been 2 to 3 shillings a day? And to give these prices their full meaning, the Massachusetts General Assembly, at this time, set the salary of a private at 18 shillings a month, that of a lieutenant at 120 shillings and that of a major general at 1,000 shillings.

Then, too, there were all the other inconveniences of war. Occupying British troops or friendly compatriots might be billeted in your house; sometimes it was complete strangers who barely spoke your language and were not overly careful of how they treated you and your possessions; even American soldiers ate and drank sometimes more than you could afford to give them. Worse, a skirmish, or just a march, might take place across your fields, and there went your crops. Even if you were spared the direct presence of war, tools broke and could not be replaced and essential supplies—salt, sugar—were available only at enormously high prices; and this was also true of fabrics of all kinds. For most Americans the war was a close physical presence, and survival could not be taken for granted.

Still, all those troubles, once they stopped, were quickly forgotten. By 1781 the war was essentially won and the cities were humming once again with business and pleasures. The French who had come early, like La Fayette, saw an America close to ruin. By the time most of his compatriots arrived, all was prospering except for foreign trade, still impeded by the British navy, and the war had resumed its proper eighteenth-century character as a limited confrontation between two armies which left most everyone else unaffected. By 1782 or 1783 the lives of the populations of Providence or Philadelphia were hardly more transformed, in their daily details, than those of the courtiers at Versailles. And, perhaps fittingly, both governments were struggling hard to meet their expenses.

To many people, most of them French, the war was only incidentally a disruption of life in the colonies; more important, it was a theatrical experience and a fashion which soon turned into a new ethic. Few officers who came returned unchanged.

At first the Revolution had attracted mostly profiteers, men who were so dishonored or so thoroughly ruined in their own country that they were willing to try anything anywhere, men of notorious incompetence who thought to find employment where they were not so well known, or swindlers pure and simple who counted on the naïveté of a fledgling nation.

[3] By comparison, ten years later, when prices in general were higher, butter was only 6 shillings a pound.

By 1777, after a number of unpleasant experiences, the Americans and their Congress were prepared to look askance at any foreign volunteer. La Fayette and the people who followed him changed all that: the Marquis, as he was soon universally called,[4] may have come for the wrong reasons, but come he did, and with his own money. At first everyone thought he was just another crook; but when it became apparent that he was really rich and wanted no cash, but a command, people melted; soon he had become Washington's favorite. After France had officially entered the war, the new wave of French officers was greeted with open arms.

At first the revolutionary character of the war was not apparent to them. To be sure, the Americans were revolting against their King, but then, he was so far away; when they won, they would probably just choose another sovereign: it was nothing like the English revolution in the course of which Charles I lost his head. Many, after meeting Washington, assumed he would be the first King of the United States. Then, too, even though the seat of war was so far away—and this gave it an exotic, unreal quality—the French expected it to be fought in a civilized manner, with a long winter break during which they would return to the pleasures of Paris and the court.

By the time they returned to France they were changed men—not in their daily habits but in their political conceptions. They had seen real democracy, freely elected assemblies governing the states and the Union, a press unfettered and able to say anything it wished, a people taking up arms to defend its freedom and putting them down again as soon as that result had been achieved. More important, perhaps, they lived in a Republic which was respectful of wealth and property, where all men were equal before the law but where money determined precedence and influence.

It was also a country where they had been greeted with open arms, feted, applauded and praised; where virtuous women smiled chastely on them and lionized them. Thus they had every reason to like what they saw: it was right—Rousseau could vouch for that; it was pleasant; it gave them that wonderful feeling of having selflessly come to the help of a downtrodden but worthy people, and succeeded; and it showed clearly that, except for a few unimportant details, they had little to lose if they brought democracy back to their own country. In fact, since they had money and experience, they could expect to play leading roles in a new constitutional France.

They had, of course, brought much to America. French funds and French forces were essential and they themselves opened American eyes to a whole new view of the world. Before they came, there was grumbling about incipient luxury; after they left, luxury had become a necessity. American horizons were broadened; new, more polished manners began to catch on, new books were read. A real exchange took place, with the Americans receiving the graces of an expiring culture and the French taking back with them the principles which they were to apply in the early phases of their own revolu-

[4] As one French observer remarked with awe: "They call him just the Marquis and everyone knows who they mean: he is the only marquis in the American army."

tion. Thus, more than a disruption, the war was a broadening experience which altered both partners.

This was all the more true because a number of Frenchmen, during the war and after, came as observers rather than combatants. It was still possible to travel through a war unhampered and to observe battles as a civilian. To those visitors, the events were a kind of splendid theater; and while some of the officers leaped upon pen and paper, so did the observers, who ranged from an adventurous abbé to a daring political publicist, Brissot, with a sharp eye and a thorough mind. They all reported at length, not just on the physical characteristics of the new country but also on its political institutions. They attended the debates of Congress and the state legislatures and were able to watch at first hand the functioning of a government without king or nobles.

As so often, they reverted to familiar clichés to convey new impressions. When Washington retired to Mount Vernon at the end of the war, he was a new Cincinnatus; the American people were new editions of Brutus, striking Caesar that they might be free. Clichés are catching; patriotic acts of selflessness, perhaps too good to be true, were extolled and endlessly publicized.

A good example of this is the farmer whose two sons, having been sent to join the army, soon deserted and came home again. The indignant father, in true Roman fashion, put his country before his family and took his sons back to the regiment they had fled. Its colonel, instead of having the deserters shot, pardoned them as a reward for the father's heroic act; and, as his sons were led back to the ranks, the father, thanking the colonel, said he had not expected such magnanimity and felt the kindness done him was more than he deserved. The story was told and retold. The French were just as impressed as the Americans, and the father's virtue was praised to the sky. Hearing this edifying story, one wonders just how the sons felt as they were being marched back to their regiment.

The war did not always give rise to such virtuous feelings; indeed, there would have been no need to praise the father's patriotism so highly if it had been commonplace. In fact, desertions were frequent and numerous, and very naturally so: there is a wide margin between wanting to fight for freedom and actually doing so under difficult circumstances. The army was always short of money and supplies, and, while giving one's all in battle may be exhilarating, trudging day after day through bare country without enough food and dressed in insufficient clothes is, in the end, a good deal harder. The simple, natural fact is that, all the French paeans notwithstanding, many American soldiers thought about their comfort before their country.

Another, perhaps more unpleasant consequence of the war, and one the French seem to have either missed or ignored, was the rise of a new kind of intolerance. To a European eye, the United States might seem, as Ségur wrote about Philadelphia, "a noble temple to tolerance," and in fact religious persecution had completely ceased; but this was a brand-new attitude, and the Quakers, for instance, had fresh memories of a very different situation. Now it was the Tories who bore the brunt of public anger. Understandably, perhaps, in a country fighting for the very right to exist, anyone who manifested pro-English feelings was considered a traitor and often treated as such. Like most revolutions, the American was led by a convinced minority; in those pre-poll days it was difficult to ascertain just what the great mass of the people thought; in all probability, most of them were "undecided," or even in favor of the status quo, though this may have changed as the war continued. Still, the pro-independence activists treated anyone suspected of being a Tory very much the same way the late Senator McCarthy treated those whom he suspected of being Communists in the 1950s. In 1775, for instance, the Massachusetts legislature ordered Harvard College to dismiss members of the faculty who appeared to be "unfriendly to the Liberties and Privileges" of the colonies. As it turned out, there were none; or, at least, no dismissals; but, clearly, academic freedom weighed as little then as it sometimes has since.

Some Tories simply fled, and came back after the war: that they were allowed to do so shows how quickly the new government recovered its respect for people's rights and how shallow wartime hysteria in fact was. Others, who stayed, were simply excluded from all contact with patriots: they became non-persons and could taint even the members of their families who disagreed with them. The French heard about this and took it all in stride; it was all in a good cause, and mild compared to imprisonment or exile.

—◄| |►—

Most people, throughout the war, stayed at home; a few others, who felt personally involved, went to Philadelphia or even, as envoys, abroad; but of course there could have been neither war nor victory without the army. It would be altogether beyond the scope of this book to give a history of the army during the war, but there, too, daily life went on; it is too important a part of the over-all picture to be ignored.

If you had asked just about any American, in 1783, who was responsible for the country's success, he would have answered without a moment's hesitation, as would the French who had shared in the fighting: General Washington. It really seemed as if both country and army were represented by his majestic figure. It was he who had held the troops together in their darkest hour, he who had persevered, he whose skills had been recognized even by his British opponents, he who had known just how to use the French troops sent to help him, he who had received the surrender at Yorktown, he, finally, who had returned home at the end of the war, firmly ignoring all the people who were ready to salute him as King George I of the United States.

The enormous impression Washington made on all those who met him was probably due to a mixture of his size—he was very tall and broad-shouldered—his air of quiet authority and what we would call charisma. Even the sharpest, coolest observers raved after seeing him. One of Abigail Adams' letters shows us just how far they could go. Washington, she wrote on July 16, 1775, has "dignity with ease and complacency;[5] the gentleman and the soldier look agreeably blended in him. Modesty marks every line and feature of his face. Those lines of Dryden instantly occurred to me:

> "Mark his majestic fabric; he's a temple
> sacred by birth, and built by hands divine;
> his soul's the deity that lodges there;
> nor is the pile unworthy of the god."

Coming from a woman more given to criticism than praise, this is no mean encomium. It didn't hurt, of course, that Washington was so personally disinterested as to refuse a salary. Whether or not he did, in fact, cheat on his expenses is, in that sense, unimportant: what mattered is that he gave up years of his life and endured great hardships, at no apparent gain to himself, solely to free his country.

In 1774, George Washington was just forty-two years old and, if we are to believe his portraits, rather bovine-looking; gifted with enormous physical strength—he once, in the middle of winter, swam across a river, then slept all night in clothes that had frozen solid—he was beginning to put on weight, the result of a formidable appetite. Most of the people who met him during and just after the war tended, of course, to see what they wanted to see. They had come to admire and proceeded to do so; but, if that were all, descriptions would differ, each observing what he had expected; instead, everybody agreed, so that to read one portrait of Washington is to read them all.

"His exterior appearance almost announced his history: simplicity, grandeur, dignity, calmness, kindness, firmness, all showed in his face, in the way he held himself as well as in his behavior," Chastellux wrote ecstatically. "He was tall and noble-looking; his expression was pleasant and welcoming; his smile was pleasing, his manner simple without familiarity.

"He did not display the pomp of a general in our monarchies; everything in him proclaimed the hero of a republic; he inspired respect more than he commanded it and, in the eyes of all those who surrounded him, one could read true affection and that entire confidence in a leader on which he seemed to solely base his safety. His quarters, which were a little apart from the rest of the camp, embodied the image of the order which reigned in his life, in his habits, in his behavior. . . . Everyone knew that he counted his private interest for nothing and that the general interest was his only goal. . . . He modestly tried to avoid the praise that everyone enjoyed giving him; yet no one ever knew better how to greet it and answer it."

[5] Complacency, in the eighteenth century, meant ease of manner.

The French, accustomed as they were to awkward, clumsy, rude Louis XVI, found Washington enormously polite; he talked to them as if they were equals (and, try as they might, they always thought of him as the equivalent of a king), asked about their journey, about their lives, invited them to dinner, and treated them as welcome friends. It was no wonder they were thrilled.

Everyone commented on his obvious openness and honesty—a very far cry from the habits of Versailles—and was amazed at his power over the troops, which they attributed to a mixture of skill, presence and personal sobriety. While the general did not live quite like a soldier, or even another officer, still, by any known standards, his simplicity was extreme; the least of British commanders lived ten times more luxuriously than he did, and the rank and file knew it. As for his ability to organize an improvised, ragged, undisciplined body of men into a real army, it seemed nothing short of miraculous. The vicomte de Ségur, who had acted as his father's assistant in the War Ministry, knew just what a mess a regiment could turn out to be when closely examined; and that, of course, was what he had expected to find. Instead, he wrote, "I was surprised to find an obedient army where everything gave a picture of order, reason, instruction and experience." And it wasn't done with smiles and personal charisma. Disobedient or otherwise inadequate soldiers were stripped to the waist and flogged severely. This was simply a carry-over of the British habit, but a traveler who witnessed one of these floggings was amazed at the fortitude and good temper with which it was borne. Being French, he attributed it to the tougher skin undoubtedly produced in these exotic climes; this is nonsense, of course, and the men felt every stripe just as keenly as if they had been European. But, whereas the British troops were either mercenary or men who had been pressed into service (the scum of the earth, Wellington was to call them a few years later), the Americans were volunteers. It says much for Washington and his officers that they were willing to submit to this kind of punishment.

No one man, even a genius, can run an army all by himself. Like all other great commanders, Washington relied on his officers; but they were more than just subordinates, they had become his family. He expected bravery and efficiency from them but treated them like near relations and, while he always remained a rather awesome presence to them, he also earned enormous devotion for himself. Curiously, the closest of all the officers was a foreigner, La Fayette, partly because Washington seems to have had a taste for a certain kind of aristocratic manner, partly because the Marquis was fighting, and fighting effectively, just for the love of America, but partly also because, used as he was to a court, La Fayette did not display the same awed reverence as his fellow officers. He knew how to amuse the general, how to joke with him, how to lighten his problems, and as a result developed a filial relationship with him which continued even after the war had ended.

16. The Surrender at Yorktown. *This American engraving mixes allegory—Liberty triumphant over Tyranny on the right, the Muses celebrating Independence on the left —and rearranges history. Washington, left, stands in front of Generals Lincoln, Rochambeau and Hamilton; the dashing duc de Lauzun in hussar's uniform, center, is surrounded by Generals Knox, Nelson and La Fayette, while the British officers, right, are grouped behind Cornwallis, who in reality never showed up.*

Every afternoon, after the day's work was done, Washington gathered a number of his officers around him for dinner in his tent or house. "There were twenty-five guests," Blanchard recounts. "We dined under the tent. . . . The table was served in the American style and pretty abundantly: vegetables, roast beef, lamb, chickens, salad dressed with nothing but vinegar, green peas, puddings and some pies . . . all this being put upon the table at the same time. They gave us on the same plate beef, green peas, lamb, etc. At the end of the dinner, the cloth was removed, and some madeira wine was brought, which was passed around whilst drinking different healths." At that point, Chastellux goes on to tell us, "apples were served along with a great quantity of nuts which General Washington usually eats for two hours while proposing toasts and making conversation. . . . Around seven-thirty, we would leave the table."

Half an hour later the same officers who had been present at dinner would be called back for supper. Three or four light dishes were set down on the table, along with fruit and another great quantity of nuts, while claret and madeira were again passed around and a new, endless series of toasts was offered. At eleven everyone went off to bed.

Washington and his officers used tents as seldom as possible. When the army was positioned near a small town they would always become the guests of the local householders; and, since they were constantly moving about, Washington did in fact manage to sleep in a great many different houses. In the open country, especially after 1780, the soldiers would quickly assemble wooden shacks which served as tents but were much more comfortable; their virtuosity astonished the French officers, especially because no nails or metal parts (they no longer came from England) were used. The constant difficulties of the first years had given way to relative comfort.

The same evolution could be seen when it came to supply. The ragged, hungry army of the mid-seventies, thanks in part to French money, weapons and imports, was well dressed and fairly well armed, though the shortage of ammunition continued until the end. Food was usually a minor problem; luckily, it grew everywhere and was sent in, reluctantly and often late, along with the subsidies of the several states. By 1780 the army was well provisioned, and the general was able to have between twenty and thirty guests for dinner every night.

Whenever the French who attended these dinners wrote about the war, it was always Washington who stood at center stage. That his achievements were immense no one could deny. He had created the army, kept it together through the worst difficulties and was now winning significant victories. Still, when on October 19, 1781, Cornwallis surrendered at Yorktown, he tried to ignore the Americans. It was far less humiliating to be defeated by the French, a traditional enemy, than by those ragtag rebels; so, he proposed to address the Articles of Surrender to the French commanders, Rochambeau and De Grasse. It was in large part due to Washington's personal prestige that the two men refused: Cornwallis would have to acknowledge his defeat at the hands of His Excellency General Washington.

The way in which the American commander chose to arrange the surrender was typical of that flexibility of character, that mixture of principle and kindness which all the observers remarked upon. "During the surrender negotiations, Washington, not wishing victory to be marred by persecutions, agreed to a subterfuge which allowed the British to spirit away American Tories, who would otherwise be arrested, and American deserters to the British army, who would otherwise be hanged. Captured slaves were to be returned to their owners and the British army would become, without reservations, prisoners of war. But one grievous issue did arise: Washington's insistence that 'the same honors shall be granted to the surrendering army as were granted to the garrison of Charleston.'

"When Charleston had fallen, Clinton had expressed his disdain for the rebels by refusing them the 'honors of war' traditionally accorded a defeated army which had fought well. In addition to other humiliations, the Americans had not been allowed to march to the surrender ceremonies with their flags flying. If the same strictures were applied to Cornwallis, his army would be disgraced before all Europe. But Washington was adamant."[6] In the end, Cornwallis feigned sickness and General O'Hara, his representative, was forced to surrender his sword to General Lincoln, the very officer whom Clinton had insulted at Charleston.

After that the war dragged on; it was a period of watching and waiting, with Congress reluctant to provide enough money and arms. Because De Grasse had taken the French fleet back to the West Indies after Yorktown, the British navy once more commanded the seas. The last American city in enemy hands, New York, was only given up as part of the peace settlement and Washington was frustrated of a conquest he felt sure could have been made with French help. With the departure of the British on November 25, 1783, the war was ended; and so was the general's function. On December 4, at Fraunces Tavern, near the Battery, Washington took leave of his officers. Unable to eat, he finally raised his glass with a trembling hand; then, as tears ran down his cheeks, he kissed every man in the room and left. More tears were shed, a few days later, on December 20, when he appeared before Congress at Annapolis where a great dinner and ball had been prepared. There, in a typical show of modesty, he said: "If my conduct has merited the confidence of my fellow citizens and has been instrumental in obtaining for my country the blessings of peace and freedom, I owe it to that Supreme Being who guides the hearts of all, who has so signally interposed his aid in every stage of the contest, and who has graciously been pleased to bestow upon me the greatest of earthly rewards, the approbation and affection of a

[6] James Thomas Flexner, *Washington, The Indispensable Man* (Boston, 1974).

free people." With that, he retired to private life and, making his way to Mount Vernon, arrived there on Christmas Eve. Cincinnatus, having won the war, had disdained power and returned to his plow.

It seemed almost beyond comprehension to the French officers who also went home that the general should have become just another citizen of the United States. Even if he did not choose to be the founder of a new monarchy, he could have continued the old Roman tradition according to which the victorious commander went on to rule the state. La Fayette, who would later urge Napoleon to imitate Washington, never forgot it, nor did many of his compatriots. All the French who, having survived the Revolution, still loved liberty held Washington's example up to the admiration of their people. Nearly two hundred years later it still has not been duplicated.

Four years later, in May 1787, Washington was called out of retirement to preside over the Constitutional Convention, and on February 4, 1789, he was unanimously chosen as the first President of the United States by the Electoral College. It was only just in time. Without a real federal government, the bickering states could agree on little, and the country drifted very close to catastrophe. It seemed to many here and abroad that the experiment had failed. The United States might be free, they said, but it was clearly incapable of governing itself: yet another fledgling republic was sinking into anarchy.

The adoption of the Constitution and Washington's ensuing election silenced the critics. In fact, as quickly became apparent, the United States was launched on a successful career. Long before it became reality, a few shrewd observers predicted the rise of a new power: a republic worked after all. By one of history's ironies, it proved its viability at the very time when the eight-hundred-year-old French monarchy was collapsing. For the next twenty-five years, as Europe was bathed in blood, the new American democracy established itself. In the long run, the war had changed the fate of more people than anyone could have guessed in 1783.

Chapter Sixteen

OF LAWS AND MEN:
CRISIS AND CONTINUITY

Unlike the French government, which was highly visible and all-pervasive, the administrative structure in America was weak and almost unnoticeable. Colonial governors, often unpopular, did the best they could with their limited powers. It wasn't just that they represented Britain and its taxing power: many of the people who came to the new continent were fleeing not only from religious persecution but from strong government as well. Lacking both the tradition of an authoritarian state and the need for centralized control, since there was more land than could be settled, little poverty and no fear of outside intervention, that government seemed best which governed and taxed least. And if you didn't like it where you were, it was always easy to move: the several states prided themselves on their differences.

Even when they came together, slowly and reluctantly, to support the fight for independence, it never occurred to them that they ought to give up their sovereignty. In that sense, the first Congress was not unlike the General Assembly of the United Nations: if you didn't reach a consensus, nothing would get done, since there was no forcing a state to do something it didn't like. The new nation, in fact, started out in life with a singularly inapposite name: the states were allied but hardly united.

Still, you can't fight a war against a powerful enemy from thirteen different capitals, with thirteen different armies and thirteen budgets, although that, in essence, is what the Americans kept trying to do. The Congress, born of necessity, was the weakest of governments. It could do nothing without the component states and frequently failed in its attempts at becoming a central government. As a result it was difficult to tell just where the power lay: the states, after all, went on regulating the business of daily life; they had the power to tax, to educate, to police, to define ownership, to outlaw, to print money and to raise troops.

Still, throughout the war some decisions had to be taken in common: it would have looked pretty silly for each state to issue its own Declaration of Independence; nor was it possible to send thirteen envoys to allied courts. Common sense demanded a degree of centralization; it was granted only reluctantly since, after all, the states were hardly rebelling against the Crown just to saddle themselves with another master. This attitude made for endless delays because all issues had to be negotiated; it precluded any really forceful policy and was often attended with disastrous results.

Even Washington found himself hard pressed to get anything decided by the Congress, especially when it came to the granting of supplies. Although the general deliberately planned a war of attrition as a means of mobilizing the entire country against the British, there can be little doubt that it would have ended a good deal sooner if there had not been such resistance to the concept and practice of a central government. And with the need for a consensus went vacillations in policy which often reduced generals and ambassadors to despair.

This failure to resolve the contradiction implied in the notion of thirteen united but sovereign states was especially grave when it came to finance; nearly wrecking the war effort and leaving a legacy of troubles and instability, sometimes actually causing out-and-out rebellion, the problem did not begin to be solved until the much stronger federal government created by the Constitution began to operate. It must be said, in all fairness, that the new authorities were faced with an extremely difficult situation. Already in 1770 bullion was in very short supply, and for very simple reasons.

North America, in the eighteenth century, produced neither gold nor silver and, since it was largely composed of British colonies, it had no currency of its own; so, for its everyday needs, it relied on whatever coinage was available, British or Spanish, and it used the British pound as its unit of record. Here, just as in France, there was no such thing as an actual pound: the current gold coin, the guinea, was worth twenty-one shillings.[1] There was nothing that could be done about shortages of currency: coins had to come from England or Latin America, where the Spanish had productive silver mines. Unfortunately the colonies imported more goods than they exported, so money always had a tendency to leave the country. This was partly offset by a system of letters of credit, but the shortage remained a constant problem.

Until the seventies Britain, as a government, had been spending more in America than it received; the consequent transfer of cash helped to relieve the shortage, but it stopped when the war started and the colonies suddenly found themselves with very little metallic money at a time when they had to spend more than ever before in order to support the war effort. The troops

[1] The pound was worth only twenty shillings.

had to be paid, supplies had to be bought, envoys had to be sent abroad; yet in this otherwise prosperous country there was no money. The answer to the problem was perfectly obvious: paper money would have to substitute for gold and silver. The result was disaster.

There were two ways, in the eighteenth century, of creating a paper money successfully: one was to tie it to a gold reserve substantial enough to ensure exchange back into gold whenever required; the bank notes then stayed at par. The other method, used by England after 1793, was to print money without the required gold cover; but, to offset this, the government held control over all imports and exports, thus preventing a depreciation of the pound against other European currencies and keeping the economy a closed circle within which any excess of paper could be absorbed again by taxes or the national debt. If you bought a bond, you got paper for your gold; the bond was not due for a number of years, so you couldn't ask the government to give you back your gold; but you could always sell it on the open market and get your money back that way. So what the government did by selling bonds to the public was, in effect, to create an unredeemable paper currency. Only this wouldn't work unless the people buying government paper had faith in the government's ultimate solvency and its ability to pay any due interest on time. And, obviously, you must have only one authority printing and selling the paper, and thus always controlling the amount offered to the public.

None of these conditions existed in America. There was neither gold cover, nor central bank, nor reliably solvent government (what price American paper if the English won?), nor control over the amount of paper offered the public. At first there wasn't even a currency: the United States dollar as such[2] didn't come into being until after the war. As late as 1788 it was still only an accounting unit.

Congress, in the meantime, needed money, so it printed it in large amounts; the states were just as broke, and they caught on quickly, so they kept their own presses busy. The result was a bewildering array of increasingly worthless paper moneys. Then, to add to the confusion, each state defined the dollar differently, so that its value compared to the British pound fluctuated as you traveled. In 1788, for instance, one metallic dollar was worth six shillings in Massachusetts, eight shillings in New York, seven and a half shillings in Pennsylvania, and so on down the line. And of course the key word here is metallic: the local paper currencies fluctuated far more wildly. So, supposing you had silver (a very large supposition indeed) and were trading between New York and Boston; you had to figure with the fluctuations of two virtually independent currencies which were called by the same name. This was obviously no help to commerce.

As for the paper, it went the usual way of uncontrolled inflation. The dollar was naturally supposed to stay at par: one silver dollar for one paper dol-

2 The original dollar was a Spanish doubloon.

lar; but of course, as more paper kept being printed by every government in sight, the value of the paper dollar began to drop rapidly against that of the silver dollar, creating even further confusion, since people thought of the new, impossibly high prices in terms of *real* (i.e., silver) money. In one sense they were right: since there was so little metal around, you had to use inflated paper money for your daily purchases, and chances were it had lost a good deal of its value even since you first received it. The rate of depreciation was both rapid and drastic: in 1789 in Philadelphia, for instance, it took seventy-five paper dollars to buy one silver dollar.

This often made for real distress. Many patriots had, early in the war, exchanged their silver for paper currency or government bonds; they were simply ruined. On top of that, it didn't help Congress to have all that paper when it had to purchase supplies abroad: nobody there wanted American paper; so it was back to looking for silver and gold, which were getting scarcer anyway, on the eternally valid principle that bad money drives out good. If you still had some silver you hid it, since it was gaining value every day and would automatically be worth more in the future, while the paper money you might get for it would merely continue to depreciate.

Luckily, there was the British army. In an early demonstration that guerrilla wars are unwinnable, it was supplying America with the one thing it needed most: good, solid metallic coinage. The soldiers were paid in silver, and they promptly spent it, thus adding significantly to the total amount of hard currency in circulation. When the French came, they, too, brought their money along and paid for supplies in silver and gold.

Then there were the French subsidies, amplified by the loans contracted there, in Spain and in Holland, some forty million livres altogether. Some of that had to be spent abroad for a variety of war supplies, but some made its way into the United States and was added to the monetary mass.

A major component of the general financial mess was that the several currency-issuing bodies just didn't understand what was happening: it was, after all, unprecedented. So they rushed headlong into a series of self-defeating measures. When Massachusetts, for instance, found that its paper had become worthless, it decided to issue a *new* paper which would be backed by taxes due to be collected in the future. This had several major defects. First, taxes came in fitfully and unevenly, so just what receipts might be in any given year was anybody's guess. Since no one trusted the full theoretical amount of tax money to come in, the paper's value promptly started to decline. Second, the Commonwealth announced that it would accept federal paper at par in payment for taxes or its new paper; since federal dollars were well below par, it stood to reason the new paper would follow shortly. Third, driven by necessity, the Commonwealth printed more paper than the full amount of theoretical tax receipts: since its new paper had started to lose value almost immediately, and would no longer provide the right amount of purchasing power, it was necessary to print more than originally planned, which of course only speeded up its decline. Within a very few months the new paper was quite as worthless as the old.

For many people the consequences were disastrous. If you were owed money, for instance, you could be repaid as scheduled—in paper. This was the equivalent of not being paid back at all, since most paper was worth between one and three cents on the dollar. What could you do? If you sued, you would get nowhere: you had indeed been paid back in legal currency, so you were stuck. Again, if you were a farmer, and you had sold your crop in July, but needed to buy a plow in October, you found that all your paper money wouldn't buy you a pocket knife, let alone a plow. So, duly chastened, you refused to sell your next crop for anything but silver; but, since there wasn't enough silver to go around, your crop was likely to remain in your barn.

Things were just as tough for workers: they were being paid, in paper, wages that never quite kept up with inflation. And merchants were in trouble too. When they bought goods abroad they had to pay in metal, but when they resold them here they had to accept paper, which no one abroad would take. As for people on fixed incomes, those, in particular, whose capital was invested in state or federal bonds, they suffered dreadfully.

It was, on the other hand, possible to make a handsome profit by cleverly trading in the various papers. In the case of that Massachusetts issue we just discussed, for instance, you could have bought up United States paper at, say, twenty cents on the dollar and made a beeline for the Massachusetts issuing office where you would have exchanged it for the new notes, which you could then resell at eighty-five cents on the dollar to buy goods or perhaps silver: your twenty cents would have grown to eighty-five overnight. Then there was a whole group of speculators who made it a practice to buy up the various paper currencies for a tiny fraction of the face value from people who needed real money badly. They then waited, not too patiently, until 1790–91 and found that the new United States Government was willing to reimburse them for their paper at par, or close to it. Those particular people made a very great deal of money.

Still, few people engaged in this kind of transaction, and the fluctuations of the currencies had a highly deleterious effect on the economy. It was obvious that something must be done, but no one quite knew how to do it or when, and in any event, as long as the war was going on, the first requirement, cutting down on spending, could obviously not be met.

The situation didn't improve when the war ended, either. The Congress and the states now had huge debts which must be serviced; many currencies were still being used and printed; and since it took a while for the country to recover and for trade to resume, tax receipts continued to be very small. That, of course, meant they had to be raised, again and again, making tax evasion a national pastime.

There was another important reason why the financial situation so signally failed to improve: Congress was virtually powerless. That all-important pre-requisite, a central authority able to control and manage the currency, was still missing. So the paper-money blitz continued and people began to think that America, having won the war, would soon defeat itself. This was an opinion so widely shared that Washington himself, no enemy of the Republic, expressed his fear that the country was sinking into anarchy. And not only did the states continue to print their own currencies, but they actu-ally set up their own customs and proceeded to wage something very close to economic war with their neighbors. So great was the general distrust, in fact, that, during the Constitutional Convention, several of the smaller states an-nounced that they were about to conclude foreign alliances so as not to be overrun by giants like Virginia and Massachusetts.

Of course a Constitution was finally accepted which gave the new federal government the power to tax and control over the customs; it also became the sole purveyor of the currency; but it was not until the debts of both Union and states had been examined and consolidated in 1790, following much bickering about who was to pay for what, that the flood of paper money finally began to recede. This strengthening of the central govern-ment, an obvious necessity by 1787, was also speeded along by Shays's rebel-lion in Massachusetts when the farmers rose rather than face foreclosure and the loss of their land because of non-payment of the impossible taxes made necessary by the depreciation of the paper money. Today that brief upheaval is largely forgotten, but at the time it looked like the beginning of the end, and it might well have been just that if the Articles of Confederation had lasted much longer.

This kind of fragmentation meant that people thought of themselves as citizens of Pennsylvania, or Rhode Island, or Georgia first and of the United States second. Conditions varied widely from state to state; every state had its own laws, its own political system and its own constitution which seemed much more binding than the Articles of Confederation, as well as its own, closed economy. Nobody, in the eighties, could conceive of being ruled from the as yet non-existent Washington; respective budgets give us a very clear image of this relationship.

In 1787, for instance, the budget of New York City, which was only the third largest city in America, came to a little over 24,000 New York dollars, or 200,200 shillings.[3] It worked out as follows:

Salaries	750 shillings
Elections	1,252 "
Wells and pumps	4,088 "
Roads and streets	14,682 "

[3] One shilling was worth one livre, so New York spent on itself only about a third of Marie Antoinette's dress budget.

Poorhouse[4]	75,834	shillings
Prison	18,000	"
Street lights	28,800	"
Night watchmen	38,622	"
Prisoners	7,460	"
Repairs for public buildings	6,856	"
Quays	500	"
City of New York	2,760	"
County of New York	2,600	"

This was about fifteen per cent of the first federal budget, that of 1789, when the government was established with Washington as President. By comparison, today, New York, with the largest municipal budget in the country, spends only 0.8 per cent of the federal outlay. Massachusetts, on the other hand, an important and wealthy state, collected $153,333, almost a third of the federal budget.

The main problem which had to be faced by the Congress and states alike was the crushing load of debt. Massachusetts, for instance, after passing off as much as it could to the new federal government, was still responsible for some 16,000,000 livres in outstanding, unconsolidated debt; the service for this alone came to some 800,000 livres, four times the budget of New York. As for the federal government itself, it included neither the national debt nor its service in its regular budget: the problem was so huge that it required special treatment. The figures are indeed awesome. In 1788, after some partial repayments, the United States still owed France 144,000,000 livres, Holland and Spain 360,000,000 livres, on which it had to pay five per cent interest. This alone came to a little over 20,000,000 livres a year when the total budget only reached 3,000,000 livres. On top of this, there was the domestic debt—government bonds, paper of various descriptions, and plain unpaid bills. That came to the staggering sum of 1,800,000,000 livres, and nobody saw how it could ever be paid off by a country with a population of a little over four million. In the event, the rapid rise in population, along with the coming of the Industrial Revolution and the multiplication of trade, took care of the problem; but no one in 1788 could even guess at this.

The federal budget for 1789, the very first year of the new government, was simple and small. It was financed entirely through customs receipts, a new resource that the states had only grudgingly—and partially—given up, and it included one major expenditure, military pensions, which reflected Washington's solicitude for the men who had fought under his leadership. It listed only three major items: the civil list, which provided for all gov-

4 Interestingly, then as now, New York spent the largest chunk of its budget on welfare.

ernment salaries, amounted to $254,892 (1,529,352 livres). The War Department spent $155,357 (768,222 livres). And the military pensions accounted for another $96,979 (581,972 livres), for a grand total of $507,408 (3,044,446 livres).[5] While it is not altogether fair to compare this to the French budget, since, after all, the states and cities assumed a significant proportion of public outlays, the difference is still striking: the United States Government was spending about 0.6 per cent of what Monsieur Necker was handing out at the same time. And, as a clear sign of the sobriety of the new government, the President's salary was a mere $25,000 (150,000 livres). It wouldn't have paid for a single evening's fete at Trianon.

Since the American system was so new and so shaky, a great number of tasks tackled in France by the State had been left to private enterprise or local initiative. Roads were prime examples of this. Pennsylvania imported the turnpike system from England: private investors would improve and keep up a stretch of road, then charge every traveler a fee. It was a profitable business (it still is) and, as a result, you could travel from Philadelphia to Lancaster, for instance, with ease and rapidity. Elsewhere, in places like Massachusetts, the state of the roads was left up to the townships with obvious consequences: when the town was prosperous, the road was excellent; when it was poor, the road was left unimproved and was almost impassable. And of course the United States did without a State-run engineering school like the French Ponts et Chaussées.

Aside from its tackling of the financial problem, the American system of government had at least one singular merit: it was absolutely new. Not only was there no hereditary sovereign, but every man (slaves excepted) was allowed to vote: there was no example of this in human history. Even in the very few countries where elected bodies shared power with the ruler (England, Sweden, Holland), there was no such thing as universal suffrage. There, only householders or men paying a qualifying amount of tax were considered active citizens. In America you needed only to be male and twenty-one to elect the members of the House of Representatives and those of the state legislatures, who in turn chose the United States senators. More surprising still, an elaborate system of checks and balances ensured the independence, and prevented the supremacy, of the three branches of government, thus preventing both anarchy and tyranny. The President, unlike the British Prime Minister, could not be toppled by a Parliamentary majority; but then, he couldn't dissolve the Congress. As for the judiciary, it wasn't just separate and untouchable: it was crowned by a brand-new institution, the Supreme Court, which served not only as the ultimate court of appeals (like the House of Lords in England and the King's Council in France) but also as the sole body able to decide whether or not the laws were constitutional, and so, eventually, veto them. This gave the Court a power and prestige which are still unrivaled.

[5] This is, very approximately, about 9,000,000 of our 1980 dollars.

It was no small achievement for this fledgling nation, apparently sinking into divisiveness and anarchy, to produce this unique framework for itself. More amazing still, the new Constitution worked and, with some amendments, has continued to do so for almost two hundred years. It would have been a bold man indeed who predicted this when the Constitutional Convention met in 1787.

The thirteen colonies, in 1770, had been what we would call today a third world country; their economy was primitive and based largely on simple crops—cotton, wheat, tobacco, wood, and the fruits of the hunt—furs, whale oil, cod, ivory. Industry was almost non-existent: almost all manufactured goods were imported from England; even shipping was relatively backward, though shipbuilding was a major activity thanks to the huge forests which still grew close to the coast. The war quickly made this state of affairs unacceptable; by 1790 manufactures of every kind, from iron to glass, from carriages to cotton cloth, were being started up. Already by 1782 a popular blue and white striped wool cloth was being woven in Hartford; it proved so successful that the workers could be paid an enormous wage: ten to twelve shillings a day. By 1790 the United States was actually exporting cotton and wool cloth.

In the eyes of the outside world, nothing much had changed by the time Washington took the oath of office. The United States still exported mostly crops: flour, rice, tobacco, oil, leather, fish, wood, furs. But whereas it had once had to import every kind of manufactured object, it now purchased mostly spirits, wines, tea, coffee, cocoa, sugar, molasses, salt and luxury goods. Everywhere factories were going up. By 1791 the Commonwealth of Massachusetts alone exported over two and a half million dollars' worth of goods, and Philadelphia three and a half million. Nothing could have been better for the state and federal treasuries, or for bringing bullion into the country.

This emphasis on trade was due to the rise of a new power, the banking industry. More than a convenience for their depositors, banks were also sources of the credit so necessary to an expanding society; by lending money to prospering industries they created increases in production; by giving out mortgages they helped establish a more widespread, secure system of land tenure. They also eased international trade by lending money against the value of incoming cargoes. Finally, by issuing their own notes and obligations, the banks were creating a fully secured paper currency.

By the early nineties several major banks had been founded on a new, bold principle: the banker didn't own the bank, the public did. The Bank of Massachusetts, for instance, was opened in 1784 with a capital of $4,000,000 (24,000,000 livres) obtained through the sale of eight hundred shares at $500 each. Not only did this spread the wealth—the dividends went to numerous shareholders—but it also made for safety: yearly accounts must be rendered; the way the bank was run had to be justified. And since the shareholders were pretty solid men themselves ($500=4,500 of our dollars), the bank had the backing of fairly substantial men. So there was a very powerful Bank of the United States, and a Bank of Pennsylvania, and a Bank of New York, and a Bank of North America, and so on throughout the country.

Just as important to the development of trade and industry as the free flow of money is the existence of a literate population. This may not have been the primary reason for the establishment of schools everywhere, but it certainly helped; soon almost everyone received at least some education, and all without assistance from the federal government: schools were controlled and established by the states themselves. The quality of teaching varied enormously from state to state. Massachusetts, for instance, always in a progressive mood when it wasn't a question of Sunday observance or an honest legislature, promptly established a system of free and general education: each township with a population of at least fifty families must support a school where reading, writing, spelling and arithmetics would be taught. Very soon the level of literacy in the Northeastern states was far above that of any European country.

Travelers found all this altogether admirable, although they were sometimes puzzled by the variations in standards of education as they moved across the country. Even more astounding to them was the disparity of the legal systems obtaining in the different states. While there was a small body of federal law, and a federal judiciary, most matters came under the jurisdiction of the state courts, which might or might not function in the tradition of the English common law. A crime in one state could be legal behavior in another: this made for enormous complications. And these differences were not restricted to minor questions: slavery, fast becoming a major issue throughout the civilized world, was regarded with horror and loathing in Massachusetts, where it was absolutely illegal. In Virginia, though, and a number of the other Southern states, it was not only legal but regulated, and the foundation of all prosperity. It was very hard for foreigners to understand how a country could survive when it was divided on so fundamental a question—yet it did well enough on just that basis for three quarters of a century.

Then there were all those constitutions. The very notion of constitutional law, in the eighties and nineties, was new and exciting. It was scarce and, even where it was deemed to exist, largely inchoate. Moreover, the adoption of a constitution was widely considered to be the benchmark of progress and democracy. When, in 1789, the French National Assembly started to transform the country into a constitutional monarchy, the golden age was held to have arrived at last by everyone who wasn't an extreme reactionary: nothing could go wrong when you had a good constitution, every major Enlightenment philosopher, from Montesquieu to Rousseau had made that perfectly obvious. Still, fourteen constitutions for starters might seem to indicate an excess of zeal.

They all shared a common grounding in a truly democratic ideal. The executive was always controlled by the legislature and was unable to dissolve it; in fact it was sometimes its direct emanation. Then, those democratically elected legislatures influenced the federal government through their choice of two senators per state. The executive was there to implement the decisions of the legislative. This was so obvious that President Washington was extremely reluctant ever to send a bill to Congress: it was not up to him to make the laws, only to carry them out. It should all have been perfection, but, as is so often the case, the reality was not so appetizing.

Perhaps one of the most constant themes in American history, and one which has by no means vanished today, is the corruptibility of state legislatures. This weakness has been deplored for nearly two centuries, often without much follow-up. As early as 1790 a keen and cultivated observer, the duc de La Rochefoucauld-Liancourt, who was also a fervent liberal, was able to notice, and deplore, the extreme corruption of the Massachusetts General Assembly. Far more than the Congress, the state legislatures regulated the way people did business, and it was an unfortunate fact that many of their members could be purchased for modest sums. It made obvious sense to do so: why labor under the disadvantage of strict regulation when a small investment would allow you to milk the public freely? Only, those corrupt legislatures were defining much of what the new country would be; and so, constitutions or no, the system proved to have at least one major flaw.

At the same time another enduring but, on the whole, more praiseworthy institution was born: the United States court system. That courts play an essential role in a government of laws was self-evident, and the framers of the Constitution gave much care to the structure of the new judiciary. Along with Montesquieu's plea for a strong, independent third power, there was the English tradition of decision by jury. This was enormously important: on the Continent, where judges were often incompetent and corrupt, they were also the sole arbiters of guilt and innocence: this was clearly dangerous for anyone on trial since it only took one man's prejudice to sway the verdict.

The English had long held that the right to be judged by a jury of their peers was one of their fundamental liberties. The framers of the Constitution understood this perfectly and embodied it in their own judicial construction, along with that other safety, the Supreme Court. As for the states, each had its own parallel system where most suits, in fact, were lodged. On the whole, they achieved relative simplicity. In Pennsylvania, for instance, the pyramid rose as follows: at the very bottom was a Court of Quarter Sessions in which minor matters could be tried; and, to ensure fairness, it had its own Court of Appeals. Then, for everyday suits on a higher level, there was a Court of Common Pleas. For major matters and serious criminal offenses there was the Court of Oyer and Terminer, which borrowed its law-French name from the English Assizes. Then at the very top came the state Supreme Court, which was patterned after its federal equivalent in being both the court of appeal of last resort and the final arbiter of the laws' constitutionality. While some of the details have changed since the 1790s, the basic principles, like the form of government itself, have proved fair and enduring.

The most surprising feature of the new system, however, was not its fairness but its power. The very existence of an independent judiciary, whose members could not be removed except for gross malfeasance, and who could therefore be relied on to render justice to all whatever the government might think, was in itself a major achievement. Because, on the whole, the keystone of the system, the Supreme Court of the United States, has worked out to the people's satisfaction, it is easy to overlook its revolutionary character: the acts of both elected branches of the government can be overturned by an unremovable court whose members have lifelong tenure. This is a truly regal privilege; in France only the King's Council held similar power; in England no one could reverse an act of Parliament which had received the royal assent. There were some people who, in the early years of the Republic, feared monarchical plots; in fact, the Constitution had given the country a nine-headed monarch.

As we look back to the late eighties we see not just a system of government being created practically from nothing, but also the setting of a number of enduring patterns. The constitutional separation of Church and State was not the least of these. The principle that *ejus regis, cujus religio* had become a fact of life throughout Europe. Not only did the different countries each have its state religion, but they also discriminated, more or less violently, against members of contending sects. In liberal England, Catholics suffered under civil disabilities until the 1830s; in France it took Napoleon to establish the principle that, while the State was officially Catholic, its citizens were free to belong to any cult they chose, and the separation of Church and State had to wait until 1904.

It was all the more amazing, therefore, that in the United States where, to be sure, a variety of sects proliferated, but where they all retained some link to Protestantism, religion was absolutely removed from the State's purview. As it happened, the pattern existed before 1787. Whereas in Europe the various clergies were either directly paid by the State or else lived on the income of extensive Church lands, in America the custom of having the clergyman supported by his congregation was well established. It made perfect sense: if you wanted religion, it was up to you personally to pay for it. This resulted in greater personal involvement—financial cost usually does—and greater control over the various clergymen: after all, anyone whose salary is paid by a congregation is not very likely to disregard its wishes. Another consequence was the absolute exclusion of any kind of religious persecution: neither the State, nor any of its citizens, had anything to say about how anyone worshiped his God. Finally, it was impossible for any church to form a powerful body within the State, since it had no claim to special privileges.

Just because the churches were free of both protection and interference from the government, however, does not mean they ought to be overlooked. Churches of every kind and denomination were everywhere; no small village but had at least one minister, no city without a large and varied array of religious bodies. Washington himself was a deist and carefully referred to the Supreme Being instead of God; but, in that instance, he was not at one with the rest of his compatriots. The Americans' religious fervor never ceased to astonish European visitors, nor did the strictness of their Sunday blue laws in the Northeast. As for new, ministerless sects like the Quakers, they were watched with a puzzled fascination which often turned to scorn. Still, it didn't matter: it was the absolute freedom of religion which dazzled the envious travelers.

Before 1790 there was no real social or political establishment, either, although one was rapidly being formed. There had been no central administrators before 1789. Even society, such as it was, underwent rapid transition. True, there were older families, and rich ones as well, but the war had wrought great changes. A new capitalist class was emerging in the Northeast; and when President Washington moved with the government from New York to Philadelphia and started to attend the balls, dinners and parties which so enlivened the evenings there, he often went to the houses of people whose fortunes were very recent. Setting another precedent, Washington made it plain he didn't care: what he wanted was the company of pretty women in a setting of relative luxury. In this new, egalitarian country, where you could inherit neither rank nor position, you could at least pass on your money: a new kind of establishment was in the making.

In the meantime there were a few great men who had played leading roles in the Revolution and were treated by visitors much like public monuments. The first of these, of course, was Washington. Every traveler seemed to take it for granted that he could simply appear at Mount Vernon and ask to see the general. Amazingly, they were right, and the great man saw them all, often keeping them for the night; now and again, he would lavish on an impostor the consideration with which he always treated his guests.

Then there was John Adams, who was a good deal less hospitable. Still, visitors loved to remark on the simplicity of his household: Mount Vernon, while modest by European standards, was still a fairly large house; the Adams farm at Braintree was just a plain house, with few servants and no ceremony. It seemed right for the new country, somehow, as did Adams' grumbling about the state of affairs, the aristocratic tendencies of other famous Americans and the low yield of land, only three per cent of invested capital, which would prove the ruin of agriculture and the Republic. Adams was very different from Washington but just as colorful.

Some of the great men of the Revolution were not so popular; then as now, Americans disliked levelers,[6] and that Tom Paine undoubtedly was. Already in 1782, Chastellux found that Paine was read but not trusted and was

[6] The eighteenth-century equivalent of socialists.

carefully kept out of all government activities. His appearance, we are told, was not prepossessing; he was living "in a rather messy room with dusty furniture and a big table covered with open books and unfinished manuscripts. He was dressed in a costume suitable to the room, nor did his face give the lie to the principles expounded in his works." Still, he was a curiosity, another of those monuments which the conscientious tourist must visit.

Nothing could have been more different from that messy room than Monticello. Not for nothing had Jefferson traveled in Europe, acquiring wines and knowledge; here was a house worthy of a gentleman. That its style lacks originality, that it is, in fact, a rather inferior adaptation of several English Palladian mansions, was hardly surprising in a man who would soon beg Washington to fire L'Enfant so that the most famous European façades (as drawn by T. Jefferson) could grace the streets of the new Federal City. But Monticello is the precursor of a well-known, if somewhat later, American mania of which Asheville and Newport are prime examples.

To Chastellux, busily completing his rounds, the house seemed "Italianate and rather elegant although it is by no means without faults. . . . Mr. Jefferson is the first American who consulted the Arts to know how he would shelter himself." With its park, tame deer, books, scientific instruments, European furniture, porcelain and wines, Monticello was in striking contrast to the usual simplicity of other American establishments.

As for the owner, he was "tall, with a sweet and pleasant face, but one on which intelligence and knowledge might well replace any exterior qualities; an American who . . . knows music, drawing, geometry, astronomy, physics and law, he is a statesman, a senator[7] of America who sat for two years in that famous Congress which brought forth the Revolution. . . . A governor of Virginia who held that difficult post during the invasions of Arnold, Phillips and Cornwallis; finally, a philosopher retired from the world and its business because he only likes the world when he can be useful to it. . . . I found his manner serious and even cold, but by the time I had spent two hours with him, I felt as if I had known him all my life." This feeling was confirmed when it became apparent that both men were devotees of Ossian, the supposed Scottish bard whose epic masterpiece was, in fact, a literary fraud. As for that dislike of the busy world outside, which all the visitors to American great men noticed, it luckily vanished when the new government was installed with Washington as President, John Adams as Vice-President, and Jefferson as Secretary of State.

That installation marked the beginning of a new era; by 1790 party politics were appearing; Republicans and Federalists had very different concepts of the role of the federal government, and said so in Congress and newly created newspapers. The war began to recede into the past; a new era was born.

[7] In the sense of chosen representative.

The seventies and eighties had been a period of flux, of new beginnings, of men striking out into the unknown. There was no telling, it seemed, what would happen or how it would all end; but, while the political structures underwent a radical change, many of the characteristics of American life, somewhat tempered by the war and the influx of visitors, persisted. After 1790 all that changed; politically, it was a period of consolidation; economically, of revolution. The agrarian country of small farmers so dear to Jefferson was quickly disappearing and being replaced by the twin lures of capitalism and the frontier. While in France and Naples revolutions were sweeping all before them, a parallel phenomenon could be observed in America, for almost opposite reasons. On both sides of the Atlantic, 1790 marked the end of a world.

BIBLIOGRAPHY

Harold Acton. *The Bourbons of Naples*. London, 1956.

Abigail Adams. *Letters of Mrs. Adams*. Boston, 1840.

The Adams–Jefferson Letters. University of North Carolina Press, Chapel Hill, North Carolina, 1959.

H. H. Arnason. *The Sculptures of Houdon*. New York, 1975.

Georges d'Avenel. *"Le Coût de l'ameublement depuis sept siècles,"* Revue des Deux Mondes, May 15, 1926.

Paul Avril. *L'Ameublement parisien avant, pendant et après la Révolution*. Paris, 1929.

M. Bariéty. *Histoire de la médecine*. Paris, 1963.

Pierre-Augustin Caron de Beaumarchais. *Oeuvres complètes*. Paris, 1809.

Baron de Besenval. *Mémoires*. Paris, 1821.

Charles Blanc. *Histoire des peintres*. Paris, 1862.

Claude Blanchard. *Journal 1780–1783*, tr. by William Duane. Albany, 1876.

Georges et Germaine Blond. *Festins de tous les temps*. Paris, 1976.

Dorothie Bobbé. *Abigail Adams, The Second First Lady*. New York, 1929.

Comtesse de Boigne. *Récits d'une tante*. Paris, 1907.

Marquis de Bouillé. *Mémoires*. Paris, 1821.

René Bouvier and André Lafforgue. *La Vie napolitaine au XVIIIème siècle*. Paris, 1956.

Carl Bridenbaugh. *The Colonial Craftsman*. Chicago, 1961.

Jean-Pierre Brissot. *Nouveau Voyage dans les États-Unis de l'Amérique septentrionale*. Paris, 1791.

Anita Brookner. *Greuze, The Rise and Fall of an Eighteenth Century Phenomenon*. London, 1972.

Marquis de Buffon. *Oeuvres complètes*. Paris, 1817.

Madame Campan. *Mémoires*. Paris, 1826.

Richard Cantinelli. *Jacques-Louis David*. Paris, 1930.

Henri Carré. *La Fin des parlements*. Paris, 1912.

André Castelot. *Marie-Antoinette*. Paris, 1953.

Marquis de Chastellux. *Voyages dans l'Amérique septentrionale*. Paris, 1788.

Madame de Chastenay-Lanty. *Mémoires*. Paris, 1896.

François-René de Chateaubriand. *Mémoires d'outretombe*. Paris, n.d.

Anna Francesca Cradock. *La Vie française à la veille de la Révolution*, tr. by Madame Belleyguier. Paris, 1911.

J. Hector St. John de Crèvecoeur. *Letters from an American Farmer*. New York, 1804.

La Cuisinière bourgeoise. Paris, 1779.

Louis Denis. *Itinéraire complet de la France*. Paris, 1788.

Denis Diderot. *Oeuvres complètes*. Paris, 1875.

J. R. Dolan. *The Yankee Peddlers of Early America*. New York, 1964.

Charles Duclos. *Voyage en Italie*. Paris, 1793.

Louis Ducros. *French Society in the Eighteenth Century*. London, 1926.

Charles Dupati. *Lettres sur l'Italie en 1785*. Rome, 1789.

Thomas Fairfax. *Journey from Virginia to Salem, Massachusetts*. London, 1936.

Max Farrand. *The Fathers of the Constitution*. Newhaven, 1921.

Edgar Faure. *La Disgrâce de Turgot*. Paris, 1961.

Axel Fersen. *Lettres à son père*. Paris, 1929.

James Thomas Flexner. *Washington, The Indispensable Man*. Boston, 1974.

Benjamin Franklin. *The Works of Benjamin Franklin*. Boston, 1856.

Félicité de Genlis. *Mémoires inédites*. Paris, 1857.

Ernest-Désiré Glasson. *Le Parlement de Paris*. Geneva, 1974.

M. Glotz, M. Maire. *Salons du XVIIIème siècle*. Paris, 1945.

J. W. Goethe. *Italian Journey*, tr. by W. H. Auden and Elizabeth Mayer. London, 1962.

E. and J. de Goncourt. *La Femme au XVIIIème siècle*. Paris, 1923.

Evarts Boutell Greene. *The Revolutionary Generation*. New York, 1943.

Rufus Wilmot Griswold. *The Republican Court*. New York, 1856.

Louis Hautecoeur. *Madame Vigée-Lebrun*. Paris, 1926.

Comte Félix d'Hézecques. *Souvenirs d'un page de la cour de Louis XVI*. Paris, 1873.

Victor Hugo. *Choses vues*. Paris, 1887.

Pierre Jacomet. *Vicissitudes et chutes du Parlement de Paris*. Paris, 1954.

Charles William Janson. *The Stranger in America, 1793–1806*. New York, 1935.

Marie-Henri Jette. *La France religieuse du XVIIIème siècle*. Paris, 1956.

Pierre Joly. *Jacques Necker*. Paris, 1947.

Emil Kaufmann. *Architecture in the Age of Reason.* Cambridge, Massachusetts, 1955.

Charles Kunstler. *La Vie quotidienne sous Louis XVI.* Paris, 1950.

———. *La Vie privée de Marie-Antoinette.* Paris, 1938.

Robert Lacour-Gayet. *Calonne.* Paris, 1963.

Paul Lacroix. *Le XVIIIème siècle.* Paris, 1878.

Duc de La Rochefoucauld-Liancourt. *Voyage dans les États-Unis d'Amérique.* Paris, 1799.

Marquise de La Tour du Pin. *Journal d'une femme de cinquante ans.* Paris, 1914.

Duc de Lauzun. *Mémoires.* Paris, 1858.

Hector Lefuel. *Georges Jacob.* Paris, 1928.

Pierre Lespinasse. *Lavréince.* Paris, 1928.

Marcel Marion. *Les Impôts directs sous l'ancien régime.* Paris, 1910.

Sébastien Mercier. *Tableau de Paris.* Amsterdam, 1783–88.

Lady Anne Miller. *Letters from Italy.* London, 1777.

Francisco de Miranda. *Diary, Tour of the United States.* New York, 1928.

John Moore. *A View of Society and Manners in France, Switzerland and Germany.* London, 1786.

———. *A View of Society and Manners in Italy.* London, 1795.

L'Oeuvre de Moreau le Jeune. Paris, 1880.

Morrison, Commager and Leuchtenberg. *The Growth of the American Republic.* New York, 1969.

Jacques Necker. *Compte-rendu au roi.* Paris, 1781.

Pierre de Nolhac. *Le Trianon de Marie-Antoinette.* Paris, 1924.

———. *Madame Vigée-Lebrun.* Paris, 1908.

P. de Nouvion. *Un Ministre des modes sous Louis XVI, Mlle. Bertin.* Paris, 1911.

Baronne d'Oberkirch. *Mémoires.* Paris, 1970.

Vedad Zeki Örs. *Jacques Delille, poète célèbre.* Zurich, 1936.

Charles Oulmont. *La Maison.* Paris, 1929.

Anne-Marie Passez. *Adélaide Labille-Guiard.* Paris, n.d.

Edmond Pilon. *La Vie de famille au XVIIIème siècle.* Paris, 1923.

Hester Lynch Piozzi. *Observations and Reflections Made in the Course of a Journey through France, Italy and Germany.* Dublin, 1789.

Nicolas-Edme Restif. *Oeuvres.* Paris, 1930.

Exposition Hubert Robert. Paris, Musée de l'Orangerie, 1933.

Abbé Robin. *Nouveau Voyage dans l'Amérique septentrionale.* Paris, 1782.

Jacques Robiquet. *Pour mieux connaître le palais de Compiègne.* Compiègne, 1938.

Madame Roland. *Mémoires.* Paris, 1823.

Jean-Jacques Rousseau. *Oeuvres complètes.* Paris, 1959–69.

D. A. F. de Sade. *L'aigle, Mademoiselle.* Paris, 1949.

————. *Oeuvres,* introduction by Guillaume Apollinaire. Paris, 1909.

Abbé de Saint-Non. *Voyage pittoresque de Naples et de Sicile.* Paris, 1782.

Bernardin de Saint-Pierre. *Oeuvres.* Paris, 1833.

H. E. Scudder. *Men and Manners in America One Hundred Years Ago.* New York, 1887.

Comte de Ségur. *Mémoires, souvenirs et anecdotes.* Paris, 1859.

Charles H. Sherril. *French Memoirs of Eighteenth Century America.* New York, 1915.

Henry Swinburne. *Travels in the Two Sicilies.* London, 1790.

Prince de Talleyrand. *Mémoires.* Paris, 1957.

Charles-Maurice de Talleyrand-Périgord. *Rapport fait au nom du comité de constitution à la séance du 7 mai 1791.* Paris, 1791.

Thiéry. *Guide des amateurs et étrangers voyageurs à Paris.* Paris, 1789.

Comte de Tilly. *Mémoires.* Paris, 1965.

La Vie parisienne au XVIIIème siècle, Conférences du Musée Carnavalet. Paris, 1928.

Madame Vigée-Lebrun. *Souvenirs.* Paris, 1926.

Horace Walpole. *Letters.* Oxford, 1914.

Samuel Blackley Webb. *Family Letters, 1764–1802.* New York, 1912.

George M. Wrong. *Washington and His Comrades-in-Arms.* New Haven, 1921.

Arthur Young. *Travels During the Years 1787, 1788 and 1789.* London, 1794.

INDEX